About Island Press

Since 1984, the nonprofit organization Island Press has been stimulating, shaping, and communicating ideas that are essential for solving environmental problems worldwide. With more than 1,000 titles in print and some 30 new releases each year, we are the nation's leading publisher on environmental issues. We identify innovative thinkers and emerging trends in the environmental field. We work with world-renowned experts and authors to develop cross-disciplinary solutions to environmental challenges.

Island Press designs and executes educational campaigns, in conjunction with our authors, to communicate their critical messages in print, in person, and online using the latest technologies, innovative programs, and the media. Our goal is to reach targeted audiences—scientists, policy makers, environmental advocates, urban planners, the media, and concerned citizens—with information that can be used to create the framework for long-term ecological health and human well-being.

Island Press gratefully acknowledges major support from The Bobolink Foundation, Caldera Foundation, The Curtis and Edith Munson Foundation, The Forrest C. and Frances H. Lattner Foundation, The JPB Foundation, The Kresge Foundation, The Summit Charitable Foundation, Inc., and many other generous organizations and individuals.

The opinions expressed in this book are those of the author(s) and do not necessarily reflect the views of our supporters.

CLIMATE ACTION PLANNING

Climate Action Planning

A Guide to Creating Low-Carbon, Resilient Communities

Michael R. Boswell,
Adrienne I. Greve, and
Tammy L. Seale

With contributions by Eli Krispi
Images by Dina Perkins

ISLANDPRESS

Washington | Covelo | London

Island Press is a trademark of the Center for Resource Economics.

Library of Congress Control Number: 2019933787

All Island Press books are printed on environmentally responsible materials.

Manufactured in the United States of America
10 9 8 7 6 5 4 3 2 1

Keywords: Chief resilience officer, climate action team, climate adaptation,
climate science, climate vulnerability assessment, emissions inventory, energy
efficiency, global warming, greenhouse gas emissions, local government, Paris
Climate Accord, public participation, reduction strategy, resilience strategy

Contents

Preface

In response to increasing evidence that climate change is occurring and has the potential to negatively impact human civilization, communities are engaging in climate action planning. Climate action planning is an opportunity for communities to shape their future in the face of global change, protect against climate hazards, achieve energy security, sustainably develop their economies, and ensure a high quality of life. Communities can seize this opportunity by building on existing planning and partnerships, being creative and innovative, and committing to working together for a better tomorrow for themselves and the next generations. If the world is to end the climate crisis, we will need international and national commitments and actions, but we will also need to create low-carbon, resilient communities.

This book describes the process and methods for local climate action planning. It is intended to be a practical guide, helping readers navigate the principal actions and critical considerations for managing a climate action planning process in their communities. We believe that the best climate action planning is based on sound science, public education and outreach, recognition of the global context and external constraints, awareness of the interdependent nature of local policy, and integration with existing planning policies and programs. We base this on our professional experience of working on dozens of climate action plans and greenhouse gas emissions inventories in California, our academic experience researching and publishing on the state of climate action planning practice nationwide, and our international climate action work with UN-Habitat and the World Bank. As of this writing, there is no book that addresses climate action planning as a specific area of professional practice. Our hope is to contribute to the robust development of this professional field.

The book is aimed primarily at those who have been tasked with climate action planning, whether they are local government staff members, consultants, or community volunteers. Professionals who should find the book useful include city/urban planners, regional planners, land use planners, environmental planners/managers, natural resource and conservation managers, transportation planners, city administrators, city attorneys, city engineers, emergency managers, hazard mitigation planners and managers, public works and transportation managers, architects, landscape architects, building officials, sustainability coordinators/managers, and climate action managers. In addition, the book is accessible to students in these fields and can serve as an introductory text to the field of climate action planning. The book should also be useful to anyone involved or interested in the climate action planning process, such as elected officials, environmental and planning nonprofits, advocacy groups, and members of the public.

In this second edition—the original edition was titled *Local Climate Action Planning*—we have updated scientific information on the understanding of climate change and its impacts; updated cases and examples; substantially revised chapter 4 on greenhouse gas emissions accounting to be consistent with standard protocols; added a chapter on climate change vulnerability assessment; updated chapters on low-carbon, resilient community strategies; and generally updated the book to document current best practice.

We extend our sincere thanks to all those who supported us in this effort to update the original book: Heather Boyer (our editor) and the rest of the staff at Island Press; Christine Theodoropoulos, dean of the College of Architecture and Environmental Design at California Polytechnic State University in San Luis Obispo (Cal Poly) for her encouragement and support; all our colleagues in the City and Regional Planning Department at Cal Poly for help in editing chapters and their general cheerleading; our circle of friends and colleagues pursuing climate action both professionally and personally, who have been a wonderful, supportive network that always inspires and teaches; Dina Perkins for her beautiful chapter pictures and support; and our colleague Eli Krispi, who made substantial contributions to chapter 4.

CLIMATE ACTION PLANNING

Chapter 1

Climate Action Planning

To prevent the worst impacts of climate change, we have to cut greenhouse gas emissions even as the population grows. Cities are showing that it can be done—and that the same steps they're taking to reduce their carbon footprint are also strengthening their local economies, creating jobs, and improving public health.[1]

> —Michael R. Bloomberg, former mayor of New York City, UN secretary-general's special envoy for climate action, and president of the C40 Board

The Fourth National Climate Assessment prepared by the U.S. Global Change Research Program in 2018 clearly establishes the nature of the global warming problem:

The impacts of climate change are already being felt in communities across the country. More frequent and intense extreme weather and climate-related events, as well as changes in average climate conditions, are expected to continue to damage infrastructure, ecosystems, and social systems that provide essential

benefits to communities. Future climate change is expected to
further disrupt many areas of life, exacerbating existing challenges to prosperity posed by aging and deteriorating infrastructure, stressed ecosystems, and economic inequality. Impacts
within and across regions will not be distributed equally. People
who are already vulnerable, including lower-income and other
marginalized communities, have lower capacity to prepare for
and cope with extreme weather and climate-related events and
are expected to experience greater impacts. Prioritizing adaptation actions for the most vulnerable populations would contribute to a more equitable future within and across communities.
Global action to significantly cut greenhouse gas emissions can
substantially reduce climate-related risks and increase opportunities for these populations in the longer term.[2]

Global warming is already impacting human health and safety, the economy, and ecosystems. As greenhouse gas (GHG) emissions continue to
accumulate in the atmosphere, global warming impacts will increase in
severity. The global challenge is twofold: reduce the human-caused emissions of heat-trapping gases and respond to the negative climate impacts
already being felt and the likelihood that they will worsen in the future.

The largest sources of these heat-trapping GHGs are fossil fuel–
burning power plants and fossil fuel–burning vehicles (see figure 1.1).
For the former, changes such as better technology, the development of
large-scale renewable energy, and the retirement of old, inefficient power
plants (especially those that burn coal) have an important role to play
in reducing GHG emissions. For the latter, evolving vehicle and fuel
technology and standards help reduce GHG emissions. These types of
technological evolution and large-scale energy programs are driven by
private-sector investment and federal and state government legislation
and programs. Although these efforts are important and necessary, the
problem of global warming cannot be solved without the participation
of communities, local governments, and individuals as well.

Local action is critical for the necessary GHG emissions reductions to
occur. Local governments control the vast majority of building construction, transportation investments, and land use decisions in the United

Figure ES-6: 2016 CO₂ Emissions from Fossil Fuel Combustion by Sector and Fuel Type (MMT CO₂ Eq.)

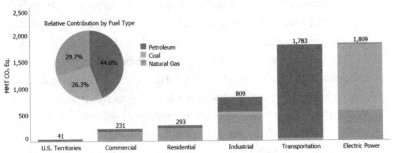

Note on Figure ES-6: Fossil Fuel Combustion for electric power also includes emissions of less than 0.5 MMT CO₂ Eq. from geothermal-based generation.

Figure 1-1 2016 CO₂ emissions from fossil fuel combustion by sector and fuel type

Source: U.S. Environmental Protection Agency, "Inventory of U.S. Greenhouse Gas Emissions and Sinks: 1990–2016" (2018), https://www.epa.gov/ghgemissions/inventory-us-greenhouse-gas-emissions-and-sinks-1990-2016.

States. Civic and business organizations, environmental groups, and citizens can join forces with local governments and commit to local action that includes energy-efficient operation of local government; energy-efficient buildings; renewable energy systems; alternatives to driving, such as buses and bicycles; and city planning that improves the quality of life and allows people to depend less on their cars. The goal is to create low-carbon, resilient communities.

Fortunately, communities all over the world are responding to the challenge of climate change by assessing their GHG emissions and specifying actions to reduce these emissions. As of early 2019, over 9,000 mayors representing over 780 million people around the globe had made a commitment to address climate change through the Global Covenant of Mayors for Climate & Energy (see box 1.1). These mayors have made commitments to reduce GHG emissions by 1.4 billion metric tons by 2030. At the 2018 Global Climate Action Summit in San Francisco, numerous mayors reported on their progress and made new commitments to accelerate their ambition in addressing climate change. The Lord Mayor Clover Moore of Sydney declared,

Greenhouse [gas] emissions in the City of Sydney peaked in 2007 and have declined every year since—despite our economy expanding by 37 percent. We've achieved this because we developed a long-term plan with ambitious targets and we determinedly stuck to that plan for over a decade. We have one of the largest rooftop solar programs in Australia, we converted our streetlights to LED and we're working with industry leaders to reduce their emissions. We lead by example and we partner with businesses and residents to help them on their journey. As the first government in Australia to be certified carbon neutral, our achievements show the

---

Box 1.1

The Global Covenant of Mayors for Climate & Energy Commitment

I, [Name], [Mayor or equivalent representative title] of [name of city or jurisdiction] commit to the Global Covenant of Mayors for Climate & Energy, joining thousands of other cities and local governments around the world currently engaged in climate leadership.

The Global Covenant of Mayors for Climate & Energy envisions a world where committed mayors and local governments—in alliance with partners—accelerate ambitious, measurable climate and energy initiatives that lead to an inclusive, just, low-emission and climate resilient future, helping to meet and exceed the Paris Agreement objectives.

Whatever the size or location, the mayors and local leaders committed to the Global Covenant stand ready to take concrete measures with long-term impact to tackle the interconnected challenges of climate change mitigation, adaptation, and access to sustainable energy.

To implement this vision, the [city/town/village/type of jurisdiction] of [name of city or jurisdiction] pledges to implement policies and undertake measures to (i) reduce / limit greenhouse gas emissions, (ii) prepare for the impacts of climate change, (iii) increase access to

---

sustainable energy, and (iv) track progress toward these objectives. Specifically, within no more than three years of this commitment, we pledge to develop, formally adopt and report on the following:

- A community-scale greenhouse gas (GHG) emission inventory;
- An assessment of climate hazards and vulnerabilities;
- Ambitious, measurable and time-bound target(s) to reduce/ limit greenhouse gas emissions;
- Ambitious adaptation vision and goals, based on quantified scientific evidence when possible, to increase local resilience to climate change;
- Ambitious and just goal to improve access to sustainable energy; and
- Plan(s) to address climate change mitigation / low emission development, climate resilience and adaptation, and access to sustainable energy, including provisions for regular (annual or biennial) progress reports.

The targets and action plans for mitigation / low emission development must be quantified and consistent with or exceed relevant national commitments defined through the relevant UNFCCC [United Nations Framework Convention on Climate Change] (Intended) Nationally Determined Contribution (NDC).

We acknowledge that there may be additional region- or country-specific commitments for us to adhere to, agreed through our local membership networks or through our direct engagement with local Global Covenant of Mayors partners.

The [city/town/village/type of jurisdiction] of [name of city or jurisdiction] acknowledges that continued membership in the Global Covenant of Mayors and associated local chapters or "Regional Covenants" as established, is contingent on complying with the above requirements within established timeframes.

Source: Global Covenant of Mayors for Climate & Energy, https://www.global covenantofmayors.org.

impact that can be had at a City level despite shocking inaction from State and National Governments.[3]

San Francisco mayor London Breed stated,

> Our greenhouse gas emissions peaked in 2000, [and] since then, we've successfully reduced them by 30% from 1990 levels, while growing our economy by 111% and increasing our population by 20%. But in order to fully realize the ambitions of the Paris Climate Accord, we must continue to make bold commitments and accelerate actions that reduce emissions and move us towards a clean energy future. That is why, in addition to formally joining the Sierra Club's nationwide clean energy campaign, San Francisco is committing to reducing landfill disposal by 50% by 2030 and ensuring all of our buildings are net-zero emissions by 2050.[4]

As of 2019, over 200 U.S. cities and counties had committed to over 500 climate actions through the United Nation's Global Climate Action portal (see figure 1.2). In the last decade, the field of climate action planning has rapidly advanced from the commitment and planning phase to the implementation phase. Many communities are now showing success in both reducing GHG emissions and becoming more resilient.

Local action is also occurring on climate adaption. One of the most notable global initiatives was 100 Resilient Cities (100RC), started by the Rockefeller Foundation. The 100RC program sought to embed the urgency of climate adaption within the broader social, cultural, and economic issues of the city. Becoming a resilient city isn't just responding to climate change; it is also addressing such issues as food security, access to jobs, and social justice to create a resilient community in the most comprehensive sense. The program provided participant cities with support for hiring a chief resilience officer (CRO), developing a resilience strategy, and accessing a global network of partners and fellow cities. Most of the participant cities have now completed resilience strategies and hired a CRO. In Norfolk, Virginia, the CRO is directing an effort "to transform an area of highly concentrated poverty adjacent to downtown into a vibrant mixed-income and mixed-use neighborhood."[5]

Figure 1-2 U.S. cities and counties committed to climate action as reported on the Global Climate Action platform (as of January 2019)

Source: United Nations Framework Convention on Climate Change, http://climateaction .unfccc.int/.

Also at the local level, many U.S. colleges and universities are leading the way in climate action planning. As of early 2019, nearly 500 U.S. colleges and universities had committed to climate action through the Second Nature Climate Leadership Network. Many of these colleges and universities have pledged to assist their local communities in pursuing their own climate action goals. There is a great opportunity for communities to partner with their local colleges and universities to share knowledge and resources and engage in collaborative planning.

The tremendous variety of efforts taking place in cities, counties, and colleges and universities to address the problem of climate change is impressive and suggestive of the need to establish "best practices" in this field of planning for GHG emissions reduction and climate change adaptation. This book provides basic guidance on conducting local climate action planning, including the preparation of climate action plans and other policies and programs. The information in the book should be useful to cities, counties, colleges and universities, tribal governments, and other local government entities, since the basic climate action planning process is the same. Although climate action is needed at higher levels of government as well—states, nations, and international organizations—this book focuses on the local level but addresses the linkages across the various scales of action.

What Is Climate Action Planning?

Climate action planning is a strategic planning process for developing policies and programs for reducing (or mitigating) a community's GHG emissions and adapting to the impacts of climate change. Climate action planning may be visionary, setting broad outlines for future policy development and coordination, or it may focus on implementation with detailed policy and program information. Although there is no official process for climate action planning, the most commonly followed has been ICLEI's Cities for Climate Protection Five Milestones.[6] A review of existing guidance and best practice shows that climate action planning is usually based on GHG emissions inventories and forecasts, which identify the sources of emissions from the community and quantify the amounts. Communities usually also identify a GHG emissions reduction goal or target. To reduce emissions and meet the reduction target, climate action planning typically focuses on land use, transportation, energy use, and waste, since these are the sectors that produce the greatest amount of GHG emissions, and may differentiate between community-wide actions (including the public's) and local government agency actions. This book refers to these actions as *emissions reductions* or *reduction strategies* rather than using the terms *mitigation* or *mitigation strategies*. Additionally, many communities now address how they will respond to the impacts of climate change on the community, such as sea-level rise, extreme heat and wildfire, and changes in ecological processes; this is usually referred to as *climate adaptation* (see box 1.2).

The outcomes of a climate action planning process can be documented, codified, and implemented in a number of ways. Many communities have chosen to adopt stand-alone climate action plans (CAPs). Others choose to integrate the developed climate action strategies into comprehensive land use plans, "green" plans, sustainability plans, or other community-level planning documents (see box 1.3). For example, New York City prepared a sustainability plan titled *PlaNYC* that addresses housing, open space, brownfields, and water and air quality as well as climate change. The City

Box 1.2

Defining Emissions Reduction (Mitigation)
and Climate Adaptation

Terminology is not consistent in climate action planning. Two
common terms are climate mitigation and climate adaptation. This
book [*Climate Action Planning*], rather than referring to mitigation
or mitigation strategies, refers to emissions reductions or reduction
strategies as the preferred terminology. Either terminology refers
to actions that reduce the net amount of GHG emissions to the
atmosphere. The objective of emissions reduction is to produce
low-carbon communities.

Climate adaptation refers to actions taken to improve a community's resilience when confronted with impacts of climate change.
This usually includes addressing sea-level rise, changes in weather
and rainfall, and increased susceptibility to natural disasters such
as wildfires, floods, and hurricanes. Climate adaptation planning
is linked very closely to hazard mitigation planning, and this often
creates confusion over terminology. To avoid this confusion, this
book [*Climate Action Planning*] uses the terms climate adaptation
and adaptation. The objective of climate adaptation is to produce
resilient communities.

Climate change is like an imminent car crash.

Mitigation is the brakes—it will reduce the magnitude of the
impact of climate change.

Adaptation is the airbags—it will soften the blow.

We need BOTH to survive the crash intact.

Source: Geos Institute and Local Government Commission, *Integrated Strategies for a Vibrant and Sustainable Fresno County* (March 2011), http://www
.lgc.org/wordpress/docs/adaptation/fresno/Integrated_Strategies_for_Vibrant
_Sustainable_Fresno_County_3011.pdf, 18.

Box 1.3

Types of Local Plans Addressing Climate Change

Communities may choose to address climate change through a variety of local planning documents. The following five are the most common types:

> *Climate action plans:* Stand-alone plans specifically addressing climate change issues and based on local greenhouse gas (GHG) emissions inventories and climate vulnerability assessments.
>
> *Sustainability and "green" plans:* Plans that address a variety of sustainability, "green," or environmental issues but include a climate action section.
>
> *Energy plans:* Plans that focus on energy efficiency and conservation but include a climate action section.
>
> *Adaptation and resilience plans:* Plans that focus on preparing for and adapting to the impacts of climate change and other community stressors.
>
> *Comprehensive/general/community plans:* Community land use plans that include an element or sections that address climate action.

---

of Hermosa Beach, California, integrated climate policy and programs throughout their community general plan. Yet others are acting more incrementally as opportunities arise to integrate climate action, such as during the update of a zoning code or when evaluating investments in coastal infrastructure.

Climate action planning can vary in role and scope based on community context and local vision. *Role* refers to the purpose that the planning serves in the community. *Scope* refers to the topics or issues that the planning process covers. Communities need to consider the following points as they make decisions about the roles and scopes of their own climate action planning. In turn, these decisions should direct the climate action planning process.

Climate action planning performs these functions in a local community:

1. Establishes actions necessary to reduce local GHG emissions and meet desired targets
2. Establishes actions for adapting to climate change–induced impacts and hazards
3. Establishes accountability for action
4. Brings stakeholders together
5. Informs the public
6. Integrates actions from various community plans
7. Integrates actions across different scales (local, regional, state, federal, international)
8. Saves money through energy efficiency and builds the local economy
9. Improves community health and livability
10. Responds to local context and conditions[7]

The following are standard contents of a stand-alone climate action plan and are instructive of what to address in any climate action planning initiative (also see box 1.4):

1. Background on climate change and potential impacts, including a climate vulnerability assessment
2. An inventory and forecast of local GHG emissions
3. Goals and objectives, including GHG emissions reduction targets
4. Emissions reduction strategies (quantified, based on the best available science, and appropriate for the jurisdiction) that cover energy, transportation, solid waste, and land use
5. Adaptation strategies (based on the best available science and appropriate for the jurisdiction)
6. An implementation program, including assignment of responsibilities, timelines, costs, and financing mechanisms
7. Monitoring and evaluation programs

Climate action planning has two technical or quantitative tasks that can be challenging to complete: GHG emissions accounting and

Box 1.4

Example of a Climate Action Plan Table of Contents

City of Encinitas, California, Climate Action Plan

1. Introduction
   1.1. Climate Action Plan Overview
   1.2. Introduction to Climate Change Science
   1.3. Regulatory Framework
   1.4. Community Action and Co-Benefits
   1.5. Climate Action Plan Update
2. Greenhouse Gas Emissions Inventory, Projections, and Targets
   2.1. Why Prepare a Greenhouse Gas Emissions Inventory?
   2.2. Baseline Inventory
   2.3. Emission Projections
   2.4. Reductions Targets
3. Greenhouse Gas Reduction Strategies, Goals, and Actions
   3.1. GHG Reduction Strategy Framework
4. Implementation and Monitoring
   4.1. Implementation Strategy
   4.2. Monitoring and Updates
   4.3. Ongoing Engagement
5. Climate Change Vulnerability, Resilience, and Adaptation
   5.1. Climate Change Effects and Vulnerability Assessment
   5.2. Current Adaptation Efforts
   5.3. Resiliency and Adaptation Strategies

Source: City of Encinitas, http://www.ci.encinitas.ca.us/Portals/0/City%20 Documents/Documents/City%20Manager/Climate%20Action/Encinitas _Climate%20Action%20Plan_Final_01-17-18.pdf1.

climate vulnerability assessment. GHG emissions accounting includes GHG inventorying, forecasting, and reduction strategy quantification. GHG inventories include identification and quantification of GHGs emitted to the atmosphere from sources within the community over a period of time, usually a calendar year. These emissions are not measured directly; instead, they are estimated based on quantifying community activities and behaviors such as the number of miles driven in vehicles and the amount of electricity consumed by residences and businesses. For example, the City of Hoboken, New Jersey, conducted a GHG emissions inventory using the ICLEI ClearPath tool and determined that the community emitted 415,423 metric tons of GHGs in 2017 (7.5 tons per capita). The emissions sources were split among the residential sector (21%), the transportation sector (33%), the industrial and commercial sector (36%), and the waste sector (10%).[8] The GHG emissions inventory also usually contains projections of future emissions that provide a basis for reduction targets and a benchmark for progress toward achieving them.

There are various approaches for inventorying GHG emissions, but a global protocol has been developed that is now in common use and is considered best practice. Moreover, communities participating in global agreements or reporting protocols may be required to use this protocol. When applied in the U.S., it is actually three related and consistent protocols depending on the use (see chapter 4 for more detail). They are

1. the Global Protocol for Community-Scale Greenhouse Gas Emission Inventories,[9]
2. U.S. Community Protocol for Accounting and Reporting of Greenhouse Gas Emissions,[10] and
3. Local Government Operations Protocol (LGO Protocol).[11]

The complement to the GHG emissions inventory is the development of GHG emissions reduction strategies. Reduction strategies are tied quantitatively to the emissions detailed in the inventory to demonstrate that they help reach emissions reduction targets. Predicting emissions reductions from reduction strategies requires that numerous assumptions be made about future local behavior and the feasibility of implementation for each strategy. For example, the City of Cincinnati, Ohio, identified a reduction strategy in collaborating with "regional bicycling advocates in order to increase bicycle use as a mode of transportation."[12] They then estimated that it would reduce annual GHG emissions by 6,300 tons per year by gathering data on existing and forecasted transportation mode share, average bicycle trip length, and vehicle emissions factors. A key assumption was that this collaboration could achieve a fourfold increase in the percentage of workers over the age of 16 that bike to work. Through future monitoring and evaluation, the City can determine the accuracy of its predictions and make necessary adjustments.

The second technical area of climate action planning is climate vulnerability assessment. This involves first identifying the climate change and associated hazards that a community will be exposed to—for example, sea-level rise, extreme heat, or flooding—and then identifying community infrastructure, assets, and functions that are susceptible to being impacted by these hazards. In addition, communities are now examining how climate impacts will affect various segments of their populations; this is referred to as *social vulnerability assessment.*

There are no formal protocols for assessing climate vulnerability, nor has a clear set of best practices emerged. Nevertheless, several states have prepared guidance and tools, most notably New York and California. The State of New York developed the New York Climate Change Science Clearinghouse to support state and local decision-making.[13] The Clearinghouse includes maps, data, and supporting tools and documents to conduct a vulnerability assessment and prepare plans and policies. The State of California developed the Adaptation Clearinghouse, ResilientCA,[14] to provide climate adaptation and resiliency resources, including the Adaptation Planning Guide and Cal-Adapt, among others. The Adaptation Planning Guide assists local governments in assessing climate vulnerability and developing adaptation plans and policies.[15]

Once GHG emissions inventories and climate change vulnerability assessments are complete, the challenge for the community will be clearer. The community can then begin developing strategies for becoming low-carbon and resilient. GHG emissions reduction strategies usually are in the areas of land use, transportation, renewable energy and clean fuels, energy conservation and efficiency, industrial and/or agricultural operations, solid waste management, water and wastewater treatment and conveyance, green infrastructure, and public education and outreach. Although these categories are fairly consistent across communities, the reduction strategies within the categories vary. Climate adaptation strategies also share common categories such as buildings and infrastructure, human health and safety, economy, and ecosystems with variation among local measures. For climate action strategies to be implementable, they must reflect the local context, including emissions sources and relative amounts, geographic location, climate and weather, natural hazards, existing policy, employment base, transportation modes, development patterns, community history, and local values and traditions. These factors inform decision-making as to which emissions reduction or adaptation strategies are most likely to be locally effective.[16]

Climate action planning often addresses the co-benefits of the emissions reduction and climate adaptation strategies. Co-benefits accrue in addition to the primary climate benefits (see figure 1.3). For example, residential energy efficiency programs often decrease homeowners' power bills, bicycling incentives promote health and recreation, and tree planting improves air quality and community aesthetics. Communities may emphasize co-benefits more than climate benefits to garner broader support for climate action planning. For example, in Knoxville, Tennessee, the award-winning Knoxville Extreme Energy Makeover (KEEM) program is an energy efficiency program aimed at assisting and educating low-income families. The program has reduced energy use, thus lowering residents' bills, and has provided numerous other co-benefits (see figure 1.4): "By investing in homes, creating jobs, supporting local businesses, teaching life-long habits, and improving energy efficiency, KEEM creates lasting and meaningful economic, environmental, and social impacts."[17]

Because climate action planning has novel technical requirements, it is becoming a specialized area of professional practice. In addition to nonprofit organizations that specialize in providing planning guidance and technical assistance—such as ICLEI–Local Governments for Sustainability, C40 Cities, and the Urban Sustainability Directors

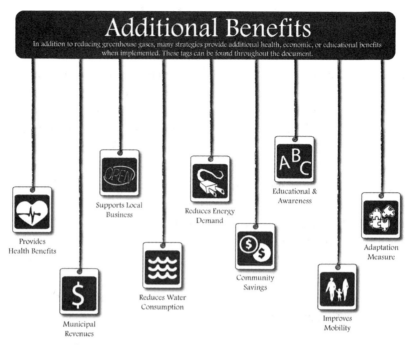

Figure 1-3 Categories of co-benefits identified in the City of San Luis Obispo, California, climate action plan

Source: City of San Luis Obispo, Climate Action Plan (2012), https://www.slocity.org/government/department-directory/community-development/sustainability.

Network—a number of consulting firms specialize in GHG emissions inventories, climate change vulnerability assessments, and climate action planning services. Many communities are creating high-level staff positions to oversee preparation and implementation of climate action and sustainability plans, policies, and programs. Professional associations are offering training and support for members specializing in climate change issues. Colleges and universities are offering classes and certificate programs, and full-degree programs are emerging. This book contributes to this emerging field by guiding climate action planners and others interested in the field through the planning process by identifying the key considerations and choices that must be made in order to ensure locally relevant, implementable, and effective climate action strategies.

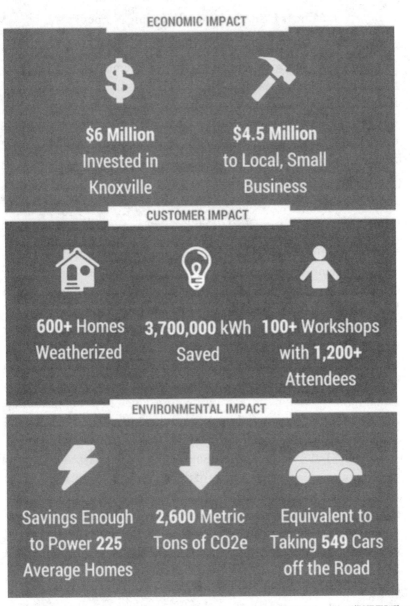

Figure 1-4 Benefits of the Knoxville Extreme Energy Makeover (KEEM) program

Source: "Knoxville Extreme Energy Makeover," City of Knoxville, http://www.knoxvilletn .gov/government/city_departments_offices/sustainability/keem.

Why Is Climate Action Planning Needed?

Climate change is a global phenomenon that cannot be adequately addressed at any one scale. Both reducing GHG emissions and adapting to unavoidable climate impacts require action at the local level as well as the state, federal, and international levels. This section summarizes the science and predicted impacts of climate change globally and in regions of the United States (appendix A provides a discussion of the science of climate change). Following these descriptions are discussions of the need for solutions at the global and local scales.

The Global Problem

Without an atmosphere and the natural greenhouse effect, Earth's average global temperature would be around freezing. When considered in this context, the greenhouse effect is a physical phenomenon on which human life and civilization and other forms of life as we know it depend. The greenhouse effect is due to the presence of carbon dioxide, water vapor, and a few other chemicals in the atmosphere (i.e., GHGs). In the manner of a greenhouse, these chemicals help trap heat and thus keep Earth's temperature within a life-sustaining range. The problem is that human activities such as burning fossil fuels in power plants and automobiles, clearing tropical forests, and operating modern agricultural systems have produced additional GHGs that are accumulating in the atmosphere and generating additional global warming (see figure 1.5).

To better understand the nature of this accumulation and its potential impacts, the United Nations Environment Programme (UNEP) and the World Meteorological Organization (WMO) established the Intergovernmental Panel on Climate Change (IPCC) "to provide the world with a clear scientific view on the current state of climate change and its potential environmental and socio-economic consequences."[18] The IPCC is an international group of over a thousand scientists who review and summarize climate science and issue periodic reports. These reports represent the consensus of these scientists as to the best knowledge we have about climate change. The IPCC, in their 2014 reports, states the following:

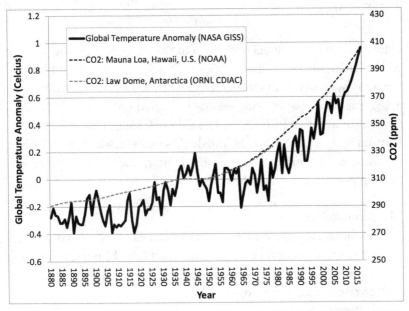

Figure 1-5 Annual global temperature anomaly (NASA GISS) and CO_2 levels from ice cores at Law Dome, Antarctica (ORNL CDIAC), and atmospheric measurements at Mauna Loa, Hawaii, U.S. (NOAA)

Human influence on the climate system is clear, and recent anthropogenic emissions of greenhouse gases are the highest in history. Recent climate changes have had widespread impacts on human and natural systems. . . . Continued emission of greenhouse gases will cause further warming and long-lasting changes in all components of the climate system, increasing the likelihood of severe, pervasive and irreversible impacts for people and ecosystems. Limiting climate change would require substantial and sustained reductions in greenhouse gas emissions which, together with adaptation, can limit climate change risks. These conclusions demonstrate that there is a global problem in both cause and effect.[19]

The Local Problem

Climate change is a global problem, but the impacts of climate change will be felt locally through disruptions of traditional physical, social, and economic ways of life. In some cases, these changes may be positive, such as the lengthening of growing seasons in midlatitudes, but in most cases, they will be negative. In 2018, the U.S. Global Change Research Program released its Fourth National Climate Assessment, which summarizes the impacts of climate change on the United States. The key findings of the report include the following:

1. Communities

    Climate change creates new risks and exacerbates existing vulnerabilities in communities across the United States, presenting growing challenges to human health and safety, quality of life, and the rate of economic growth.

2. Economy

    Without substantial and sustained global mitigation and regional adaptation efforts, climate change is expected to cause growing losses to American infrastructure and property and impede the rate of economic growth over this century.

3. Interconnected Impacts

    Climate change affects the natural, built, and social systems we rely on individually and through their connections to one another. These interconnected systems are increasingly vulnerable to cascading impacts that are often difficult to predict, threatening essential services within and beyond the Nation's borders.

4. Actions to Reduce Risks

    Communities, governments, and businesses are working to reduce risks from and costs associated with climate change by taking action to lower GHG emissions and implement adaptation strategies. While mitigation and adaptation efforts have expanded substantially in the last four years, they do not yet approach the scale considered necessary to avoid substantial damages to the economy, environment, and human health over the coming decades.

5. Water

The quality and quantity of water available for use by people and ecosystems across the country are being affected by climate change, increasing risks and costs to agriculture, energy production, industry, recreation, and the environment.

6. Health

Impacts from climate change on extreme weather and climate-related events, air quality, and the transmission of disease through insects and pests, food, and water increasingly threaten the health and well-being of the American people, particularly populations that are already vulnerable.

7. Indigenous People

Climate change increasingly threatens Indigenous communities' livelihoods, economies, health, and cultural identities by disrupting interconnected social, physical, and ecological systems.

8. Ecosystems and Ecosystem Services

Ecosystems and the benefits they provide to society are being altered by climate change, and these impacts are projected to continue. Without substantial and sustained reductions in global greenhouse gas emissions, transformative impacts on some ecosystems will occur; some coral reef and sea ice ecosystems are already experiencing such transformational changes.

9. Agriculture and Food

Rising temperatures, extreme heat, drought, wildfire on rangelands, and heavy downpours are expected to increasingly disrupt agricultural productivity in the United States. Expected increases in challenges to livestock health, declines in crop yields and quality, and changes in extreme events in the United States and abroad threaten rural livelihoods, sustainable food security, and price stability.

10. Infrastructure

Our Nation's aging and deteriorating infrastructure is further stressed by increases in heavy precipitation events, coastal flooding, heat, wildfires, and other extreme events, as well as changes to average precipitation and temperature. Without adaptation, climate change will continue to degrade infrastructure performance over the rest of the century, with the potential for cascading impacts that threaten our economy, national security, essential services, and health and well-being.

11. Oceans and Coasts

Coastal communities and the ecosystems that support them are increasingly threatened by the impacts of climate change. Without significant reductions in global greenhouse gas emissions and regional adaptation measures, many coastal regions will be transformed by the latter part of this century, with impacts affecting other regions and sectors. Even in a future with lower greenhouse gas emissions, many communities are expected to suffer financial impacts as chronic high-tide flooding leads to higher costs and lower property values.

12. Tourism and Recreation

Outdoor recreation, tourist economies, and quality of life are reliant on benefits provided by our natural environment that will be degraded by the impacts of climate change in many ways.[20]

These changes will vary regionally, so each community will experience a different mix of types and severities of impacts.

Some states have prepared similar analyses of the risks presented by climate change to assist communities in more clearly understanding their own risks. For example, Alaska identified problems such as melting glaciers, rising sea levels, flooding of coastal communities, thawing permafrost, increased storm severity, forest fires, insect infestations, and loss of the subsistence way of life as animal habitat and migration patterns shift and as hunting and fishing become more dangerous with changing sea and river ice.[21] South Carolina is concerned that climate change is a "threat-multiplier that could create new natural resource concerns, while exacerbating existing tensions already occurring as a result of population growth, habitat loss, environmental alterations and overuse."[22] In California, the combined effects of increased drought, wildfires, and floods and rising temperatures and sea levels could result in "tens of billions per year in direct costs, even higher indirect costs, and expose trillions of dollars of assets to collateral risk."[23]

At the local level, cities and counties are identifying their climate risks and developing adaptation strategies. For example, Chicago identified more intense heat waves and responded with changes to the building code, an aggressive tree-planting program, and a revised emergency response plan. Miami-Dade County, Florida, at an average of only 1.8 meters above sea level, has identified sea-level rise as a current problem that will only get worse and has established Adaptation Action Areas for planning and implementation.[24] Aspen, Colorado, is worried about economic impacts to its world-famous ski resorts. The ski season is predicted to start later and end earlier, with a decreased ability to make and maintain snow during the season.[25] For each of these communities, the local problem is very real and provides enough justification to act.

The Need for Solutions beyond the Local Level

Some aspects of emissions reduction and climate change adaptation require action at larger scales. The connected nature of materials flows (including global trade), economic markets, and information results in the need for governmental mandates on national and international scales. These policies level the playing field to alleviate the potential loss in competitive advantage by unilaterally enacting local climate policy. These larger-scale strategies also provide context for local efforts by addressing those emissions sources that fall outside local jurisdictional control.

The most widely recognized of the international efforts to address climate change is the United Nations Framework Convention on Climate Change (UNFCCC). Created in 1992, the UNFCCC now has 197 country signatories who have committed to reducing greenhouse gas emissions and acting on climate change. The history of the UNFCCC is complex, but a number of notable milestones have occurred. The first was the Kyoto Protocol, adopted in 1997. The protocol defined GHG emissions reduction targets and outlined a series of strategies to reach them, most of which are market-based mechanisms, including a cap-and-trade or emissions-trading system. The emissions reduction target, which varied slightly by participating country, averaged 5% below 1990 emissions levels by 2012. This target has been used as the basis for many local climate planning efforts. In addition, Kyoto signatories were required to measure or inventory their emissions and identify strategies to reduce them. The Kyoto Protocol has resulted in an overall reduction in emissions, but these reductions are not uniformly distributed among participating countries or emissions sectors.[26] Between 1990 and 2007, GHG emissions had dropped in some countries, but not in all. There is similar variation among emitting sector and type of GHG. Carbon markets have proved effective for curbing manufacturing emissions but have not resulted in reduced emissions from transportation or energy sectors.

In December 2015, after numerous failed attempts to establish a post-Kyoto agreement, 195 nations—including the U.S.—reached consensus on the Paris Agreement. The basis of the Paris Agreement is a goal of limiting the global average temperature increase to below 2°C and ideally 1.5°C. National governments will achieve this goal by making commitments (called "nationally determined contributions") to take certain actions and achieve certain reductions over time. The Obama administration signed the Paris Agreement and made a commitment to reduce GHG emissions to 26–28% below 2005 levels by 2025, but in 2017, President Trump announced his intention to remove the U.S. from the Paris Agreement.

At the national level in the United States, legislative acts, executive orders, court decisions, and agency rule making have defined the nation's climate change policy. Perhaps most notable have been the decision by the Environmental Protection Agency (EPA) to consider carbon dioxide a pollutant to be regulated, the Clean Power Plan, rule making on automobile efficiency and gas mileage standards, and the failure of Congress to pass a cap-and-trade bill that would further regulate GHG emissions from big industries and utility providers. On climate adaptation, little federal policy direction exists, but President Obama created the Interagency Climate Change Adaptation Task Force to provide recommendations to his administration on this issue. The bottom line is that the U.S. federal government has been doing little on climate change, and the current administration has further reduced federal action in this area.

State-level actions are too numerous to list here. According to the Center for Climate and Energy Solutions, 10 states have carbon pricing (mostly cap-and-trade), 20 have GHG emissions reduction targets, 34 have climate action plans, and 21 have climate adaptation plans. In addition, 26 states have renewable portfolio standards (RPS), which require utilities to produce a certain portion of their electricity from renewable sources.[27] Communities should consult state agencies when doing their own local planning; they may provide information or the opportunity for multiscale coordination of climate action.

These international, national, and state-level actions affect local communities, so it is important that they are considered when developing emissions reduction and climate adaptation strategies. Legislative actions or government programs that increase fuel efficiency, increase renewable energy, incentivize energy-efficient buildings, or mitigate natural hazards provide a foundation on which local climate actions may build.

The Need for Local Solutions

Although solutions for climate change are needed at all levels of government, there is a clear need for action at the local level. Globally, cities consume 75% of the world's energy and emit 80% of the GHGs.[28] These emissions come from the cars and trucks we drive; the houses and buildings we heat, cool, and light; the industries we power; and the city services on which we depend. The impacts of climate change will be felt most severely at the local and regional levels as cities become threatened by rising sea levels or increased risk of flood, drought, or wildfire, for example. Changing the way we build and operate our cities can reduce GHG emissions and make cities more resilient against the impacts of climate change.

Several studies have shown the necessity of action at the local level to reduce GHG emissions. In a study of the Puget Sound region of Washington State, researchers determined that an aggressive set of assumptions about future mandated state or national fuel-efficiency standards (a 287% increase in fleet-wide fuel economy) would still require actions to reduce the number of vehicle miles traveled (VMT) by 20%.[29] Reducing VMT is largely a function of land use planning and alternative transportation availability, which are mostly controlled by local governments. In another study, researchers showed that to reach necessary GHG emissions reductions in the United States, part of the reduction must come from a decrease in "car travel for 2 billion, 30-mpg cars from 10,000 to 5,000 miles per year" and a cut in "carbon emissions by one-fourth in buildings and appliances projected for 2054."[30] These reductions can come from local communities reducing

VMT and requiring that new buildings meet strict energy codes and existing buildings be upgraded.

In the United States, local governments have primary control over land use, local transportation systems, and building construction. Each of these areas is a critical component of climate action planning. Of course, most communities already have plans, policies, and programs that address these issues. For them, climate change is perhaps a new motivation or provides a different approach for pursuing good community planning.

Regardless of the specific purpose or variation of local climate action planning, it is an acknowledgment of the local responsibility for addressing part of the climate change problem (see box 1.5). In fact, one could argue that cities are leading the way in the United States. Federal and state action has been slow to emerge, but many cities are well into implementation of climate action and already helping solve the global problem and ultimately their own local problems.

Why Do Local Climate Action Planning?

We offer eight possible reasons for local climate action planning. Communities may acknowledge all or some of them, and there are likely additional reasons:

- *Global leadership:* Communities acknowledge an ethical commitment as a global citizen to help solve the climate change crisis.
- *Energy efficiency:* Communities want to increase energy efficiency and save money.

Box 1.5

"Why Waiting Is Not an Option," from the City of Cambridge, Massachusetts, 2002 Climate Protection Plan

Because climate systems are complex and we can't predict the nature and extent of the impacts with certainty, some people advocate

---

delaying action. Unfortunately, waiting to resolve the scientific uncertainties in predicting climate could be disastrous.

To slow and eventually reverse global warming, we must lower the concentration or total amount of greenhouse gases in the atmosphere. This means that not only do we have to lower the rate of greenhouse gas emissions, but we have to reduce the total quantity of emissions until they are lower than the rate at which nature removes carbon from the air. Otherwise, the concentration of carbon dioxide and other GHGs will continue to rise as will temperatures. Currently, the rate of human-made GHG emissions is roughly double the rate of removal. Consequently, emissions must fall by at least half to stabilize GHG concentrations at current levels, and even more to lower the concentration. Scientists indicate that ultimately emissions need to fall to 75% to 85% of current levels.

Waiting to take action is dangerous because of the nature of GHGs. When carbon dioxide emitted by a motor vehicle, building furnace, or power plant enters the atmosphere, it will stay there for a long time—50 to 200 years. This means the warming trend cannot be reversed quickly. The longer the wait, the worse the problem becomes.

While uncertainties in predicting how climate will change in the future may cause scientists to overestimate the impact, there are also uncertainties that may cause them to underestimate the impact. For example, it is unlikely that nature will continue to absorb carbon dioxide at current rates; the latest science suggests it will absorb less as natural systems become saturated, and that several factors limit the ability of plants to take up more CO_2.

This plan proposes that rather than gamble that the scientific community is wrong about climate change, Cambridge takes action to reduce emissions by taking advantage of existing technology and resources.

Source: City of Cambridge, Massachusetts, Climate Protection Plan (2002), https://www.cambridgema.gov/~/media/Files/CDD/Climate/climateplans/climate_plan.pdf.

- *Green community:* Communities want to create a sustainable or green image for the community, possibly to promote tourism or economic development.
- *State policy:* Communities want to be consistent with state policy direction, sometimes due to incentive programs or looming mandates.
- *Grant funding:* Communities want to gain access to funding that depends on having climate action policies and programs in place.
- *Strategic planning:* Communities want the opportunity to organize disparate sustainability, green, and environmental policies under one program for ease of management and implementation.
- *Public awareness:* Communities want to raise public awareness of the climate change issue and build support for more ambitious future efforts.
- *Community resiliency:* Communities that have recognized their vulnerability to the impacts of climate change are seeking greater resilience.

What Is Happening in Climate Action Planning?

Climate action planning is occurring all over the United States in a wide variety of communities. As noted earlier, there are over 200 U.S. cities and counties committed to climate action. The communities doing climate action planning are a diverse bunch and defy the typical stereotypes of liberal or green. They range from small towns to global cities and include communities in all four U.S. regions and nearly every state. They are places varying from Des Moines, Iowa, a Midwestern city known for its financial sector and majestic state capitol, to Atlanta, Georgia, a major metropolis that is a hub of the economy in the southeast U.S. and the birthplace of Martin Luther King Jr. and the civil rights movement. They include San Luis Obispo, California, a small city that is home to the highly regarded California Polytechnic State University, and Charleston, South Carolina, a historic community on the Atlantic Ocean. There is no typical climate action planning community.

To further illustrate the diversity of climate action planning in the United States, four cases of local climate action planning are presented here, and chapter 9 provides in-depth examinations of seven other communities. These communities are very different from each other, but they have all decided to address the problem of climate change and create low-carbon, resilient communities. They illustrate the kinds of climate action planning under way, the level of innovation occurring in communities, and the range of challenges and opportunities present in communities.

The City of Des Moines, Iowa

Des Moines is a capital city of 217,000 people located in central Iowa along the banks of the Des Moines and Raccoon rivers. It demonstrates a Midwestern pragmatism toward addressing a global challenge in a way that makes sense to and supports the community. In 2016, Mayor Frank Cownie committed the City to reducing its energy consumption 50% by 2030 and becoming carbon-neutral by 2050. The following year, Mayor Cownie joined the Global Covenant of Mayors, committing to set targets for greenhouse gas emissions reductions, conduct a climate vulnerability assessment, and implement mitigation and adaptation measures.

The City's focus has been on energy efficiency and includes these notable actions:

- In 2007, the City Council adopted the Energy Efficiency and Environmental Enhancement Policy.
- The City Council committed to reducing greenhouse gas emissions 28% by 2025 in the *Des Moines Strategic Plan 2015-2020-2031*.
- In 2016, the City of Des Moines became part of the City Energy Project.
- The City of Des Moines is leading by example by
    - benchmarking energy use in 30 of the largest and most often occupied city buildings,
    - developing a municipal building energy efficiency plan to improve efficiency in underperforming buildings, and
    - continuing to measure and manage energy and water efficiency for ongoing improvements.[31]

They have also launched the Energize Des Moines Challenge. The goal is to reduce energy and water consumption in the nearly 900 buildings greater than 25,000 square feet. Building owners and managers who choose to participate in the challenge must benchmark their energy use, identify and implement energy conservation measures, and report progress. Participants receive technical support from the Energize Des Moines team and the utility provider MidAmerican Energy. This is good for the City's goals and good for businesses' bottom lines.

The City has also established the Citizens' Taskforce on Sustainability to engage the community and advise the City on issues of climate change and the broader issue of sustainability. They have partnered with organizations such as 1000 Friends of Iowa, Greater Des Moines Habitat for Humanity, Iowa State University, and the Martin Luther King Jr. Neighborhood Association. They have supported the City in its launch of a climate action planning process.

The City of Atlanta, Georgia[32]

Atlanta is a capital city of 420,000 at the center of a metro region of over 6 million. The City has followed an uneven path toward climate action as it learned more about itself and the best way to make real change. In 2010, the Atlanta Mayor's Office of Sustainability began the process of creating a citywide climate action plan. They prepared a GHG emissions inventory, conducted stakeholders participation sessions for over 300 individuals representing a diverse set of community interests, and developed strategies in 10 action areas. In 2015, the City adopted the *Climate Action Plan* and set out to implement the key strategies, including several energy initiatives that began in the prior decade.

The following year, in 2016, the City became a member of 100 Resilient Cities and hired its first chief resiliency officer. The Office of Sustainability was also reorganized and renamed the Office of Resilience (under the mayor's office). The first order of business was to collect input from more than 7,000 residents from 40 public events, conduct 25 Neighborhood Planning Unit meetings, and work with a 100-member advisory group composed of the business, faith-based, nonprofit, academic, and civic engagement communities. This incredible public participation effort resulted in the creation of the *Resilient Atlanta* plan, which "serves as a roadmap to better prevent and adapt the city to the challenges of the 21st century, which include extreme climate events such as major floods or heat waves, terrorist threats, and long-term chronic stresses such as income inequality, lack of affordable housing, or the effects of climate crisis."[33] Notably, the plan goes beyond just climate change and addresses a host of short- and long-term stressors for the city. In the *Resilient Atlanta* plan, we see the increasing integration of climate action with broader city goals. It now serves as an overarching plan for coordinating a variety of climate and energy plans and strategies such as the *Climate Action Plan* and the *Clean Energy Atlanta* plan.

The goal of the *Clean Energy Atlanta* plan is for city operations to achieve 100% clean energy by 2025 and community-wide 100% clean energy by 2035. There are many possible pathways to achieving the 100% clean energy goal, but all are a combination of three key strategies: consuming less electricity through investing in energy efficiency, generating electricity from renewable sources, and purchasing renewable energy credits. Atlanta has responded to opportunities to broaden climate action beyond just GHG emissions reduction; it is striving to create a low-carbon, resilient community.

The City of San Luis Obispo, California[34]

San Luis Obispo is a small city of 47,000 on the Central Coast of California. The City has been addressing climate change in various ways since 2006 but recently made bold decisions to accelerate climate action. In 2008, the City joined ICLEI–Local Governments for Sustainability and the following year completed its first GHG emissions inventory. In 2012, the City adopted its first climate action plan with a goal to reduce emissions to 1990 levels by 2020. In 2017, the City adopted "climate action" as a "Major City Goal" to direct policy and budgeting decisions. The plan and goal facilitated a number of actions:

- hiring of a full-time sustainability manager
- establishing a "green" team for implementation

- committing to create a community choice energy program
- updating the climate action plan
- formalizing a partnership with the community climate coalition

The city sustainability manager is a full-time position within the city manager's office. The responsibilities are for the overall administration, development, and management of environmental sustainability and climate action policies and programs. The location within the city manager's office ensures that climate action is seen as a citywide initiative, not just the purview of the community development or public works departments. The City has also formed a Green Team made up of representatives from city departments to assist the sustainability manager in planning and implementation.

In late 2018, the City became a formal partner in Monterey Bay Community Power. In California, local governments may form their own collectives for purchasing energy to provide to local residents and businesses rather than having them get power from private utilities. This way they can accelerate the purchase of renewable and low-carbon energy sources faster than state mandates on the private utilities and retain greater control for local energy rates and choices. Many California communities are now doing this, and San Luis Obispo's plan is to move quickly to 100% carbon-free electricity.

Most recently, Mayor Heidi Harmon and the city council unanimously voted to pursue a carbon-neutral goal by 2035 for the City; this is one of the most aggressive city goals in the world. The City has begun the process of updating its climate action plan to build on its numerous successes and achieve its goal of carbon neutrality. The City will partner with a community-led climate coalition to develop and implement the plan.

The City of Charleston, South Carolina[35]

Charleston is a midsize city of 135,000 people with a historic waterfront downtown. In October 2015, the city experienced significant flooding associated first with Hurricane Joaquin and then later in the month with a peak astronomical tide. The hurricane did not make landfall, but it dropped over 11 inches of rain in 24 hours and a total of 20 inches of rain over several days. The high tides later in the month peaked at nearly nine feet, impacting an already drenched city. The following year, in October, Hurricane Matthew swept over the city, dropping as much as 11 inches of rain, driving over six feet of storm surge, and breaching a flood wall. Currently the city averages 11 tidal flooding events per year, and this is forecasted to increase to nearly 180 events per year by 2045. Charleston is already experiencing natural disasters that have been exacerbated by climate change, and the future looks daunting, especially if hurricane intensities increase with warming oceans.

Yet the City is not discouraged. In 2016, they adopted their first *Sea Level Rise Strategy* and are in the process of updating it. The first strategy identified 76 actions, of which 27 are in progress. The City has begun to better educate the public on the challenge, develop better tools for monitoring and forecasting flooding, develop in a more resilient manner, and prepare for better emergency response. In addition, it is investing $235 million in improving its old, undersized flood drainage system. It has also hired its first chief resiliency officer to help guide and oversee much of the climate action work. It has worked closely with NOAA on technical studies in particular to use the NOAA Sea-Level Rise Viewer for impact assessment and scenario planning.

The City isn't only focused on responding to the impacts of sea-level rise; it has also sought to reduce emissions through the creation of the *Green Charleston Plan*. The plan is truly a community effort: "All told, more than 6,000 person-hours have been dedicated to this plan by more than 800 representatives of local and regional businesses, agencies, and organizations. More than two dozen City staff members contributed their expertise. Participants were professionally and politically diverse. The process was inclusive, with newcomers continuing to join the group until the plan's completion."[36] The plan establishes GHG emissions reduction goals of 30% by 2030 and 83% by 2050 and includes quantified reduction strategies to get to the 2030 goal.

To make all this work for everyone in the community, the City established the Resiliency & Sustainability Advisory Committee, made up of community stakeholders, to advise the city council. The City is taking the problem of climate change seriously and leveraging all available resources to develop and implement solutions.

Overview of the Book

This book describes the climate action planning process and methods for achieving low-carbon, resilient communities. The book is a practical how-to guide that directs the reader through principal steps and critical considerations. At the end is a list of additional resources on climate action planning. In the book, we advance the theory that the best climate action planning process is based on sound science, public education and outreach, recognition of global context and external constraints, and integration with existing policies and programs.

Chapter 2 lays out a framework for getting started on climate action planning, including identifying issues of community commitment and partnerships, determining costs and timing, staffing, creating a climate action team, and auditing existing policies and programs.

Chapter 3 establishes principles and practices for developing community participation methods, including the important task of educating the public about this new and challenging public policy issue.

Chapter 4 describes best practices for GHG emissions accounting and includes advice on choosing software, acquiring and managing data, developing inventories and forecasts, and establishing emissions reduction targets.

Chapter 5 focuses on a process for identifying and evaluating measures to reduce the amount of GHGs the community is emitting. The chapter includes numerous examples of how tailoring measures to particular community contexts and capabilities is the key to successful implementation.

Chapter 6 details a process for conducting a climate change vulnerability assessment, laying the foundation for eventual adaptation strategy development. The chapter addresses climate impacts, community assets, and vulnerable populations.

Chapter 7 addresses climate adaptation strategy development, shows the link between resilience and local hazard mitigation planning, and summarizes adaptation strategies commonly used to address climate impacts, including examples from communities preparing for the short- and long-term impacts of climate change.

Chapter 8 provides guidance on successful plan implementation, including timing and financing measures and monitoring outcomes.

Chapter 9 presents seven case studies that show how communities have put this all together to develop effective climate action strategies.

Chapter 10 presents our closing thoughts about the potential for local climate action planning to positively transform the way we live, work, and play.

Finally, there are two appendices that address the science of climate change and public participation.

Chapter 2

Creating a Framework for Community Action

G etting started can be the most challenging step of any new planning process. Although climate action planning includes many of the traditional steps in a comprehensive planning process, it presents a set of distinct challenges. Climate action planning requires greenhouse gas (GHG) emissions accounting, including inventories, forecasts, and quantification of reduction strategies. It also requires a climate change vulnerability assessment. Climate action strategy development requires technical expertise and detailed data from a variety of sources not usually drawn upon for many types of local plans, which places an added informational and organizational burden on climate planning efforts.

It is important that a community completes several preliminary steps in the climate action planning process before working on the core components. These preliminary steps warrant special consideration, as they will serve as the foundation for the overall climate action planning process. Communities can usually initiate and complete these steps without external assistance from technical experts or consultants. The steps presented in this book are based on traditional steps for comprehensive planning and include observations from a review of climate action planning processes and evolving best practices. They are primarily written for an audience of local government professionals leading a climate action planning effort but are readily transferable to other organizations that may be leading the effort.

This book proposes a three-phase climate action planning process: phase 1, "Preliminary Activities"; phase 2, "Climate Action Strategy Development"; and phase 3, "Implementation and Monitoring" (see box 2.1). Although the steps are presented in numerical order, many of them overlap or are iterative; thus they should be applied as general organizing principles rather than a stepwise "cookbook" for planning. This chapter provides an overview of the phases and describes phase 1 (except public education and outreach, which are covered in chapter 3). Phase 2 is described in chapters 4, 5, 6, and 7, and phase 3 is described in chapter 8.

In phase 1 ("Preliminary Activities"), the community makes a clear commitment to climate action; builds community coalitions and partnerships; establishes the goals of the planning process; assembles a climate action team; makes logistical choices such as identifying a funding source, a timeline, and a manager (e.g., city, consultant, stakeholder, task force); develops a public outreach and education program; and conducts an audit of existing community policies and programs. The order of these preliminary tasks is not critical and will vary based on community needs. For example, in some communities, political commitment may be secured after partnerships have been formed. In others, time and funding considerations may affect the goals.

In phase 2 ("Climate Action Strategy Development"), the community conducts a baseline GHG emissions inventory, develops an interim forecast of future GHG emissions, conducts a climate change vulnerability assessment, establishes a vision and goals (including GHG emissions reduction and adaptation targets), and develops, evaluates, and specifies climate action strategies. This phase is usually iterative; often the GHG emissions forecast is adjusted based on the policy audit, and the goals may be adjusted as the community evaluates potential strategies.

In phase 3 ("Implementation and Monitoring") the community develops and administers an implementation program, implements the adopted policies and strategies, monitors and evaluates implementation, reports

---

Box 2.1

Climate Action Planning Process

Phase 1: Preliminary Activities

1. Make a community commitment.
2. Build community partnerships.
3. Establish planning process goals.
4. Assemble a climate action team (CAT).
5. Consider the logistics of the planning process.
6. Establish a public education and outreach program.
7. Audit existing community policies and programs.

Phase 2: Climate Action Strategy Development

8. Conduct a baseline GHG emissions inventory and interim forecast.
9. Conduct a climate change vulnerability assessment.
10. Formulate vision, goals, and targets.
11. Develop, evaluate, and specify climate action strategies.

Phase 3: Implementation and Monitoring

13. Develop and administer an implementation program.
14. Monitor, evaluate, and report implementation.
15. Modify and update the strategies.

---

progress to the community and any reporting platforms, and then modifies and updates the strategies based on the evaluation and the changing policy environment. The last two steps are critical but often overlooked.

These three phases of the climate action planning process reinforce each other. When moving through these steps, it is important to adhere to principles for a good planning process, such as transparency and documentation, participation, justification, and consistency (see box 2.2). Given this is a new area of planning, communities need to be willing to experiment, innovate, change course, admit failures, and promote successes. The freedom to develop and implement aggressive, innovative emissions reduction and climate adaptation strategies in phase 2 relies on the strength of the organizational steps taken in phase 1 and the feedback loop provided by phase 3. Experimentation and innovation are only possible with careful monitoring and a firm commitment to revise and adapt strategies based on observed effectiveness.

Make a Community Commitment

Chapter 1 outlined several reasons a community may want to pursue local climate action planning. These include the critical nature of the global climate change problem and the need for immediate action. Some communities act out of self-preservation, some from external mandates, and some due to a sense of responsibility to the global community. Regardless of the reason, the commitment to climate action planning should be established through a formal mechanism. Many communities have accomplished this by the mayor signing the Global Covenant of Mayors for Climate & Energy Commitment (or previously, the U.S.

Box 2.2

UN-Habitat's Guiding Principles for City Climate Action Planning

Ambitious

Setting goals and implementing actions that evolve iteratively towards an ambitious vision

Inclusive

Involving multiple city government departments, stakeholders, and communities (with particular attention to marginalized groups), in all phases of planning and implementation

Fair

Seeking solutions that equitably address the risks of climate change and share the costs and benefits of action across the city

Comprehensive and Integrated

Coherently undertaking adaptation and mitigation actions across a range of sectors within the city, as well as supporting broader regional initiatives and the realization of priorities of higher levels of government when possible and appropriate

Relevant

Delivering local benefits and supporting local development priorities

Actionable

Proposing cost-effective actions that can realistically be implemented by the actors involved, given local mandates, finances, and capacities

Evidence-Based

Reflecting scientific knowledge and local understanding, and using assessments of vulnerability and emissions and other empirical inputs to inform decision-making

Transparent and Verifiable

Following an open decision-making process, and setting goals that can be measured, reported, independently verified, and evaluated

Source: United Nations Human Settlements Programme (UN-Habitat), *Guiding Principles for City Climate Action Planning, Version 1.0* (Nairobi, Kenya: Author, 2015).

Mayors Climate Protection Agreement) and joining a national or international organization such as ICLEI or C40 Cities, by elected officials passing resolutions, or by community leaders issuing proclamations supporting the commitment to addressing climate change. These are all positive steps for a community, but it is important that they move beyond symbolic gestures and rhetoric to specific action.

In addition to formally committing to address climate change, two steps are necessary to move forward with planning. First, the local government must establish work program priorities and then commit staffing, funding, and resources to climate action planning. Whether the local government is leading the planning effort or not, its commitment is necessary. The second is to secure formal commitments of funding, technical expertise, or political support from relevant private and nonprofit organizations. The cooperation and coordination of local government and community partners constitute a successful formula that has been used by most communities engaged in climate action planning.

Build Community Partnerships

Communities engaging in climate action planning should develop partnerships with entities such as government agencies, community associations and nonprofits, colleges and universities, and neighboring communities (see below). Partners can help with data collection, community education and outreach, stakeholder mobilization, implementation, and monitoring (see box 2.3). They may also help reduce the costs of planning by donating volunteer hours, providing needed expertise on specific issues, and enhancing the effectiveness of implementation. A successful planning process built on partnerships can also increase the visibility and credibility of climate action. This helps with implementation in the community.

Potential Community Partners for Climate Action Planning

Government Agencies
• regional and environmental, transportation, and planning agencies
• public health agencies
• water resources agencies

Community Associations and Nonprofits
• chambers of commerce (representing local employers)
• builders' associations
• realtors
• environmental groups
• homeowners' associations
• green building groups
• bike and pedestrian advocacy groups
• private utilities

Colleges and Universities
• city planning departments
• architecture and landscape architecture departments
• public policy and administration departments
• geography departments
• business departments
• agricultural departments
• engineering departments
• science departments

Neighboring Communities
• cities
• counties
• townships
• indian tribes
• special districts and authorities
• military bases
• federal lands
• state lands

When identifying potential partnerships, communities should look to existing planning or implementation partnerships as a starting point. For example, many cities already have formal partnerships among public, private, and nonprofit transit, housing, and social service providers. Also, some communities participate in county and regional cooperative efforts on transportation planning and funding, emergency management and

Box 2.3

Partnership Examples

The City of Aspen (Colorado) created a community partnership as part of the Canary Initiative (City of Aspen Climate Action), which includes 13 organizations, including Aspen Global Change Institute, Aspen School, District Black Hills Energy, Colorado Communities for Climate Action, Citizen's Climate Lobby, Colorado Compact of Communities, and the Community Office for Resource Efficiency. These organizations served to help create, update, and implement strategies in the City's climate plan.[1]

The City of Cleveland developed an extensive network of collaborators to develop and implement its 2018 climate action plan. These collaborators included a group providing technical expertise, over 300 local community leaders, and a climate action advisory committee that included religious, educational, governmental, and nonprofit organizations. These collaborators play a critical role in the envisioned implementation by providing feedback, education and outreach, and funding.[2]

The City of Reno, Nevada, has taken action in recent years focused on sustainability, climate adaptation, and greenhouse gas reduction. To identify strategies and implement actions, several partnerships have been established; for example, the City is working with the local utility on energy efficiency. These efforts also include a focus on workforce development and social justice pursued through partnerships with the University of Nevada–Reno,

1. City of Aspen, *Climate Action (Canary Initiative)* (2017), https://www.cityofaspen.com/518/Climate-Action-Canary-Initiative; City of Aspen *Aspen's Climate Action Plan* (Aspen, CO: Author, 2017), 55, https://www.cityofaspen.com/DocumentCenter/View/1893/Aspens-Climate-Action-Plan-2018-2020.
2. City of Cleveland, Climate Action Plan (Cleveland, OH: Author, 2018), 82, https://drive.google.com/file/d/1Z3234sMp7S7MjaXvMgcZtcAaYs4x2oHE/view.

the Washoe County School District, and the Economic Development Authority of Western Nevada (EDAWN).[3]

The City of San Luis Obispo adopted an aggressive GHG reduction goal—carbon-neutral by 2035—in 2018. In support of this aim, a community climate action coalition was established and filled with interested, committed community members. Shortly after being established, the coalition, now called the SLO Climate Coalition, signed a memorandum of understanding with the City and was assigned a city council member to serve as a liaison. The task force serves in educational and motivational roles in the city and has become a key collaborator with the City staff as they develop strategies to reach the City's goals.[4]

3. Randy Rodgers, "Reno Brings Sustainability to the Wild West," Sustainable City Network (2019), https://www.sustainablecitynetwork.com/topic _channels/policy/article_75f2b638-0496-11e9-8cbc-8b88b60233b9.html.
4. SLO Climate Coalition, *San Luis Obispo (SLO) Community Climate Action Task Force Charter* (2018), 3, http://www.slocity.org/home/ showdocument?id=19346; City of San Luis Obispo, *SLO Climate Coalition* (2018), https://www.slocity.org/government/department-directory/ city-administration/sustainability/slo-community-climate-task-force.

hazard mitigation, air quality, public health, and stormwater management. These partnerships can be leveraged to assist in climate strategy preparation and implementation. They also ensure alignment with other local and regional efforts. This consistency increases the likelihood of successful implementation.

Once potential partners are identified, it is reasonable to consider the pros and cons of the partnership and ask the following questions:

- What is their reputation?
- What experiences have other groups had working with them?
- How may they affect the legitimacy or respectability of the planning process?
- What resources do they bring—knowledge, data, money, labor?

Choosing the Type of Partnership

Partnerships in climate action planning must define responsibilities. There are a variety of questions regarding responsibility, including the following: (1) Who will be responsible for managing the climate action planning process? and (2) Who will be responsible for implementation? These roles can be filled by a local government agency or a nongovernment community-based organization and may be shared or divided between process management and implementation. The advantages of a government-led approach are that local governments have regulatory and taxing authority and usually the legitimacy to successfully implement strategies. The disadvantage is that the process may become enmeshed in local government politics, may be superseded by other local priorities, or may succumb to fiscal pressures. The advantages of a nongovernment-led approach are the potential to build strong grassroots support and relief from the potential legal or political complications. The disadvantages are the lack of a clear implementing authority and the potential for conflicts between disparate community organizations. Regardless of this choice, local governments and community-based organizations should seek each other out, settle the responsibility issue, and commit to a partnership.

In many communities, umbrella groups form around the issue of climate action planning. These may be government-appointed task forces or committees (mayor-appointed groups are common) or selforganized. They may be focused on technical expertise in areas such as climate science, city planning, alternative transportation, energy efficiency and renewable energy, public health, emergency management, and finance. Or they may be focused on bringing together diverse stakeholders within the community, such as environmentalists, business and industry representatives, energy and utility providers, developers and builders, alternative transportation advocates, and homeowners' associations.

The role of each partner should be established early in the process to avoid confusion, duplication, and turf battles. There are numerous roles to play that can be clarified by asking the following questions:

• Will partners have an advisory role? In this case, their role is to assist in developing the strategies and to review and comment on proposals.

- Will partners have an oversight role? In this case, their role is to critically review proposals, make decisions, and provide a final endorsement of the approach.
- Will partners provide technical or implementation assistance? Partners may have specialized knowledge in an area critical to the preparation of climate action strategies, or they may have experience in implementing community programs.
- Will partners provide funding? Partners may have funding available for strategy preparation or implementation.
- Will partners conduct education and outreach efforts? Partners can use their networks, memberships, and community standing to provide education and outreach during both planning and implementation.

PARTNERSHIPS WITH COMMUNITY AND NONPROFIT ORGANIZATIONS

Community and nonprofit organizations often partner with government agencies to prepare and implement climate strategies. Community organizations may include nonprofits, advocacy groups, foundations, and business associations. These organizations often fill a critical role in strategy development because many of the GHG emissions reduction and adaptation strategies rely, at least in part, on behavior change, such as increased bicycle ridership, which reflects overall community awareness and acceptance of alternatives. Close alliances with or support from key local organizations can be critical to building community support for such changes in daily patterns. During strategy formulation, carefully selected local organizations are in an ideal position to provide feedback on measures most likely to be effective. They can assist with outreach and communication to people who might not normally participate in community planning or who may not be aware of climate change issues. In addition, many partners are well positioned to aid in the outreach programs that ensure long-term implementation.

PARTNERSHIPS WITH COLLEGES AND UNIVERSITIES

Since many colleges and universities have prepared plans to address climate change on campus, communities should check in with them to see if the measures being pursued can be coordinated. Colleges and universities can serve as sources of information and provide technical assistance in preparing GHG emissions inventories, vulnerability assessments, and climate action strategies. For example, students from the University of Michigan completed a GHG emissions inventory for the City of Detroit.[1]

Partnerships with Neighboring Communities

Partnering with neighboring communities presents unique challenges and opportunities. Communities can differ in politics, priorities, demographics, wealth, size, government structure and capacity, and a variety of other factors. But collaborating offers an opportunity to share resources, save money, and coordinate on difficult regional issues. In South Florida, the counties of Miami-Dade, Monroe, Palm Beach, and Broward partnered to form the Southeast Florida Regional Climate Change Compact and prepared a regional climate action plan (RCAP), completed in 2012. RCAP 2.0 was released in 2017, drawing on lessons learned over the prior five years and providing a tool for local communities in the region with a broad set of best practices that can be incorporated into local action.[2]

Pros of Partnership with Other Communities
- sharing of knowledge and resources
- potential to save money through efficiencies in planning, strategy development, and implementation
- coordination of actions that address intercity and regional issues, such as transportation

Cons of Partnership with Other Communities
- dependence on other jurisdictions and loss of some control
- inconsistency in vision and policy direction

Establish Planning Process Goals

Communities must determine what they want to achieve through a climate action planning process. Clear definitions of goals in combination with local knowledge such as values, capabilities, politics, and available resources help a community determine the best course of action to achieve those goals. A community may pursue a stand-alone climate action plan or may choose not to develop a separate plan but to integrate climate action strategies into its comprehensive land use plan, sustainability plan, or other planning and policy documents. This can vary from integrating climate action strategies throughout existing chapters, to developing a climate change chapter, to creating an appendix or addendum. All these choices carry different benefits and challenges, meaning the status of the climate action strategies and their positions relative to other local plans and policies must be made based on local context, including existing policy, political climate, and the time and funding available for planning.

As climate action planning becomes more common, communities are considering whether to integrate strategies into their comprehensive land use plan (also called "general plans" and "city master plans"). Updating a comprehensive plan can be a lengthy process. If a jurisdiction would like to ultimately integrate climate policy into its comprehensive plan but does not have the time or funding to do so, in the short term, climate action strategies can be developed that specifically identify areas of the comprehensive plan that should be revised in the future. This does not imply that a community must wait to implement emissions reduction or climate adaptation strategies until the appropriate sections of a comprehensive plan are due for revision. Many of the strategies common to a comprehensive plan already serve to reduce GHG emissions and foster community resilience so that the existing plan may serve as a basis for action.

In addition to the issue of whether to create a stand-alone climate action plan is the decision of whether to prepare strategies that address only local government (i.e., municipal) operations or to prepare a plan that is community-wide. Local government operations strategies only address those things that local governments have direct control over, such as public buildings, government vehicle fleets, public transit, and water and sewer infrastructure. Although local government operations strategies can be a great way to get started and can serve as an example to the community, they only address a very small percentage of a community's total emissions (typically 3% to 8%). This book assumes and advocates for the preparation of community-wide strategies that address both local government operations and community-wide emissions sources, such as residential and commercial energy use, private vehicle use, and industrial and agricultural operations.

Based on the various considerations for the role of climate action planning, a few typical approaches have emerged:

- *Developing a climate action plan as a unifying document:* A community's lack of a climate action plan does not necessarily indicate a lack of action. Many cities have taken aggressive action focused on emissions reduction and climate adaptation through a suite of independently adopted policies. For example, a community may already have a green building ordinance or a renewable energy program. In cases where cities have an array of existing climate-related local policy, a climate action plan can be viewed as a unifying document. In this case, a climate action plan can bring together existing policies under an overarching community goal and guide the development of future policy.

- *Developing a climate action plan as a new policy direction:* In direct contrast to cities that fit in the preceding description, some cities may have no adopted plans or policies that directly address GHG emissions reductions and climate adaptation. In these cases, a climate action plan serves to identify a new policy direction by identifying overarching emissions reduction and climate adaptation goals, policy focus areas requiring feasibility assessment, and extensive education and outreach to the community to build support for future policy development, such as integration into comprehensive plan updates.

- *Developing climate action strategies as a component of a larger sustainability effort:* Climate action strategies, when viewed in the larger context of environmental policy, are narrow in focus. Prior to the emergence of climate action planning, many cities pursued sustainability goals. Climate action strategy development can be viewed as one aspect of an overarching sustainability program.

- *Developing climate action strategies as an additional section or component of a comprehensive community plan:* Implementable climate strategies must be consistent with other local policy. Many climate strategies directly impact building codes, land use patterns, and circulation. The integration of climate-related strategies with local policy such as a comprehensive plan can occur in a variety of ways. Climate change can be identified as an additional component of a comprehensive plan.

Assemble a Climate Action Team (CAT)

Climate action planning is a data-intensive planning process that relies on a number of government agencies or departments and organizations, many of which are unaccustomed to being directly involved in the planning process. Regardless of who is identified to prepare the GHG emissions inventory, vulnerability assessment, and climate action strategies—local government staff members, consultants, or community organizations—one of the first steps in the climate action planning process is the establishment of a forum for interactions between the primary planners and other local government staff members. The ease and accuracy of the GHG emissions inventory, vulnerability assessment, and strategy implementation will rely, in part, on the quality and continuity of the collaboration between primary planners and staff members.

This collaboration can be developed through the establishment of a CAT. The CAT plays two critical roles in the climate action planning process. The first is provision of data needed to complete the GHG emissions inventory and vulnerability assessment. With the completion of these, the role of the CAT changes to advising GHG emissions reduction and adaptation strategy development, assessing feasibility, and in the long-term, implementing the chosen strategies. Thus the CAT serves in both a technical capacity and a policy capacity.

Through a CAT, tasks such as staff education, data collection, operational documentation, and long-term plan implementation and monitoring are completed. Because the establishment of a CAT is an integral part of plan development and implementation, it is critical to assemble the team strategically. This section details CAT formation and the initial steps necessary to lay the groundwork for conducting a GHG emissions inventory, a vulnerability assessment, and subsequent strategy development and implementation.

Team Members

A CAT consists primarily of government staff from a variety of departments that oversee day-to-day operations and activities, including fleet management, accounts payable and contracts, parks and recreation maintenance, facility management, building permit approval, emergency management (including policy and fire), utilities, and long-range planning. Individual members must be well integrated into their respective departments to facilitate and monitor data collection and review materials. Members of a CAT should have some combination of the following characteristics or knowledge areas: (1) familiarity with department operations that will allow for easy identification and collection of the data needed for the GHG emissions inventory and vulnerability assessment, (2) knowledge of department operations and budget procedures to evaluate climate action strategies, and (3) the authority to implement strategies identified in the strategy development process. In a given department, this may require several people.

Identifying departments for inclusion on the CAT begins with identification of needed information and responsibilities. Table 2.1 is a partial list of information to aid government agencies in identifying departments and personnel for the CAT. Based on local context, additional staff and information may be required, such as jurisdictions that include an airport. Staff may not be able to provide all information needed for the emissions inventory and vulnerability assessment. In some cases, a local agency may choose to include members from a partner organization identified as integral to plan development.

The size of the CAT should be limited (e.g., fewer than 20 members) to ensure that the team can foster open dialogue and timely review and response to requests. All staff members who will participate in the strategy development and implementation need not be on the CAT. The CAT should include staff members who are best able to transmit information to colleagues and identify departmental information sources and have an overall understanding of department operations.

In most departments, the best initial point of contact is the director or manager. The director is able to oversee long-term implementation of strategies and, in the short-term, is best positioned to identify the staff who are able to provide the data needed for an emissions inventory or vulnerability assessment. Involvement of department directors or managers also helps ensure the cooperation of all staff within a given department. As the process evolves, staff below the director may play a more direct role in generating data and disclosing operational procedures.

Table 2.1. Needed expertise of a climate action team

Category	Access to data for greenhouse gas emissions inventory	Knowledge of local government policies and operations
Facilities	Energy use (electricity, natural gas) Year built Square footage Number of employees Hours of operation Traffic signal energy use Quantity, location, bulb type, and energy use of streetlights, parking lot lighting, security lighting	Operational procedures Planned and completed energy or water efficiency upgrade Facilities proposed for closure or construction Critical node identification Emergency procedures
Government fleet (including police, fire, transit, general vehicle pool)	Miles traveled Gallons of fuel used Vehicles by make/model/year Refrigerant use/maintenance	Maintenance schedule Fleet replacement/conversion schedule
Employee travel behavior	Daily commute distance Commonly used routes Business travel type and mileage	Daily commute distance Commonly used routes Employee commute reduction programs
Transportation	Vehicle miles traveled on local streets Traffic signal and streetlamp energy use	Transportation infrastructure design guidelines and maintenance Long-term planning (all modes including bicycle and pedestrian infrastructure) Critical node identification

(*Continued*)

Table 2.1. Needed expertise of a climate action team (*Continued*)

Category	Access to data for greenhouse gas emissions inventory	Knowledge of local government policies and operations
Water and wastewater Facilities proposed for closure or construction	Treatment and conveyance energy use Volume treated and conveyed	Pump, blower, and lift station efficiency Critical node identification Emergency procedures
Solid waste	Volume and/or weight delivered to solid waste facility Disposal associated emissions (e.g., landfill methane production) Transport distance	Local diversion rate Existing waste diversion program effectiveness
Parks and recreation	Fuel type and amount for maintenance equipment (mowers, blowers, etc.) Size of area maintained (i.e., park and open space acreage) Water use Fire management activities	Open space and park area and use Maintenance schedule Irrigation infrastructure type Urban forest management Recreational program administration Wildfire procedures and preparation
Administration/finance	Invoices for vendors related to refrigerant replacement, waste haulers, and others as needed Lists of equipment and vehicles Mileage and destinations for employee travel	Cost feasibility evaluation Budget Capital improvement plan/program

(*Continued*)

Table 2.1. Needed expertise of a climate action team (*Continued*)

Category	Access to data for greenhouse gas emissions inventory	Knowledge of local government policies and operations
Long-range planning	Build-out year or horizon year for the comprehensive plan Baseline year of the comprehensive plan Planning area and/or expansion area included in the comprehensive plan	Planned future development Comprehensive plan build-out assumptions Existing policy consistency
Development review		Building and project permit approval process
Economic development		Identification of economic constraints and opportunities

Source: Adapted from ICLEI, *Cities for Climate Protection: Milestone Guide* (Oakland, CA: Author, n.d.); California Air Resources Board, *Local Government Operations Protocol for the Quantification and Reporting of Greenhouse Gas Emissions Inventories Version 1.0* (Sacramento, CA: Author, 2008).

While local government organization structures vary, the following sections include some of the key departments that should be participants in a CAT. These departments are critical not only to the development of a GHG emissions inventory and vulnerability assessment but to long-term implementation of emissions reduction and climate adaptation strategies. The following can be tailored based on government agency size and function, operational control, and organizational structure.

UTILITIES

Most jurisdictions provide all or a portion of basic services such as water, power, and solid waste services through a utilities department, making this department a critical member of the CAT. A utilities department is often the data source for energy use (electricity and natural gas), critical points of vulnerability, and operational procedures. This includes the building operations, the treatment and conveyance of drinking water and wastewater, traffic signals and streetlights, and solid waste generation. CAT members from a utilities department should be aware of operational changes such as the use of motion detectors or thermostat regulation that were implemented as cost-saving measures. If there is a community-owned utility for power, then the department should have access to data on community-wide use of electricity and existing safety procedures. Other information useful to the CAT is the success of existing programs such as recycling and educational programs.

Transportation and Engineering (Public Works)

In the United States, transportation-related emissions are one of the largest contributors to GHG emissions.[3] The transportation department is critical to assembling accurate data for the emissions inventory, particularly estimates of vehicle miles traveled (VMT) on local streets and specifying the ways in which climate impacts may disrupt transportation. In addition, transportation CAT members should be able to provide VMT, fuel use, and cost information for local government fleet vehicles. In the long-term, CAT members should have the authority to change vehicle purchasing procedures to more fuel-efficient models. They will also be key in developing and implementing strategies for the community's transportation infrastructure and management.

Community Development (Planning and Building)

The community development or planning and building departments must be included on the CAT. Depending on who is developing the inventory and plan, community development staff may be tasked with CAT coordination, ensuring that there are no gaps in data or implementation, and overseeing information-gathering efforts that span multiple departments such as employee commute data. Community development staff are also best positioned to aid in the development of the policy audit described later in this chapter. In addition to a coordination role, this department oversees updates to and implementation of a community's comprehensive land use plan and zoning codes. Also, the community development department often houses development review and permitting functions. It is through this process that strategies such as impact fees, energy efficiency programs, or green building programs (for greenhouse gas reduction and adaptation needs) may be implemented; therefore, community development is a critical adviser in the development of these and similar strategies.

PARKS AND RECREATION

Parks and recreation departments often maintain a vehicle fleet, operations and maintenance equipment, parks and recreation facilities, and the structure of parks for natural system health and reduction of hazards such as fire. The parks and recreation staff are often charged with the maintenance of community green spaces such as parks, open spaces, and vegetated areas in the streetscape. Parks and recreation staff help assess fuel, water, and energy efficiency and conservation practices. They also identify opportunities for GHG emissions reductions from parks and open spaces, provide sequestration through tree planting, enable local food access through community gardens, identify potential sites for local alternative energy generation, and manage landscapes for water retention, flood attenuation, and fire reduction.

PARTNER ORGANIZATIONS

Depending on jurisdiction size, services (e.g., water, waste, transit) may be provided by outside suppliers. In this case, data and long-term implementation require the involvement of staff from regional providers or agencies. In addition, partner organizations may have particular expertise that will strengthen plan elements. Where deemed appropriate, a representative from these organizations can be invited to the CAT.

Role of the Team

The CAT's primary role is to contribute to the GHG emissions inventory, vulnerability assessment, policy audit, and strategy development and implementation. Each of these tasks is detailed in a subsequent chapter. However, prior to beginning the climate planning tasks, there is a series of educational steps intended to prepare staff for the climate action planning process. This educational process is ongoing and iterative. It begins as soon as CAT members are identified and recruited.

Potential members may be skeptical of new policy relating to climate change or may feel uncomfortable with increased demands on staff time. The formality required for this initial outreach varies. Greater effort is required to clarify expectations and needs for a department that is hesitant to participate.

The CAT provides a forum for collaborative learning and a support network for staff as they face data acquisition and policy development challenges. While departments will be providing data, they are also expected to disclose operational information that allows the planners to accurately project emissions, quantify GHG-reducing actions already being implemented, identify vulnerabilities, and understand the adaptive actions already being implemented. The process of disclosing current GHG-reducing and adaptive actions allows departments to learn from each other and bolsters participants' confidence in the process. In many cases, these actions are adopted to improve efficiency or to lower costs rather than lowering GHG emissions or adapting to climate change. Identifying these actions clearly demonstrates to participants that climate action planning is compatible with local operations. For example, the City of Benicia, California, established an interdepartmental team dubbed the Green Team. This team included representatives from all City departments. One of the activities organized by the team was a speaker series open to all City staff covering topics related to climate change. These presentations served to raise staff awareness of the intention and utility of climate action strategies.

While the education process is ongoing, there are a few early steps critical to ensuring all participants have a shared understanding of the process and the role of the CAT. These key phases in the CAT educational process are briefly described here.

CLIMATE CHANGE SCIENCE AND POLICY OVERVIEW

Awareness of climate science, emissions-reducing strategies, and climate adaptation strategies will vary among members of a CAT. A critical first step is ensuring a common knowledge base, shared vocabulary, and collective understanding of context. This broad overview can be conducted solely for the CAT or as a series of workshops open to all government staff. These workshops or meetings should cover basic climate science (see appendix A); federal, state, and local policy; and the context in which the jurisdiction sees climate strategies in relation to other local policy. This staff preparation also lays a foundation for future engagement of the community, particularly the potential presence of climate change skeptics or deniers.

CLIMATE ACTION PLANNING PROCESS

It is critical that all participants understand the overall climate action planning process. Throughout the presentation of the process, the role of the CAT should be clearly articulated so that participants are aware of the areas to which they will be contributing. The intention is to provide an overview of the process from project inception to implementation and monitoring. It should provide a clear understanding of the relationship between a GHG emissions inventory, vulnerability assessment, policy audit, and strategy development. It should also cover the time horizon expected for implementation and periodic monitoring and reporting. It is here that the link between basic climate science, policy, emissions estimates, and projected impacts can be made tangible for CAT participants. A presentation of the preliminary strategy development timeline should also be included at this point to clearly communicate the commitment duration expected of CAT members.

GHG EMISSIONS INVENTORY

The details of GHG inventory development are covered in chapter 4. During this introductory process, it is critical to communicate the intent and role of the GHG emissions inventory. An overview of the expected data needs can also be covered. Gathering the data for the emissions inventory can be labor-intensive, with data kept in disparate locations. Obtaining information is easiest if the participating departments understand the needed level of detail and the data's intended use. This can be accomplished through a presentation detailing the GHG emissions inventory process, with specific examples demonstrating the use of requested data. Increased knowledge of the process also allows departments to evaluate if more appropriate or additional staff are necessary for CAT membership.

CLIMATE CHANGE VULNERABILITY ASSESSMENT
Chapter 6 covers the steps and details of a vulnerability assessment. When establishing the CAT, it is critical that the content, role, and intent of a vulnerability assessment be communicated. The vulnerability assessment requires all CAT members to consider their individual department responsibilities to allow identification of the community functions, structures, and individuals that may be affected by climate impacts. This understanding prepares CAT members for the information they will have to collect, some of which may require tracking down colleagues to gather data or gain understanding.

Consider the Logistics of the Planning Process

Communities deciding whether to develop a climate action plan or set of climate action strategies will want to consider factors of cost, time commitment, and needed expertise. GHG emissions inventories require data collection and analysis, specialized software, and personnel with knowledge of government operations and community energy, transportation, and infrastructure data. Vulnerability assessments require climate data acquisition and interpretation and personnel with enough knowledge of government operations and community function to be able to determine how climate impacts may affect them. Development of emissions reduction and climate adaptation strategies may require community education and participation. It will also require specialized knowledge of transportation, energy, building and development, utilities, hazard mitigation, and finance.

Costs Associated with the Planning Process

Communities will vary in their choice of planning process and approach to climate action, so costs will vary. Most of the costs associated with climate action planning come from key activities such as preparing a GHG emissions inventory. Doing this work in-house can save money, but the specific, technical nature of the work may be challenging and lengthy for staff members. Conversely, hiring a specialized consultant can deliver sophisticated and timely results but can be difficult for communities with a limited budget. Table 2.2 provides rough time estimates if done in-house, assuming an initial learning curve, and rough cost estimates if an experienced consultant is hired. The following sections describe key factors that will affect time and cost.

LEVEL OF PUBLIC EDUCATION AND OUTREACH

Since climate change and climate action planning may be relatively new concepts in some communities, a more extensive public education and outreach effort can be required. In addition, the issue of climate change

Table 2.2. Estimates of staff hours or consultant fees needed to complete major climate action planning tasks

Task	Staff hours	Consultant fee
Standard, protocol-compliant GHG emissions inventory and forecast (community-wide)	150 to 200 hours	$5,000 to $15,000
Comprehensive climate change vulnerability assessment	300 to 600 hours	$20,000 to $75,000
Limited public outreach and participation	60 to 100 hours	$10,000 to $20,000
Extensive public outreach and participation	600 to 1,000 hours	$40,000 to $80,000
Development of climate action strategies	80 to 100 hours	$10,000 to $15,000
Quantification of GHG emissions reduction strategies	6 to 15 hours per strategy	$700 to $1,800 per strategy
Implementation and monitoring program	40 to 80 hours	$5,000 to $15,000
Preparation of a full climate action plan (generally includes all of the above plus process management)	1,000 to 2,500 hours	$50,000 to $300,000

Note: These are rough estimates and can vary significantly based on size of the community, availability of data (especially on climate impacts and transportation), existing knowledge of the staff, region of the U.S., and level of detail desired.

is a politically charged one that may raise the level and intensity of participation. Many communities have chosen to spend significant up-front time in educating the community and elected officials on the science of climate change and the climate action planning process. This can be one of the largest time commitments for a community pursuing climate action strategies and can thus drive costs toward the high end of the range. Chapter 3 provides additional detail on development of a public education and outreach process.

PARTICIPATION OF ADVISORY GROUPS

Many communities have chosen to establish formal advisory groups for their climate planning process. Similar to public education and outreach, the role, membership, number, and schedule of the advisory groups will determine the level of staffing necessary. Some advisory bodies may consist of technical experts who are simply reviewing and commenting on drafts and thus require relatively little staff time. Others may be more policy oriented, may require detailed staff reports, and may hold open debates, thereby demanding significant staff time. In some cases, advisory bodies develop a life of their own and exceed initial estimates of staff time commitments.

STATUS AND CONTENT OF THE GHG EMISSIONS INVENTORY AND VULNERABILITY ASSESSMENT

Best practice requires that climate action strategies be based on a GHG emissions inventory and vulnerability assessment. The level of data collection, management, and analysis required is significant. The choices about content and level of detail of the inventory and vulnerability assessment affect costs. Communities will vary in the quality and accessibility of their emissions data and availability of the data needed for the vulnerability assessment. Chapter 4 provides additional detail on development of a GHG emissions inventory, and chapter 6 describes the vulnerability assessment process.

SPECIFICITY OF CLIMATE ACTION STRATEGIES

Climate action strategies vary in their degree of specificity. This is partly based on whether the community is pursuing a more visionary approach or one more focused on implementation. Development of emissions reduction strategies may include quantification, comparison of costs and benefits, and assessment of feasibility. Similarly, adaptation strategies can compare cost, duration of implementation, period of time until a climate impact is experienced, and feasibility. Each of these would require additional time in preparation. Chapter 5 provides additional detail on development of GHG emissions reduction strategies, and chapter 7 discusses adaptation strategy development.

DEGREE OF CONTRIBUTION BY THE CLIMATE ACTION TEAM (CAT)

A CAT provides two benefits that will affect the time and cost of the process. First, CAT members facilitate a positive and cooperative relationship with their departments. This is necessary because climate action planning requires data that may be difficult or time-consuming to provide and that departments may not be used to providing. Second, they have the technical depth of knowledge to contribute to the development of the GHG emissions inventory, vulnerability assessment, and new policies and programs.

LEVEL OF INTEGRATION INTO OTHER PLANNING DOCUMENTS

As already discussed, climate action strategies may be consolidated in a stand-alone climate action plan or can be integrated with other plans and policy documents such as a comprehensive or general plan, a sustainability plan, an energy plan, a zoning code, or a budget. Integration will require additional time to ensure consistency, including amendment of existing plans and documents that may require additional informal and formal review.

LEVEL OF REVIEW REQUIRED

In some states, the climate action strategies may require review in addition to the standard local government resolution. For example, climate action plans prepared in California are subject to environmental review under the California Environmental Quality Act. In Florida, strategies that are integrated into a comprehensive plan will require a plan amendment that is subject to state- and regional-level review. These additional levels of review extend the time frame for adoption and will result in additional costs.

LEVEL OF CONSULTANT SUPPORT

It is increasingly common for communities to hire consultants to assist in or manage the process. Some communities hire consultants to prepare an entire plan, while others will only hire them for specific tasks. When doing the task mostly in-house, common tasks to hire out include the GHG emissions inventory (due to its technical complexity), the vulnerability assessment (due to its reliance on climate change science), and the public education and outreach program (due to the need for specialized expertise).

Time Needed for the Full Climate Action Planning Process

Based on the foregoing process steps and factors, the full process will usually take one to one and a half years. Table 2.3 shows time estimates for each of the process steps. Since some tasks can be completed concurrently, the overall timeline is shorter than the sum of the individual tasks.

Funding Options for Climate Action Planning

A critical issue for climate action planning is how it will be funded. Although some communities have enlisted significant volunteer support for the effort, particularly from colleges and universities, there will likely be some costs incurred. But for most communities, the costs discussed at the top of this section will have a significant impact on the scope and quality of the climate action planning effort. There are several possibilities for funding, including local government general funds, private foundation donations and grants, and state and federal grant programs, but these change often. Communities are best advised to explore all opportunities and talk to other communities about how they funded their planning processes.

Table 2.3. Climate action planning time frame

Phase/task	Time to complete
Phase 1: Preliminary Activities	**3–6 months**
1. Make a community commitment.	1–2 months
2. Build community partnerships.	Ongoing
3. Establish planning process goals.	1–2 months
4. Assemble a climate action team (CAT).	2–3 months
5. Consider the logistics of the planning process.	1–2 months
6. Establish a public education and outreach program.	Ongoing
7. Audit existing community policies and programs.	2–3 months
Phase 2: Climate Action Strategy Development	**9–18 months**
8. Conduct a baseline GHG emissions inventory and interim forecast.	4–6 months
9. Conduct a climate change vulnerability assessment.	4–6 months
10. Formulate vision, goals, and targets.	2–3 months
11. Develop, evaluate, and specify climate action strategies.	6–8 months
Phase 3: Implementation and Monitoring	**Ongoing**
13. Develop and administer an implementation program.	Ongoing
14. Monitor, evaluate, and report implementation.	Every 1–2 years
15. Modify and update the strategies.	Every 2–5 years

Audit Existing Community Policies and Programs

The policy audit assesses preexisting policies, programs, and procedures for consistency with community goals for GHG emissions reduction and adaptation to climate impacts. For example, many communities already have policies and programs aimed at promoting transit use, bicycling, and walking—the same types of goals that may be found in a climate strategy. By going through the audit process, a community can establish the local policy context in which measures must be devised, adopted, and implemented. The policy audit is also a chance for a community to describe the great things it is already doing to address GHG emissions reduction and climate adaptation.

The audit provides useful information for several climate action planning activities. First, many communities will have implemented activities between the baseline emissions year identified in the inventory and the current year. The policy audit provides the information necessary to estimate emissions reductions achieved in that time and forecast the long-term reductions likely to result from those activities. Second, this information can help a community set more realistic emissions reduction targets that account for existing and proposed policies that reduce GHG emissions. Third, the policy audit shows where the community has the adaptive capacity to address climate impacts and where policies are maladaptive. Fourth, the policy audit lets the community clearly identify the gaps in its current policy and program framework. Thus the strategy development process can focus on filling these gaps.

The policy audit typically assesses the local government's policy and operational procedures that may or may not be formally documented. A thorough policy audit requires close collaboration with the CAT, whose members aid in the identification of relevant policy documents and disclose operational procedures. In addition, though not yet common, a community may wish to account for nongovernmental programs that reduce GHG emissions or reduce community vulnerability, such as LED lightbulb giveaway programs from electricity providers or emergency kits and evacuation educational programs offered by nonprofits. The audit seeks to identify policies or programs that already serve to reduce GHG emissions, increase local resilience, and identify policy or programs incompatible with the goals of addressing emissions reduction and climate adaptation. It is best to organize the audit into sections that generally reflect those in the emissions inventory (i.e., transportation, water, energy, etc.) and vulnerability assessment. This division helps in confining assessment to policy that directly impacts emissions sources and climate vulnerability. The following sections explain the local government policies and operations audit.

Adopted Policy

Adopted policy refers to plans, ordinances, and other local government laws that directly influence GHG emissions or adaptive capacity. The content of these policy documents falls into three broad categories: supporting policies that act to reduce GHG emissions, supporting policies that act to reduce local vulnerability to climate impacts, and potentially conflicting policies that either directly conflict with these goals or prevent actions focused on achieving them (see box 2.4). *Supporting policy* identifies positive actions the community is already taking that could be enhanced. *Potentially conflicting policies* identify those areas where plans or other city policies will require amendment to become compatible with climate action goals. It is critical that the evaluation be limited to actions that directly impact GHG emissions and climate vulnerability. It is quite easy, through a series of hypothetical scenarios, to tie any local government policy to GHG emissions or climate vulnerability. The inclusion of farfetched causal links makes the audit convoluted and more difficult to use. It is critical that each policy be tied to items in the GHG emissions inventory and the vulnerability assessment. Table 2.4 lists several of the documents most likely to be important components of an audit of adopted policy.

Identifying current policy is the first step in conducting the audit. Existing policy that supports GHG mitigation and climate adaptation must be further divided based on the level of implementation. Policy that has been or is currently being implemented should be separated from adopted policy that has not been funded or implemented. Implementation can be assessed through examination of funding allocation in the local government budget, periodic reports on implementation of plans, and feedback from the CAT. The CAT is a critical check in ensuring that this division is done accurately.

Operational Procedures

Many of the actions taken by local agencies to address climate change are enacted not only for environmental reasons but also in the interest of efficiency and cost savings. This information can only be obtained through close interaction with the CAT. Many of the procedures may be standard protocol for individual departments. This will include the maintenance schedule for municipal structures, which may entail actions such as replacement of heating, ventilating, insulating, and air

Box 2.4

Example of Supporting and Potentially Conflicting Policy

Policies such as those that encourage energy efficiency and promote walking, biking, or public transportation over automobile trips will directly reduce greenhouse gas emissions. In a few cases, a city's policies and programs support actions that may generate additional emissions, such as those that encourage vehicle travel.

Supporting: General Plan Policy X.X: No urban development beyond the urban growth boundary shall be served by city water and/or sewer services.

This policy is one that ensures dense development, curbing commute distance. Because this action directly influences resident vehicle miles traveled, it should be included in the audit as a supporting policy.

Supporting: Comprehensive Plan Policy X.X: Grading on slopes greater than 30% should not be permitted.

Not grading on steep slopes reduces the risk of landslides and severe erosion hazard events. These two outcomes can increase with climate change, and limiting the slopes where grading can occur reduces local vulnerability to these impacts.

Potentially Conflicting: General Plan Policy X.X: Maintain at least Level of Service D on all city roads, street segments, and intersections.

The most common way to improve roadway Level of Service is to increase capacity, often with an increased number of lanes. While such actions may increase vehicle speeds in the short term, which reduces emissions, in the long term, it can increase vehicular traffic.

Table 2.4. Summary of some of the documents most commonly included in a policy audit

Plans	
Comprehensive Land Use Plan (general plan) Parks, Trails, and Open Space Master Plan Urban Water Management Plan Bicycle and Pedestrian Master Plan Transit Plan Area Plan Downtown Mixed-Use Plan Local Hazard Mitigation Plan	Plans are necessarily broad; therefore, focus should be placed on the lower levels of policy hierarchy (policies and programs as opposed to goals or objectives). The goal is to identify plan elements that directly influence emissions reduction or increase community resiliency from climate change.

Standards, ordinances, programs, and policy	
Zoning Code Green Building Ordinance Water-Efficient Landscape Standards Tree Ordinance Environmentally Friendly Purchasing Policy Traffic Calming Program Floodplain Ordinance	These are the regulations that implement the plans. In these documents one may find the specifics lacking in the plans. The specificity of these regulations allows the assessment to be more nuanced.

Memoranda, feasibility assessments, and other nonbinding statements	
Community Garden Memorandum Energy Efficiency Status Memorandum Feasibility Assessments	While these documents are not enforceable policy, they do provide a good indicator of city perspective and awareness. For example, a city that has conducted a feasibility study on local renewable energy generation may not have installed any renewable energy projects, but the study may signal a political willingness to do so.

conditioning systems or the addition of motion sensors for lighting. It will also include the vehicle fleet turnover schedule and purchasing policy. In many cases, saving money on energy to operate buildings and fuel to power vehicles is motivating these choices, and staff may not initially recognize the benefit in terms of GHG emissions or climate adaptation. Another area to evaluate is employee programs such as transit incentives, office education programs, and environmentally friendly purchasing programs.

Many of the operational procedures will be revealed during the development of the emissions inventory and vulnerability assessment, but some of these programs may have been created in the time since the baseline year. In other cases, they may not be actions that directly affect these reports. For example, an emissions inventory will include energy consumed by municipal buildings. But whether the energy use data are higher or lower than normal due to an education campaign or installation of motion detectors for lighting is irrelevant to the accuracy of the inventory. When strategies are being developed, these data are critical for choosing strategies that reduce energy use.

From Policy Audit to Strategy Development

The policy audit containing a review of adopted policy, guidance documents, and department operations should be submitted to the CAT as well as the departmental staff. This serves as a final check on accuracy by those tasked with implementing the reviewed plans, guidance, and protocols. This also serves to ensure that members of the CAT share a common basis for strategy development, review, and implementation. The policy audit should set the stage for strategy development by identifying areas in which short-term strategies can be most effectively pursued and also where there are gaps in or conflicts with current policies. The policy audit data inform the prioritizing of strategies.

Next Steps

Each community will need to tailor these preliminary activities to its own needs and interests. It is good practice to talk to similar communities that have gone through the climate action planning process about how they got started and what they would do differently in hindsight. Communities that work through the issues raised in this chapter will find that the rest of the planning process will go more smoothly and that the final strategies developed to address climate change will better serve the community.

Chapter 3

Community Engagement and Collaboration

Climate action planning should include community engagement and collaboration. The United States is a democracy in which the public has a right to participate in the activities and decisions of the government. On a more practical level, many aspects of climate action require community members to voluntarily change behavior in areas such as choice of transportation mode and home energy usage, and local organizations are needed to support these changes. Successful implementation of greenhouse gas (GHG) emissions reduction and adaptation strategies in a community relies on direct engagement with the public and other community entities throughout the planning process. Community engagement and participation can result in a better process and outcome, legitimize the process in the eyes of the public, gain "buy-in" from the public, and ultimately build social capital in the community to support implementation. Public participation has become standard practice in climate action planning. Moreover, in many communities, public task forces are the main drivers of climate action planning and implementation.

Because participation is regularly included in all types of planning processes, the field of planning has a well-developed theoretical understanding of the roles, assumptions, and characteristics of varying depths of participation. Best practice calls for establishing opportunities for the public to participate in the planning process. In some communities, however, there may be a reluctance to include the public given concerns that an uninformed public could slow down or derail the planning process or a perception that the public isn't interested in participating.

As to the first concern, it is true that a quality public participation program will often take more time, but it is also true that it can improve the implementation and ultimate effectiveness of the plan. As to the second concern regarding the level of public interest, there is good evidence that the public and other community entities (e.g., small businesses) are interested in participating in deciding the future of their communities.[1] They are not apathetic or unconcerned; they simply want assurance and ongoing reinforcement that their input is meaningful. Most people have very busy lives, and taking a night off to attend a meeting about climate action planning may not be a priority, especially if they don't believe their concerns will be considered.

Talking about Climate Change with the Public

Communicating with the public about climate change can be more challenging than many other planning endeavors. Climate change generally has a lower level of public interest than other public policy issues. According to several recent polls, public opinion regarding climate change is divided and fluid.[2] A slight majority of Americans tend to believe that human-caused global warming is occurring, although this majority is considerably greater among young people. Most Americans in general think the government is doing too little to protect the environment and support policies on renewable energy, energy efficiency, and hazard mitigation. One of the first tasks of the climate action planning team is to determine the views of their intended audience. If there is not a good sense of the public's opinion, then a community survey may be useful.

Research has identified the range of views community members may have regarding climate change. A report from Yale and George Mason universities provides national averages for how a community may be differentiated based on members' beliefs. The report identifies "Six Americas":

The Alarmed (21%) are fully convinced of the reality and seriousness of climate change and are already taking individual, consumer, and political action to address it.

The Concerned (30%)—the largest of the six Americas—are also convinced that global warming is happening and a serious problem but have not yet engaged the issue personally.

Three other Americas—the Cautious (21%), the Disengaged (7%) and the Doubtful (12%)—represent different stages of understanding and acceptance of the problem, and none are actively involved.

The final America—the Dismissive (9%)—are very sure it is not happening and are actively involved as opponents of a national effort to reduce greenhouse gas emissions.[3]

While the distribution of these views will vary by community, all communities will likely contain some portion of the public and decision-makers in each group.

The planning team must be prepared to communicate with each of these groups. The Alarmed and Engaged will need little information on the science of climate change and will instead mostly focus on any information that lets them better understand options for reducing GHG emissions and adapting to climate change; they are ready to act. The Cautious and Disengaged, if they can be reached, may need information focused on the impacts of climate change on them and their communities. The Doubtful and Dismissive may need information on the basic science and evidence of climate change. A clear message for climate action planners that comes from the surveys is that considerable uncertainty exists, and many Americans feel they need more information to better understand and judge the issue.

There is some debate, though, as to whether a better understanding of the science will sway opinions. Perhaps, for community members that could be categorized as Doubtful or Dismissive, the best strategy is to point out and focus on the range of co-benefits that result from climate action rather than try to convince them of the science. In some communities, climate action is given a different name that focuses on sustainability, energy, or "greening" the community. For example, the City of Cincinnati,

Ohio, calls their climate action plan the *Green Cincinnati Plan*. It may be possible that community members with divergent views of climate change may reach consensus on the need for action in some sectors if the co-benefits are made clear. It is the job of the participation facilitator to aid community members in identifying such common ground.

To address these concerns, it is important to establish three content goals for communicating climate change science and climate action planning to the public:

- Clarify consensus on, and uncertainties in, the science.
- Explain why the problem is important, especially to them personally.
- Explain that the problem is solvable.

Each of these content goals relies on the planning team's ability to effectively communicate science to citizens.

Approaches to Public Participation

There are generally three approaches to structuring public participation with considerable variation in the specific language (e.g., task forces, working groups, boards, commissions, committees):

- community leader groups, task forces, steering committees, or commissions
- public task forces, working groups, or advisory boards
- community workshops

In the "community leader group" approach, a select group of community leaders and specialists representing such areas as government, business, industry, science, agriculture, schools and higher education, and environmental and community groups are assembled to guide the planning process. Members of these groups are usually selected or appointed by elected officials, often a mayor, and the groups usually range in size from 10 to 40 people. Although there may be other opportunities for the public to be involved in the planning process, the community leader group provides the primary method of participation for the diverse interests in the community. The planning team serves as staff for the group and makes most of the day-to-day decisions affecting the development of climate action strategies, with higher-level visioning and messaging left to the community leaders. The sectors represented by the group are usually viewed as critical collaborators for effective implementation. One caveat here is that if a group is small and not representative of the interests of most of the community, it may not achieve its goals. The group may need to create opportunities for input from more diverse voices from the community. This approach was exemplified by the City of Cincinnati. The mayor appointed 30 community leaders representing government, corporate, academic, nonprofit, faith, and community perspectives to offer guidance on the process, community engagement, and content of the plan.

The "public task force" approach is more inclusive and usually much larger than the community leader approach. The participants generally include representatives from community groups listed in the community leader approach, but its membership is likely broader in representation and will include ordinary citizens. The group is often self-selected or voluntary rather than appointed by elected officials, though elected officials may confirm or authorize creation of the group. The assembled task force does much of the work of developing and vetting climate policies and actions and may be broken into subcommittees by sector or strategy area. The task force may also report to an organizing or steering committee (or even a community leader group). The planning team provides support for the task forces and depends on them to do the heavy lifting on plan development. This approach was exemplified in San Luis Obispo, California, where a grassroots citizens group, the San Luis Obispo Climate Coalition, began working on assisting the City with implementation of its climate action plan and was later formally recognized and supported by the city council. Membership is open to the community.

In the "community workshop" approach, there is no standing task force or committee; instead, public participation is primarily accomplished through a series of community workshops or forums where anyone may participate. Participation rates and participants will vary from meeting to meeting. Meeting information may be supplemented with online forums and surveys to include participation from those unable to attend the meetings. The planning team has primary responsibility for plan development and uses the meetings to share information and ideas, assess preferences from the community, and receive feedback on proposed strategies.

In some communities, public participation is minimal and may only be done to meet the legal requirements of the adopting organization. If the plan is being prepared or adopted by a governmental agency, there are likely state or local laws with specific minimum requirements for public participation. Most states have laws that require a government agency to notify the public of pending actions (usually with a legal notice in the newspaper at minimum) and to hold open public hearings where the public may provide testimony. This is usually seen as an absolute minimum for public participation in climate action planning. Best practice is to exceed this minimum with more inclusive and meaningful forms of participation.

These do not constitute all the possible approaches for public participation. There are many ways to engage the public, and many communities choose to combine or modify elements of the three common approaches.

The following section examines five choices for participation programs and explains their relevance to each of the three recommended approaches.

Critical Choices in Designing a Public Participation Program

A series of critical choices must be made in designing participation programs:

1. *Administration:* whether or not to prepare a participation program and how to staff involvement efforts.
2. *Objectives and purpose:* what the participants are being asked to do and whether to educate, seek their preferences, and/or grant them direct influence.
3. *Stage:* when to start encouraging citizen participation in the planning process.
4. *Targeting:* which types of stakeholder groups to include in participation efforts.

5. *Techniques:* what types of participation approaches to employ and what types of information and dissemination processes to incorporate into participation activities.[4]

These choices should be made based on a review of practices in the field and adherence to the Department of Energy's "characteristics of highly effective public participation programs." Such programs

- have a clearly defined expectation for what they hope to accomplish with the public;
- are well integrated into the decision-making process;
- are targeted at those segments of the public most likely to see themselves as impacted by the decision (stakeholders);
- involve interested stakeholders in every step of decision making, not just the final stage;
- provide alternative levels of participation based upon the public's level of interest and reflecting the diversity of those participating;
- provide genuine opportunities to influence the decision; and
- consider the participation of internal stakeholders as well as external stakeholders.[5]

These criteria can be used to design and evaluate a public participation process. Appendix B provides a model approach for a public participation program that can be tailored based on the public participation approach desired and addresses these program choices and criteria.

Administration

Assuming a community has chosen to have a public participation process, the first issues to address are staffing and budget. Staff identification and budget needs are based on the desired scope of the participation program and should be part of the initial climate action planning timeline and overall budget. The staff and allocation of funds should allow for flexibility in the participation process. Issues or stakeholder groups not identified during the initial planning phase may emerge. In this case, the staff and funds allocated for participation should be able to accommodate the inclusion of additional information or events (e.g., meetings, workshops).

Equally important as having adequate staff hours and funding is choosing the person or organization that will oversee, convene, facilitate, and record outcomes. The participation process can be led by the planning entity that is overseeing climate action planning (e.g., a city, county, or consultant), or an outside entity can be brought in. This outside entity can be a local nonprofit organization or a consultant specializing in community participation. Use of a local entity can either build or threaten community trust depending on the manner in which the organization is viewed, particularly by the stakeholder groups targeted by the participation process. An outside consultant may benefit from being seen as neutral, but a lack of familiarity may result in reluctant participation by stakeholders.

Participation events bring together a collection of stakeholders with potentially divergent views. The organizing entity must have the facilitation skills to ensure that all participants feel involved and heard, particularly for participation efforts that seek to not only inform but also solicit feedback. The views expressed must be recorded so that participants can evaluate whether they have been accurately heard and the feedback can be referenced in the future. In addition to facilitation skills, the individual or group that leads participation events should have a clear understanding of climate science and the climate action planning process. This is important, as community concerns and desires for the future may not appear directly related to GHG emissions or climate impacts. A good facilitator can aid in public understanding by explaining these connections. The oversight and facilitation of these events need not be undertaken by a single individual. A team approach may best provide the skills necessary to meet participation goals.

Objectives and Purpose

The initial tasks of designing the participation program are to identify the desired outcomes, define the depth of participation, and establish the level of commitment being made to the public. The range of participation options varies based on the manner in which a community addresses these considerations (see figure 3.1). The depth of participation is determined by

	Inform	Consult	Involve	Collaborate	Empower
Participation Goal	To provide information on climate change, CAP development, and local options.	To gain feedback on local goals and proposed strategies.	To be involved throughout the CAP process to assure community concerns are understood and considered.	To facilitate community collaboration in each aspect of CAP devleopment including goals & strategy development.	To grant final decision-making to the community.
Commitment to Participants	Will be kept informed.	Will be kept informed with local concerns & aspirations acknowledged & opportunities for feedback provided.	Will work to ensure that local concerns & aspirations are directly reflected in the strategies developed and the role of input in the decisions is clearly communicated.	Will seek consensus on identificaion of local needs, planning process, and CAP strategies.	Will decide the strategies to be implemented.
Example	Fact Sheets Websites Reports Press Release Mailers Exhibitions/Speakers Citizen Academy	Exhibitions Public Hearing Workshop Survey Comment Boards	Visioning Workshop Focus Groups Survey	Visioning Workshop Focus Groups	Visioning Workshop Task forces

Figure 3-1 Range of public participation options

Source: Modified from "Spectrum of Public Participation," International Association for Public Participation, http://www.iap2.org/.

(1) the extent of the opportunities offered to those who choose to participate and (2) the weight given to the views expressed by participants.[6] Another way to conceptualize depth of participation was established in Sherry Arnstein's famous Ladder of Citizen Participation.[7]

The ladder has eight rungs for each level of public participation, and these are grouped into three categories: citizen power, tokenism, and nonparticipation. The level of public influence or control in the planning process is highest toward the top of the ladder and decreases toward the bottom:

- citizen power
  - citizen control
  - delegated power
  - partnership

- tokenism
  - placation
  - consultation
  - informing
- nonparticipation
  - therapy
  - manipulation

Arnstein proposed that for any planning process, the following question could be asked: Where does the power to control the planning process reside? Or alternatively, At what level (or to what depth) is the public participating in the planning process? Based on the ladder analogy, she established that citizens who were being placated or manipulated through participation schemes were at the bottom of the ladder, whereas citizens who were given full partnership and power in planning and decision-making were at the top of the ladder. She suggested moving up the ladder as much as possible when involving the public in community issues. Each community must decide its own desired level of participation, then clearly communicate to members of the public their role in the process and the commitment being made regarding their role and the use of their input.

Depending on the goal of a participation process, a community can develop a program using one or more of the three approaches to participation (community leader groups, public task forces, or community workshops) and select complementary levels of opportunity and event types. For example, if the goal is to inform, then a basic information distribution campaign through mailers or press releases may be sufficient. If the goal is to consult or involve, then the community workshop approach may produce the best results. If the goal is to collaborate or empower, then either the community leader group or public task force approach may create the most effective partnership. Communities with multiple goals for their public participation programs may find that blending one or more of the approaches would provide a robust and comprehensive approach.

Stage

Deciding when to include the public in the climate action planning process will be partially determined by the objectives discussed in the previous section; the greater the depth of participation, the greater the need to include the public early and often. Early on, there may be a need for a kickoff meeting. Once the planning is under way, there may be a need for periodic meetings or events. Once draft strategies are completed, there may be a need for final meetings leading up to adoption by the relevant organizations or local governments. Each of these three stages—kickoff, planning, and adoption—should be considered for public participation.

During the kickoff phase, public participation will usually focus on education and outreach. Since many in the public are unfamiliar with climate action planning, the participation process should begin by educating stakeholders about climate change and climate action planning. Moreover, participants should understand why climate action planning is needed and why it is relevant to their lives, with a focus on co-benefits. In addition to education and outreach, it may be necessary to convene the public to actively engage in a visioning process. *Visioning* is the collective exercise of describing the desired outcome or a desired future that climate action could help achieve (see box 3.1). For example, a vision statement might include the idea that the community prioritizes transportation systems for bicyclists and pedestrians. Finally, the kickoff meeting can be used as an opportunity to recruit members of the public to serve on public task forces.

The planning phase usually focuses on having the public participate in the development of ideas for GHG emissions reduction and adaptation strategies. This phase can vary in length and is often iterative. Brainstorming and other idea-generating efforts would be facilitated during this phase, including ongoing education about issues and updates on the planning process. The ideas generated through the brainstorming process can be developed into preliminary strategies. These strategies can be presented back to the community to ensure that the ideas expressed in the brainstorming and other events were accurately understood. This is also a good time to identify any gaps that the community sees in the potential suite of strategies.

Box 3.1

Vision Statements for Climate Action

Flagstaff, Arizona

Vision for 2050

Our vision for the future is that the Flagstaff community proactively preserves the natural environment, works towards carbon neutrality, and enhances the quality of life for all residents while ensuring equity, self-sufficiency, and climate resiliency.

Source: City of Flagstaff, Climate Action and Adaptation Plan (2018), https://www.flagstaff.az.gov/ClimatePlan.

Evanston, Illinois

Evanston 2050 Vision

The City of Evanston's Climate Action and Resilience Plan Working Group has a vision for the future and has set forth a path to reach that vision. This is what they foresee:

By the year 2050, Evanston has achieved carbon neutrality; all buildings are "high-performing" in terms of energy and water efficiency; all energy produced and consumed is from clean and renewable sources; a Zero Waste Strategy has been implemented and achieved; half of all trips made in Evanston are by transit, walking or bicycling; all vehicles and equipment rely on zero-emission technology; and the urban canopy is healthy and growing in size, adapted to the 2050 climate.

Green infrastructure is distributed equitably throughout the community, increased precipitation is captured by rain gardens and naturally filtered into the soil, the transition to zero emissions vehicles has improved air quality, the boom in renewable energy installations has solidified Evanston as a regional leader and expert in renewable energy and local food options are accessible and affordable to residents in every neighborhood. By 2050, Evanston will be a climate-ready and resilient City that has successfully prioritized the needs of its most vulnerable while combating climate change.

To realize this vision, the City of Evanston (City) is committed to taking immediate and decisive action to reduce the community's impact on climate change and to prepare the community to adapt and become more resilient to the changing climate and its effects. The City has set ambitious targets to combat the effects of climate change, achieve carbon neutrality by 2050 and make significant reductions in greenhouse gas (GHG) emissions in the short term. The Climate Action and Resilience Plan (CARP) will chart a path forward to meet those commitments and targets. The plan is divided into five sections with two supporting appendices.

Source: City of Evanston, Climate Action and Resilience Plan (2018), https://www.cityofevanston.org/home/showdocument?id=45170.

Berkeley, California

Vision for Year 2050

- New and existing Berkeley buildings achieve zero net energy consumption through increased energy efficiency and a shift to renewable energy sources such as solar and wind.
- Public transit, walking, cycling, and other sustainable mobility modes are the primary means of transportation for Berkeley residents and visitors.
- Personal vehicles run on electricity produced from renewable sources or other low-carbon fuels.
- Zero waste is sent to landfills.
- The majority of food consumed in Berkeley is produced locally—that is, within a few hundred miles.
- Our community is resilient and prepared for the impacts of global warming.

> • The social and economic benefits of the climate protection effort are shared across the community.
>
> *Source:* City of Berkeley, Climate Action Plan (2009), https://www.cityofberkeley .info/climate/.

The adoption phase occurs when the climate action strategies are nearing completion. This stage usually garners the most attention from the public and thus may be the point of most controversy. A greater depth of participation in the earlier stages can serve to limit the level of controversy in this stage. In the adoption stage, draft strategies are available, and the public will react to the information that they contain. Participation efforts should again focus on education and outreach. In addition, the entity that is leading the participation efforts should be prepared to facilitate and mediate meetings and disputes about the contents and direction of the strategies.

Targeting

In the targeting stage, it is important to ask, Who is the public that is involved? Are they representative of the elite, such as community leaders in business and the nonprofit sector with access to considerable resources, or are they representative of the general public?

In the community leaders approach, it is most challenging to ensure that all community interests are represented. Establishing who is on—and not on—the task force could become a contentious and politicized issue.

In the other two approaches, public task force and community workshop, where meetings are generally open to all comers, this issue may be seen as less of a concern—but this would be a mistake. A well-known phenomenon in local government is the lack of diversity at open public meetings. Meetings can be dominated by well-organized community groups and skew significantly on key demographics such as age, income, and housing tenure (renter vs. owner). Achieving diverse community participation requires good outreach efforts and the surveying (formally or informally) of key demographics at meetings to check on representativeness (see table 3.1). If a community has members with first languages other than English, then consider having translated materials and simultaneous translation available at meetings. In addition, diversity in meeting structure, location, and date and time can engage a greater portion of the community.

Techniques and Information

The question of which participation approaches to employ is challenging due to the wide variety of choices. This section presents a selection of

Table 3.1. Issues affecting public participation rates

Demographic	Issues
Age	Retirees may be more likely to participate during the day or early evening. Working-age adults and students may not be able to participate during the day.
Family status	People with younger children may not participate due to time needs of the children.
Income	People working two jobs or unable to afford child care may not participate. People may not have access to the internet to participate.
Race/ethnicity/ culture	People in the minority or who have been traditionally disenfranchised may be skeptical of participating. Some cultures are uncomfortable or unfamiliar with participation in community affairs.
Language	People for whom English is a second language may not know about meetings or may believe they cannot participate, especially if translation services are not available.
Housing tenure	People who rent may miss notices mailed to property owners or utility payers. They may also feel they are outsiders.
Residency	New members of the community may not yet be engaged with community planning efforts.

techniques split loosely into two categories: (1) basic techniques that should be employed in all public participation programs and (2) advanced techniques that can be useful in some public participation programs (see table 3.2).

Basic Techniques That Should Be Employed in All Public Participation Programs

Early in the participation process, the community needs to be notified that climate action planning is being pursued. Only after community members are aware of the problem being addressed and the local strategy being employed will they feel compelled to participate in the process. The goal of the basic techniques is to communicate climate science, anticipated local climate impacts, and the climate action planning process. The intended outcome should be increased community understanding of the issue, local needs, and the local planning process to address the needs. This is also the best time to publicize the participation events and anticipated role of the participants.

Information documentation includes the provision of hard copy and web-based plans, reports, and the like. Hard copies of planning documents should be available at city hall and public libraries at a minimum. The creation of a web site can support this process by serving as a repository for all information relating to the planning process. The site should include presentations, materials, and press releases produced for the meetings as well as versions of the strategies for public review. The site and all materials

Table 3.2. Techniques for public participation

Basic techniques	Advanced techniques
Information documentation	Visioning
Media and public relations	Focus groups
Social marketing/media	Questionnaires
Educational meetings and workshops	Computer-based polling
	Citizen academies
Exhibitions and events	Competitions and challenges
Public hearings	Speakers' bureaus and ambassadors
Mail and email notices	Roving workshops and pop-ups
	Digital platforms

should have a consistent look and feel to them that defines them as being materials representing the project. A website should be accompanied by distribution methods that effectively reach community members who do not have easy internet access. Materials should be created in different languages for community members who do not speak English.

Media and public relations campaigns engage the media and inform the public through newspaper ads, television ads, press releases, mailers, community calendars, op-eds or letters to the editor, and websites.

Social marketing/media refers to the use of internet-based social networking and digital communication platforms, such as blogs, collaborative software, and social media sites (e.g., Facebook, YouTube, Instagram, and Twitter). These platforms can be used to keep the public informed, facilitate involvement, or solicit input, especially from younger members of the community who may be less likely to participate in other ways. Developing and posting messages on these platforms can encourage conversation on the issues as well as promote the public meetings. Key community-based organizations with a vested interest in climate action can be "friended," "liked," or "followed" to promote the meetings and other participation events. There are a number of issues with using social media, including the potential for bullying and spreading of disinformation, so these should be pursued with caution, and communities should consider establishing a manager or moderator for social media feeds.

Educational meetings and workshops provide opportunities for members of the public to learn in depth about climate change and climate action planning and engage in dialogue with experts and fellow citizens. These can range from large, well-publicized meetings intended to attract a cross section of the community to smaller meetings for specific groups or neighborhoods.

Exhibitions and events provide opportunities to display information in public areas, including informational booths at farmers' markets or other regular community events, explaining the plans, processes, and locally important issues. These displays can also be used to gauge public opinion and gather feedback on potential strategies. These opinions can be gathered by having a staff member on hand to answer questions and solicit feedback or through use of a comment board or other self-service means of expressing views.

Public hearings at meetings of elected and appointed boards can also be used as a forum to solicit formal feedback from the public in a manner that becomes part of the official local government record.

Mail and email notices can raise awareness and inform community members on the planning process as it progresses. Regular email notices are a simple and low-cost tool to engage community members who are unable to regularly attend participation events such as workshops. Email addresses of interested stakeholders can be gathered through other outreach tools such as social media, websites, workshops, and exhibitions.

Advanced Techniques That Can Be Useful in Some Public Participation Programs

Some participation programs seek not only to educate the community and raise awareness but also to solicit more detailed feedback on various aspects of climate action. The feedback can occur at all stages of the planning process, from visioning for the community to individual concerns or specific strategies. These techniques often work best when accompanied by many of the basic techniques just described.

Visioning is a public meeting process that asks citizens to create a vision for a desired future state of their community. Visioning exercises require the public to think less about immediate problems and constraints and instead imagine how they would like their community to be in 20 to 50 years. A vision then becomes a long-range goal or aspiration that a community can move toward through deliberate action. The outcomes from a visioning meeting can help focus climate action strategy development and identify key co-benefits.

Focus groups are small selected groups used to gauge public interests and opinions. A community using this approach could conduct a series of focus groups with key stakeholder audiences (e.g., the agricultural community, local builders) with the goal of gathering detailed and specific feedback. Focus groups can also be used at general stakeholder meetings where community members can divide according to interests, expertise, or areas of concern. Stakeholder discussions can focus on proposed methods to reduce GHG emissions and adapt to climate change. These discussions should be facilitated to encourage substantive discussions of policy implications and benefits within each sector, with the goal of achieving consensus on policy direction for each area of climate action.

Questionnaires or surveys can be conducted through a website, mailed as hard copies, or delivered in person. This tool can be used to assess community habits and values, as well as gather feedback on potential strategies. The intended use of the survey results will determine the need for a statistically valid survey or a more qualitative, informational survey.

Computer-based polling is a type of questionnaire or survey that can be administered in real time during a meeting to provide instant feedback from an audience. Meeting participants can be given small remote devices (they look like small television remotes) that they use to respond to questions (there are also smartphone apps such as PollEverywhere .com that can do this, but they depend on everyone having such a device). The computer collects the public responses and immediately calculates and displays summaries of them. Real-time polling is also anonymous, which often neutralizes extreme positions and provides equal participation to all participants.

Citizen academies are training courses provided for community members that allow for a greater level of detail and depth than can be provided through workshops. For climate action planning, a citizen academy could address climate science, emissions reduction and climate adaptation strategies, local government policy and planning, and "green" living. Experts could be brought in to teach different parts of the course; local colleges and universities are often an excellent resource.

Competitions and challenges can take many forms. Friendly competition or prizes can help encourage attendance at participation events. Games can provide an engaging and fun context in which community members can be introduced to new concepts or examine the pros and cons of proposed strategies.

Speakers' bureaus and ambassadors, organized in advance of community workshops or town hall events, can enable the planning team to connect with key stakeholder groups on important issues and help inform citizens about the local issues related to climate change and land use planning. A speakers' bureau may consist of staff, representatives of key stakeholder groups, or a combination of staff and stakeholders. Key candidates for the bureau are those community stakeholders who are willing to be the plan's ambassadors. The objective of the speakers' bureau is to provide peer-to-peer and informal outreach for the plan. Speakers would receive key talking points, a presentation template, and training on desired presentation approaches as well as planning objectives.

Roving workshops or "pop-ups" are miniworkshops or events that are conducted in the community at places where people tend to congregate—for example, churches, schools, grocery stores, parks, and community events such as parades or street fairs. The idea is to go to the public rather than trying to make the public come to you. The activities are designed to be interactive and fun for the public and easy to transport and manage for the planning team. They are intended to go beyond *exhibitions and events* (discussed earlier), which provide no or limited public input, and instead engage the public in a constructive dialogue with planners and each other.

Digital platforms provide the public with a convenient opportunity to participate in climate action planning. Full-service platforms provide opportunities to post information, solicit input, facilitate dialogue and idea discussion, and conduct voting or polling. These tools can support many of the other identified public participation techniques. Some of the more popular platforms include MindMixer, Crowdbrite, OpenIDEO, MetroQuest, GO CO$_2$ Free, and Bang the Table.[8] These platforms can be expensive, so communities should make sure they are getting a product that works for them and increases the diversity of participation. Considering what portion of the community may have no or limited access to the internet is important. Good questions to ask of vendors include the following: How do you get people to the site and keep them engaged? How do you manage online bullying and abuse? What kind of data or output is provided? How can the platform support in-person participation strategies? Is there a mobile app version?

Public Participation in Implementation

Many, if not most, climate action strategies require individuals, families, and businesses to change their behavior. It is one thing to provide additional bicycle lanes in a community; it is another to get people to drive their cars less and ride their bicycles more. Changed behavior cannot be accomplished through a few public service announcements or brochures available at the local library. Successfully changing behavior requires a sustained and multipronged effort to continue engaging the public in the issue of climate change.

Strategies based on behavior change should include a discussion that identifies how the public will be involved in implementation. Long-term participation in implementation is an area that can often be best addressed through partnerships with local nongovernmental organizations. In some cases, funding can be provided to support these activities. For example, a bicycling advocacy organization is well positioned to carry out ongoing education and periodic community events. A local utility provider is also able to support energy conservation and efficiency programs through grants, rebates, and loan programs. Partnerships also offer the opportunity to sustain implementation through collaborative funding. Nongovernmental organization partners may be able to leverage or secure funds that are not available to government agencies and, in turn, support implementation.

In most communities, reducing GHG emissions and adapting to climate change require changes in business-as-usual behavior. Collaboration, education, and engagement are essential to creating low-carbon, resilient communities.

Chapter 4

Greenhouse Gas Emissions Accounting

With contributions by Eli Krispi

Greenhouse gas (GHG) emissions accounting is a set of methods and approaches for quantifying GHG emissions in support of climate action planning, implementation, monitoring, evaluation, and reporting. It is mostly a technical exercise requiring data collection, analysis, and management and usually follows established protocols and uses specialized software and databases. GHG emissions accounting is now a specialized area of practice and even has a professional certification through the World Bank.[1] GHG emissions accounting is generally divided into three distinct areas: inventory, forecast, and reduction strategy quantification.

Principles of GHG Emissions Inventories

The technical definition of a community GHG emissions inventory is an accounting of GHGs emitted into (and, in some cases, removed from) the atmosphere by a community over a period of time, usually a calendar year. The inventory provides the baseline or existing condition from which to measure progress toward a GHG reduction target. It is a form of gathering quantitative data to support planning, similar to transportation studies that quantify the amount of traffic on roadways or housing studies that quantify the housing stock and assess its affordability.

A GHG emissions inventory can be likened to an assessment you might do to begin a weight loss plan. First, you may weigh yourself and do an overall health assessment. You may consider your weight, cholesterol level, and percentage of body fat. Then you determine the sources of your calories and nutrients: cereal for breakfast; a burger, fries, and soft drink for lunch; and pasta, salad, and a glass of wine for dinner. You will use the information gathered in this inventory to understand where your calories come from and to change your intake of food and nutrients for a healthier future. In the same way, a community needs to understand its current emissions level, how community choices affect that level, and how it can change.

At the community scale, inventories focus on identifying sources and estimating quantities of GHG emissions from each source. The primary sources are motor vehicles that directly consume fossil fuel as well as buildings and operations that consume fossil fuels directly (e.g., gas for heating and cooking) and indirectly (e.g., fossil fuels needed to generate electricity).

There are a number of other sources of GHG emissions at the community level, but transportation and energy sources emit the majority of GHG emissions in most communities. GHGs are not measured directly; instead, they are calculated based on measurements of a certain activity, such as how much electricity and natural gas is used in the community, how much people drive, and how much waste is generated. Each of these can be measured or estimated for a community and then converted to GHG emissions using standardized tools and databases. Because GHGs are calculated in this indirect fashion, they should be considered estimates, not exact measures. Box 4.1 provides an example set of estimates relating GHG emissions to community actions. By following appropriate protocols, these estimates can be sufficiently accurate for climate action planning.

A typical GHG emissions inventory will report the total annual emissions attributed to the community and a breakdown of their sources. Table 4.1 is an example from Placer County, California, which displays the conversion factors used to calculate GHG emissions.

Box 4.1

Conversion of Greenhouse Gas Emissions to Familiar Equivalents

One thousand metric tons (MT) of CO_2 emissions is approximately equivalent to the following:

- CO_2 emissions from 112,524 gallons of gasoline consumed
- CO_2 emissions from 2,315 barrels of oil consumed
- CO_2 emissions from the electricity use of 174 homes for one year
- CO_2 emissions from burning 5.5 railcars' worth of coal
- annual CO_2 emissions of 0.0003 coal-fired power plants
- CO_2 emissions from 40,880 propane cylinders used for home barbecues
- greenhouse gas emissions avoided by recycling 350 tons of waste instead of sending it to the landfill
- carbon sequestered by 16,535 tree seedlings grown for 10 years
- carbon sequestered annually by 210 acres of pine or fir forests
- carbon sequestered annually by 8 acres of forest preserved from conversion to cropland in one year

Source: "Greenhouse Gas Equivalencies Calculator," U.S. Environmental Protection Agency, https://www.epa.gov/energy/greenhouse-gas-equivalencies-calculator.

These are a combination of standard unit conversions and conversion factors derived from data specific to Placer County. These factors are used to quantify the GHG emissions produced by a community. Table 4.2 is an example of a standard summary of total emissions attributable to a community. The table shows emissions in metric tons of carbon dioxide equivalents (CO_{2e}). As discussed in appendix A, not all GHGs are equivalent to CO_2 in their global warming potential, so they are usually converted to the same units. The table also shows the breakdown by the four most common sectors: residential energy, nonresidential energy, transportation, and waste. In some inventories these sectors are further

Table 4.1. Example of conversion and emissions factors used by Placer County, California, to calculate community-wide GHG emissions

Quantity	Value	Notes
Standard unit conversions		
1 pound (lb.)	0.0004536 metric tons (tonnes)	Engineering standard
1 short ton (ton)	0.9072 metric tons (tonnes)	Engineering standard
1 metric ton (tonne)	1.1023 short tons (tons) 2,204.62 pounds (lbs.)	Engineering standard
1 kilowatt hour (kWh)	3,412 Btu (Btu)	Engineering standard
1 therm	100,000 Btu (Btu)	Engineering standard
Placer County—sample CO_2 (only) emissions factors		
1 megawatt hour (MWh) of electricity	404.51 lbs. CO_2	PG&E 2015 emissions factor certified by the California Climate Action Registry
1 MMBtu of natural gas	53.02 kilograms (kg) CO_2	USCP, appendix C
1 vehicle mile traveled (passenger car)	0.323 kilograms (kg) CO_2	CARB EMFAC 2014 County Emissions Inventory Model

Note: The emissions factors used by Placer County are average estimates of the greenhouse gases (CO_2 specifically in this example) produced by a unit of natural gas, electricity, and VMT within Placer County in the year 2015. The full set of emissions factors are documented in the inventory: https://placer.ca.gov/sustainplacer.

Abbreviations: MMBtu, million British thermal units; PG&E, Pacific Gas & Electric (utility); CARB, California Air Resources Board; EMFAC, motor vehicle emissions model; USCP, U.S. Community Protocol; VMT, vehicle miles traveled

Source: Placer County, *Community-Wide and County-Operations 2015 Greenhouse Gas Emissions Inventories* (2015).

Table 4.2. Example of community-wide greenhouse gas emissions inventory summary

Sector	Metric tons CO_{2e}/year	Percent of total
Residential energy	49,178	18.4
Commercial/industrial energy	54,619	20.4
Transportation	150,663	56.4
Waste	12,777	4.8
Total community-wide emissions	**267,237**	**100**

subdivided (e.g., separating nonresidential into commercial, industrial, and agricultural), and some communities also break down total emissions by fuel type (e.g., gasoline, natural gas, coal).

Local governments most commonly use two types of inventories: a community-wide inventory and a local government operations inventory. It is considered best practice to conduct community-wide inventories that include assessing local government operations as a distinct subset of the total emissions.[2] Local government operations typically comprise between 3% and 8% of community-wide emissions. Some communities do not break out local government operations. Conversely, some communities choose to inventory only local government operations emissions. Usually this is because they are adopting reduction targets and emissions reduction strategies for local government operations only.

Current best practice suggests that communities should prepare a baseline GHG emissions inventory prior to the development of a climate action plan or climate strategies. Communities that are members of ICLEI–Local Governments for Sustainability[3] or signatories to the Global Covenant of Mayors for Climate & Energy[4] commit to doing so. Though preparing an inventory is good practice, a community does not need to know its specific GHG emissions to know that taking actions to improve energy efficiency and conservation and reduce fuel consumption are prudent cost-saving measures that also provide community quality of life benefits. The GHG emissions inventory is a detailed, technical exercise that will take time and expertise beyond the capacity of some communities, but there are good reasons to undertake this task. Additionally, there are numerous resources available to help local governments prepare inventories, including those provided in the "Additional Resources" chapter at the end of this book.

The most effective GHG emissions reduction strategies are tied specifically to sources of GHG emissions identified and quantified in an inventory, with an emphasis on reducing emissions from a community's largest sources of GHGs. The most effective strategies will also quantify the expected GHG reduction benefits and contribution of the strategies toward achieving the overall reduction target. According to the U.S. Environmental Protection Agency, communities use GHG inventories to do the following:

- identify sources of emissions and their current magnitude within an area
- identify and assess emissions trends
- establish a foundation for projecting future emissions
- provide a basis for future reduction targets
- set a benchmark for tracking progress toward a reduction target
- quantify the benefits of proposed emissions reduction strategies
- provide a basis for developing a climate action plan[5]

Inventories form the basis for decision-making; they should be transparent and reproducible and should follow established protocols. This will also ensure consistency and comparability with future updates and other inventories. There are five accounting and reporting principles to ensure that "GHG data represent a faithful, true, and fair account" of a local government's GHG emissions:

1. *Relevance:* The GHG inventory should appropriately reflect the GHG emissions of the community and should be organized to serve the decision-making needs of users.
2. *Completeness:* All GHG emission sources and emissions-causing activities within the chosen inventory boundary should be accounted for. The inventory should clearly explain why any sources of emissions were excluded or why any additional sources beyond those in the community were included.

3. *Consistency:* Consistent methods should be used in the identification of boundaries, analysis of data, and quantification of emissions to enable meaningful trend analysis over time, demonstration of reductions, and comparisons of emissions. Any changes to the data, inventory boundary, methods, or any relevant factors in subsequent inventories should be disclosed.

4. *Transparency:* All relevant issues should be addressed and documented in a factual and coherent manner to provide a trail for future review and replication. All relevant data sources and assumptions should be disclosed, along with specific descriptions of methodologies and data sources used.

5. *Accuracy:* The reported GHG emissions in an inventory should be as accurate as possible. The calculation of GHG emissions should not be systematically over or under the actual emissions. Accuracy should be sufficient to enable users to make decisions with a reasonable assurance as to the integrity of the reported information. Uncertainties in the quantification process should be reduced to the greatest extent possible.[6]

It is important to keep in mind that while GHG emissions inventories based on current best practices are quite robust, they are still estimates with a degree of error. Preparers should not spend substantial energy trying to account for the last 1% of emissions or estimating to significant digits that are not warranted by the many assumptions and estimates that make up the inventory calculations.

The Basic Inventory Process

The process of preparing a GHG emissions inventory entails a number of decisions and procedural steps that have been codified through a variety of GHG emissions inventory protocols and related software developed by national and international organizations. The basic steps for conducting a GHG emissions inventory in most protocols are as follows:

1. Data collection
2. Emissions calculations and reporting

3. Emissions forecasting
4. Emissions reduction target setting

This book does not provide a step-by-step explanation of how to conduct a GHG emissions inventory. Communities should refer to the chosen protocol manual for guidance. Instead, this book answers the following questions:

1. Who will prepare the inventory?
2. What is the appropriate methodology or protocol?
3. How should a baseline year be established?
4. What is the scope of the inventory?
5. What is a GHG emissions forecast?
6. How are emissions reduction targets selected?

Preparing the Inventory

Communities have several choices as to who will prepare the GHG emissions inventory. Local government staff members, community volunteers, college faculty members and students, and consultants have been the most common choices. These vary by cost, experience and aptitude, and accountability. Preparing an inventory is detailed, time-consuming work that requires strong math and logic skills, solid organizational capabilities, and a willingness to deal with uncertainties and assumptions. If the GHG reduction strategies will have a legal status, the inventory will need to be as accurate as possible, thoroughly documented, and defensible. A community will have to consider all these factors and make the best choice for its own circumstances.

Inventory Methodology/Protocol and Software

Protocols establish what will be measured in an inventory and how it will be measured. There are a variety of GHG assessment protocols for businesses, governments, individuals, and other organizations, and some adventurous communities have created their own approaches by mixing and modifying a variety of existing protocols. Although this may work for some communities, most communities should use the widely adopted, standard protocols when they are able to, although some may need to rely on other methods if they have an emissions source that is not covered. The most common protocols for communities are the Local Government Operations Protocol, the U.S. Community Protocol for Accounting and Reporting of Greenhouse Gas Emissions, and the Global Protocol for Community-Scale Greenhouse Gas Emission Inventories.[7] These pertain to the two types of emissions inventories mentioned previously—local government operations inventories and community-wide inventories, respectively.

Local Government Operations Protocol

The Local Government Operations Protocol (LGO Protocol)[8] was developed in 2008 through the collaboration of the California Air Resources Board, ICLEI, the California Climate Action Registry,[9] and The Climate Registry.[10] The LGO Protocol is a tool for accounting and reporting GHG emissions across all of a local government's operations and is intended for use by local governments throughout the United States, Canada, and Mexico. The LGO Protocol is based on the Greenhouse Gas Protocol: A Corporate Accounting and Reporting Standard developed by the World Resources Institute and the World Business Council for Sustainable Development (WRI/WBCSD). The protocol is a guidance document available for use by any local government engaging in a GHG inventory exercise. It brings together GHG inventory guidance from a number of existing programs—namely, the guidance provided by ICLEI to its Cities for Climate Protection campaign members, the guidance provided by the California Climate Action Registry and The Climate Registry through their general reporting protocols, and the guidance from the State of California's mandatory GHG reporting regulation.

U.S. Community Protocol for Accounting and Reporting of Greenhouse Gas Emissions

The U.S. Community Protocol for Accounting and Reporting of Greenhouse Gas Emissions (U.S. Community Protocol) was released by ICLEI in 2012. It is a tool for accounting and reporting community-wide GHG emissions designed to complement the LGO Protocol. The U.S. Community Protocol is tailored for use in U.S. communities.

Global Protocol for Community-Scale Greenhouse Gas Emission Inventories

The Global Protocol for Community-Scale Greenhouse Gas Emission Inventories (Global Protocol; GPC) was released in 2015 through a partnership of the World Resources Institute, the C40 Cities Climate Leadership Group, and ICLEI–Local Governments for Sustainability.[11] It provides a framework for communities to determine and report their GHG emissions. The Global Protocol is applicable to communities around the world and includes additional GHG sectors, such as land use changes and crop cultivation, that are not included in the U.S. Community Protocol.

Greenhouse Gas Inventory Software

There are two basic options for using the protocols to conduct the inventory and deal with the necessary calculations. The first is to use the detailed information in the protocols on data needs, assumptions, transformations, and calculations to manually construct an inventory spreadsheet in one of the commonly available spreadsheet programs, such as Microsoft Excel, Apple Numbers, or Google Sheets. Anyone who chooses this route should be very comfortable with spreadsheets and with math. The protocols provide sufficient detail and direction to do this successfully. This approach offers more flexibility to adjust the data and assumptions for the local context. There are also accessibility benefits to using commonly available spreadsheet software.

The second option is to use a GHG emissions inventory software package or online platform. ICLEI–Local Governments for Sustainability's ClearPath tool has become one of the most widely used software platforms for this purpose. It allows users to calculate the GHG emissions of a community by entering activity data and using either customized emissions factors or default factors that are already included in the platform. The inventories prepared in ClearPath are compliant with the U.S. Community Protocol and the Global Protocol. ClearPath reports emissions from the three major GHGs (CO_2, CH_4, and N_2O) as well as combined carbon dioxide equivalent units (CO_{2e}). A professional version of the platform also allows users to forecast multiple emissions scenarios and track their GHG reduction progress over time. Access to the basic version of ClearPath is free to any U.S. community that is a signatory to the Global Covenant of Mayors, and access to ClearPath Pro is free to California communities through the Statewide Energy Efficiency Collaborative. Access by others requires an ICLEI membership or the purchase of an annual subscription.

Choosing Protocols and Software

The selection of a protocol, methodology, and software will depend on the purpose of the inventory and the resources available to the jurisdiction. The decision will depend on city staff support, budget allocations, time constraints, and the availability of other resources or services, such as consultants, volunteers, nonprofit organizations, or college faculty and students. Consultants or other organizations may develop tools and/or software tailored to the jurisdictions' needs. In addition, local governments must consider any regulatory mandates or guidance from state or regional agencies when applicable. It is generally recommended that communities follow the U.S. Community Protocol and the Global Protocol. Also, any communities that have signed pledges, joined organizations such as C40 or the Global Covenant of Mayors, or committed to external reporting may be required to use certain protocols and tools.

Establishing a Baseline Year

The GHG emissions inventory requires the choice of an initial inventory year, usually referred to as the "baseline year." Communities should select the most recent calendar year for which consistent, comprehensive, and reliable data can be collected. The LGO Protocol recommends that local agencies select a baseline year that is "typical" and not a year in which emissions were influenced by unusual conditions such as extremely high or low economic growth, abnormal weather, or other outliers. Another issue may be whether the community wants to be consistent with state or neighboring jurisdictions' baseline years. If the community wants to be consistent with another adopted GHG reduction target, such as a statewide reduction target, it should consider using the same baseline as the adopted goal. In addition, if a community has implemented several emissions reduction strategies, it may want to choose a year far enough in the past that the impact of recent GHG emissions reduction strategies can be clearly seen. Finally, if a community has been implementing climate action strategies for a while, it may want to conduct two inventories: one for a baseline year and one for the current year so that it can see its progress. These should be at least five years apart to see meaningful differences.

Inventory Coverage

The typical sectors of a GHG inventory are residential energy and non-residential energy, waste, and transportation. Other sectors, depending on the community, may include agriculture, water and wastewater, and off-road equipment. The seven greenhouse gases that should be quantified from these sectors and included in a GHG emissions inventory are carbon dioxide (CO_2), methane (CH_4), nitrous oxide (N_2O), hydrofluorocarbons (HFCs), perfluorocarbons (PFCs), sulfur hexafluoride (SF_6), and nitrogen trifluoride (NF_3). Other GHGs may be inventoried; however, methodologies for other GHGs may not be in the most commonly used protocols. According to the common protocols, emissions of CO_2, CH_4, and N_2O from fossil fuel combustion, electricity generation (the indirect emissions associated with electricity used in the community), waste disposal, and wastewater will be the most significant sources of GHG emissions in community-wide and local government operations inventories. Table 4.3 shows an example from Placer County, California, of a detailed breakout of community-wide emissions and the data sources.

Inventories must be clear about the sources of emissions included and excluded, as these sources will form the basis of reduction measures. The inventory is conducted by compiling activity data describing energy

Table 4.3. Placer County, California, 2005 and 2015 greenhouse gas emissions inventory

Activity/sector	2005 Equiv. CO$_2$ (metric tons)	2015 Equiv. CO$_2$ (metric tons)	Percentage change	Data sources
Residential				
Electricity use	181,107	110,380	−39	PG&E; SMUD; NV Energy / Liberty Utilities; CEC
Electricity T&D losses	10,110	6,893	−32	USEPA eGRID
Natural gas use	98,045	91,812	−6	PG&E; Southwest Gas
Propane use	49,979	33,591	−33	USEPA; EIA; U.S. Census
Fuel oil / kerosene use	1,810	674	−63	USEPA; EIA; U.S. Census
Wood use	5,012	8,038	60	USEPA; EIA; U.S. Census
Subtotal residential	*346,063*	*251,389*	*−27*	
Nonresidential				
Electricity use	140,981	87,325	−38	PG&E; SMUD; NV Energy / Liberty Utilities; CEC
Electricity T&D losses	7,004	5,297	−24	USEPA eGRID
Natural gas use	59,691	39,356	−34	PG&E; Southwest Gas
Subtotal nonresidential	207,676	131,979	−36	

(*Continued*)

Table 4.3. Placer County, California, 2005 and 2015 greenhouse gas emissions inventory

Activity/sector	2005 Equiv. CO_2 (metric tons)	2015 Equiv. CO_2 (metric tons)	Percentage change	Data sources
Transportation				
On-road passenger vehicles	145,693	151,441	4	VMT: Fehr and Peers Fuel Use: CARB EMFAC
On-road light-duty trucks and SUVs	218,484	208,116	−5	VMT: Fehr and Peers Fuel Use: CARB EMFAC
On-road heavy-duty trucks	161,260	144,049	−11	VMT: Fehr and Peers Fuel Use: CARB EMFAC
Off-road vehicles and equipment	9,786	9,413	−4	VMT: Fehr and Peers Fuel Use: CARB EMFAC
Subtotal transportation	*535,222*	*513,019*	*−4*	
Water, wastewater, and solid waste				
Subtotal water and wastewater	18,034	11,548	−36	Water and wastewater service companies, utilities (PG&E, NV Energy), USCP and CA Water Boards defaults, EPA/CA DOF/ U.S. Census population data

(*Continued*)

Table 4.3. Placer County, California, 2005 and 2015 greenhouse gas emissions inventory

Activity/sector	2005 Equiv. CO_2 (metric tons)	2015 Equiv. CO_2 (metric tons)	Percentage change	Data sources
Subtotal solid waste	65,577	87,526	33%	CalRecycle Disposal Reporting System, Landfill gas capture data from facilities
Agriculture				
Rice cultivation	201,029	135,244	–33%	Crop reports
Equipment use	26,547	26,475	–0.3%	CARB
Other agriculture and livestock	38,304	22,273	–41%	DFA; DPR
Forest management open burning (nonbiogenic)	2,462	2,462	0%	DFW
Subtotal agriculture	*268,341*	*186,454*	*–31%*	
Grand total	**1,440,913**	**1,181,915**	**–18%**	

Abbreviations: CA DOF, California Department of Finance; CARB, California Air Resources Board; CEC, California Energy Commission; DFA, California Department of Forestry & Agriculture; DFW, California Department of Fish & Wildlife; DPR, California Department of Pesticide Regulation; eGRID, Emissions & Generation Resource Integrated Database (Environmental Protection Agency); EIA, U.S. Energy Information Agency; EMFAC, Emissions Factors; PG&E, Pacific Gas & Electric; SMUD, Sacramento Municipal Utility District; USEPA, U.S. Environmental Protection Agency; USCP, U.S. Community Protocol

Source: Placer County, *Community-Wide and County-Operations 2015 Greenhouse Gas Emissions Inventories* (2015).

and fuel use and waste generation (see table 4.4 for typical activity data sources) and multiplying the activity data by emissions factors for each type of energy used and each waste disposal site and technology. Protocol methodologies direct the application and selection of emissions factors. Emissions are reported in terms of activity data, metric tons of each GHG, and metric tons of CO_{2e}. Converting emissions of non-CO_2 gases to units of CO_{2e} provides a comparison of GHGs on a common basis (i.e., on the ability of each GHG to trap heat in the atmosphere). Non-CO_2 gases are converted to CO_{2e} using internationally recognized global warming potential (see appendix A).

Emissions are quantified and tracked separately, and the results are presented in inventory reports by sector and source. Some communities will also present emissions by scope, which is one way to help reduce the possibility of double counting and misrepresenting emissions when reporting while still allowing all policy-relevant information to be captured. In addition, tracking emissions sources separately allows decision-makers to tailor reduction strategies. Three classifications—scopes 1, 2, and 3—are used to categorize emissions sources when preparing an inventory using a scope framework. The scopes vary slightly when applied in the context of government operations and community-scale inventories (see table 4.3 for examples). Among the most commonly used protocols, the LGO and Global protocols both use a scope-oriented framework, while the U.S. Community Protocol does not. Scopes are defined by the LGO Protocol and Global Protocol as follows:

• Scope 1 emissions are all direct GHG emissions (with the exception of direct CO_2 emissions from biogenic sources). These are primarily emissions from motor vehicles and stationary sources such as power plants or factories located within the community.
• Scope 2 emissions are indirect GHG emissions associated with the consumption of purchased or acquired electricity, steam, heating, or cooling from power plants located outside of the community.
• Scope 3 emissions are all other indirect emissions not covered in Scope 2, such as emissions resulting from the extraction and production of purchased materials and fuels, transport-related activities in vehicles not owned or controlled by the reporting entity (e.g.,

Table 4.4. Example of greenhouse gas emissions sectors, units of measurement, scope, and data source

Sector	Information	Unit of measurement	Emissions scope	Activity data source
Residential	Electricity consumption	kWh	Scope 2	Local utility provider
	Natural gas consumption	Therms	Scope 1	Local utility provider
Commercial and industrial	Electricity consumption	kWh	Scope 2	Local utility provider
	Natural gas consumption	Therms	Scope 1	Local utility provider
Transportation	Local road VMT	Annual average VMT	Scope 1	State database or local travel model
	Highway and interstate VMT	Annual average VMT	Scope 1	State database or local travel model
Solid waste	Solid waste tonnage sent to landfill from activities in jurisdiction	Short tons	Scope 3	Local landfill operator(s) or state reports
Off-road equipment	Emissions from off-road equipment and vehicles	Tons/year of N_2O, CO_2, and CH_4	Scope 3	State model or local estimates
Agriculture	Emissions from cattle and sheep	Head of cattle	Scope 3	County crop report
	Emissions from fertilizer use	Pounds of nitrogen	Scope 3	County crop report
Aircraft	Emissions in the landing and take-off operations (LTOs) zone	Grams of N_2O, CO_2, and CH_4	Scope 3	Local airport operator / aircraft operations study

Abbreviations: CH_4, methane; CO_2, carbon dioxide; kWh, kilowatt-hours; N_2O, nitrous oxide; VMT, vehicle miles traveled employee commuting and air travel), outsourced activities, waste disposal, and so forth.

Data for Scope 3 emissions can be difficult to obtain, and their accuracy is questionable. Also, Scope 3 emissions are more economically and culturally complicated and less amenable to emissions reduction strategies (because they include things like household purchasing decisions and global manufacturing chains). However, there is increasing attention to overcoming these limitations for Scope 3 emissions, and improved data analysis methods are making it easier for communities to accurately assess these emissions through what are commonly called consumption-based inventories (see box 4.2). For example, the Global Protocol requires communities to account for and report Scope 3 emissions associated with some energy, transportation, and waste-related activities.

In some cases, not all sources of GHG emissions may be included in an inventory. There are several reasons emissions may be excluded. Often, data needed to determine emissions may not be available and there is no reasonable way to estimate the data. In other cases, the effort required to accurately assess emissions from a small source may be so considerable that it is not worth going through a lengthy and intensive effort if the overall impact on the inventory will be small (such sources are called "de minimis" and generally should be no more than 5% of the total estimated emissions). The inventory report or documentation should clearly note any emissions that are not included as well as the reason for leaving them out. The U.S. Community Protocol recommends a simple notation key for describing these excluded sources:

- *IE—included elsewhere:* The emissions are accounted for in the inventory but are treated as part of another activity.
- *NE—not estimated:* The emissions are not estimated.
- *NA—not applicable:* The activity is occurring, but no emissions are attributed to the community.
- *NO—not occurring:* The activity does not take place in the community.

Occasionally, an inventory will report GHG emissions even if the calculations are known to be inaccurate or if the emissions occur in but

Box 4.2

Consumption–Based GHG Emissions Inventories

A Consumption-Based Emissions Inventory (CBEI) assigns responsibility to the final consumer for lifecycle GHG emissions of consumed goods and services. Upstream embedded emissions within goods and services, use emissions, and downstream disposal emissions are all assigned to the final consumer within the subject jurisdiction. Consumption inventories usually focus on household and government consumption because most business consumption is for the purpose of production of goods and services.

Consumption inventories usually do not include production-related emissions within the jurisdiction except to the extent that within-jurisdiction production serves in-jurisdiction consumption. Consumption inventories have been prepared for relatively few municipalities to date, and California does not have a consumption inventory for the state as a whole.

Consumption inventories for embedded emissions in goods and services are usually based on regional economic consumption data, combined with national/international state lifecycle emissions factors, for a standard list of products or product bundles. While consumption inventories will sometimes use local or regional data on economic consumption, factors for upstream GHG emissions usually employ state and national average activity and emissions intensity data, compared to the more local data commonly used for production-based and activity-based inventories.

Source: Definition from Association of Environmental Professionals, California Chapter, Climate Change Committee, *Production, Consumption and Lifecycle Greenhouse Gas Inventories: Implications for CEQA and Climate Action Plan* (August 2017); see also C40 Cities, *Consumption-Based GHG Emissions of C40 Cities* (March 2018).

are not attributable to the community. These emissions are presented but are not counted toward the community's total emissions or used to establish reduction targets. This is often done because decision-makers or community members are curious about these emissions even if they are not appropriate to include in the total inventory. Such emissions are called "informational items."

The designation of an inventory's coverage also has a relationship to the spatial boundaries of the inventory. Before collecting data, inventory preparers must identify spatial boundaries for the inventory and include all important sources of GHG emissions occurring within these boundaries. Community-wide inventories are typically based on the local government's political boundary. A jurisdiction may elect to inventory emissions outside of its political boundary. The most common reason to inventory emissions outside of a political boundary is to be consistent with a comprehensive plan that may establish planning area boundaries for future land use beyond the community's current political boundaries. If this is done, it should be explained in the inventory. The standard use of political boundaries for community-wide emissions can be confusing when one is preparing an inventory using a scope-based framework and is considering Scope 2 emissions. In some communities, electricity is produced within the political boundaries of the jurisdiction, which would be a Scope 1 emissions source, but in most, it is produced outside of the community and is thus a Scope 2 emission. Either way, the activities that create the demand for the electricity—powering homes and businesses—do occur within the political boundaries of the jurisdiction and should be inventoried. This distinction of Scope 1 and Scope 2 emissions and political boundaries is certainly a debatable area of GHG emissions inventory practice, so whatever choice a community makes about this should be documented and justified.

Local government operations emissions include emissions arising from the use and operations of all facilities, buildings, equipment, and activities that are owned, operated, or managed by the local government. These are usually within the political boundaries of the jurisdiction, but some may exist outside the jurisdiction. For example, a local government may own a landfill or a water supply and transmission pipes outside its political boundaries. Since all emissions that are a consequence of the local government's operations must be included, these types of facilities and operations would be as well. The LGO Protocol provides clear guidance on criteria for operational or financial control:

> A local government has operational control over an operation if the local government has the full authority to introduce and implement its operating policies at the operation. One or more of the following conditions establishes operational control:
>
> • Wholly owning an operation, facility, or source; or
> • Having the full authority to introduce and implement operational and health, safety and environmental policies (including both GHG- and non-GHG-related policies). . . .
>
> A local government has financial control over an operation for GHG accounting purposes if the operation is fully consolidated in financial accounts. The LGO Protocol strongly recommends the use of the operational control approach to defining a jurisdiction's boundary for the local government operations inventory.[12]

Greenhouse Gas Emissions Forecast[13]

It is common practice to prepare a GHG emissions forecast once the inventory has been completed. GHG forecasts are projections of possible future GHG emissions from all sectors of the inventory. Local forecasts for population, jobs, and housing are used to develop a forecast of future emissions; this is referred to as the business-as-usual (BAU) forecast (see figure 4.1). The BAU forecast can be thought of as what the emissions would be in the future if nothing new was done to try to reduce them. The development of the BAU forecast is often accompanied by the setting of a GHG emissions reduction target for the forecast year. The difference between the likely increase in emissions estimated in the BAU forecast and the emissions reduction target establishes the amount of emissions reduction that must be accomplished through climate action strategies or through other means, such as state regulations. This is sometimes called the "reduction wedge" due to its appearance when graphed (see figure 4.1).

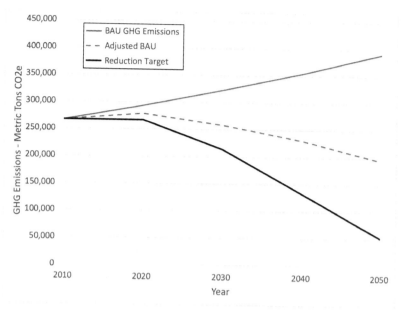

Figure 4-1 Example of a community-wide greenhouse gas (GHG) emissions forecast and reduction target. The upper line, business-as-usual (BAU), indicates the projected emissions if no additional actions to reduce emissions are taken. The middle line, adjusted BAU, represents the local consequences of state and federal policy such as fuel-efficiency regulations, renewable energy portfolio requirements, and energy-efficient building standards. The bottom line represents a community's adopted GHG emissions reduction target. The wedge that is the difference between BAU and the reduction target represents the amount of emissions that must be reduced in a given community through a combination of local, state, and federal actions. The difference between the adjusted BAU and reduction target identifies the reductions to be achieved through local climate action.

Selection of Forecast Year(s)

During the selection of a baseline year, it is common practice for a municipality to select one or more forecast years. Forecast years are usually at least five years from the baseline year, with 10 to 20 years being common. The first principle is that the forecast years should be consistent with the emissions reduction target years (described later in this chapter). Other considerations include the availability of a jurisdiction's forecasts for population, jobs, and housing and the relationship of the inventory to other long-range planning documents or regulations. For example, most municipalities in California use 2020 and 2030 as forecast years to be consistent with the goals of California's Global Warming Solutions Act and its subsequent implementation documents. The choice of a forecast year or years for the inventory also essentially establishes the planning horizon.

Adjusting the Forecast

Some GHG emissions forecasts show an adjusted BAU forecast. Since the forecasts for population, jobs, and housing used to develop the standard BAU forecast are typically simple extrapolation models based on historic data, they do not capture more complex factors that may affect these community measures. These factors are usually referred to as external (or exogenous) factors, since they are not accounted for within the simple extrapolation model.

There are several types of external changes that will affect future levels of GHG emissions in a community: technological, social/behavioral, legislative and regulatory, demographic, and economic. Issues for technological innovation and change include automotive technology and fuels, electricity generation and fuels, and building technology. Social/behavioral changes may include commuting habits, household energy use, and purchasing habits. Potential legislative and regulatory changes may include cap-and-trade legislation, renewable energy portfolio standards, and fuel-efficiency standards (e.g., the Corporate Average Fuel Economy [CAFE] federal standard). Demographic changes that may influence GHG emissions include population growth, poverty level, and housing tenure and occupancy. Long-term GHG emissions may also be influenced by economic changes in gross domestic product, industrial and manufacturing mix, and balance of trade. This sampling of issues shows that considerable uncertainty exists in forecasting future levels of GHG emissions, particularly at the community level.

Two common solutions when dealing with uncertainty in forecasting are either to ignore it and use the original BAU forecast or to develop multiple forecast ranges or scenarios. The problem with the former is that change seems almost certain at this point. For example, vehicle miles traveled (VMT) has become increasingly difficult to predict. After multiple decades of steady growth, in the mid-2000s, VMT went down, then leveled off. Just when it appeared that VMT, especially per capita, was on a long-term flat trend, it started going up again. And the rapid changes in mobility—Lyft/Uber, scooters, bicycling, and possible autonomous vehicles—have made predicting future VMT almost a guessing game. Emissions forecasts that assume long-term trends will persist and do not consider the potential for dramatic changes over the short term may have important policy consequences.

The policy implications of ongoing external change that decreases or increases GHG emissions could include the setting of unduly aggressive or conservative reduction targets, "sticker shock" reactions to how much effort would be required to meet aggressive reduction targets, or despondency created from a sense that the future growth of emissions is inevitable. Additionally, assuming no external changes puts communities in the position of misjudging the level of local GHG emissions reductions needed. Too little reduction and the community misses its reduction target. Too much emissions reduction and the community may incur high costs (an economically inefficient outcome) or bear an unfair share of state and national reduction targets. Yet this is the most common assumption made.

The problem with addressing uncertainty by developing multiple forecast ranges or scenarios is that making assumptions about future changes in the areas listed would likely exceed the capability of most local governments. Moreover, no standardized approach for addressing this has been developed for community-level emissions inventories.

The issue of external change is one of the most difficult technical issues in GHG emissions forecasting. Guidance is poor and often conflicting; moreover, the rapid rate of technical, legislative/regulatory, and social change makes it challenging to adjust BAU forecasts to account for change. Yet these changes will have a significant impact on the ability of communities to develop mitigation actions to adequately account for their share of needed GHG emissions reductions. In fact, some communities are counting on this external change to help them achieve their targets. The best current advice is for communities to identify future emissions reductions resulting from statewide policies such as requirements for vehicle fuel mileage or targets for electricity production from low-carbon fuel sources. If the state has a climate action plan or similar document, these types of policies may be specified and linked to forecasted GHG emissions reductions. Since federal policy appears uncertain at this time and the rate of technology change is very difficult to predict, it is not recommended to adjust the BAU forecast based on these factors. In the future, better assistance from federal and state agencies on this issue is needed.

Selection of Emissions Reduction Targets

The emissions reduction target is the quantity of GHG emissions the jurisdiction wants to reduce by the forecast year. The reduction target is typically expressed as the percentage by which emissions will be reduced relative to a baseline year (e.g., 15% reduction from the 2015 baseline level by 2030). A jurisdiction may select more than one reduction target. Reduction targets may be short term, midterm, or long term—or all three. The period will influence the range of actions and policy options used to achieve them. A local government may set a long-term goal but also have shorter-term targets that serve as incremental steps toward that goal. Communities may also have sector-specific targets or goals in addition to overall community-wide reduction targets. Target setting may include consideration of targets adopted by other levels of government, neighboring or peer communities, feasibility of achievement or implementation, scientific studies and reports, and the urgency of the issue. Separate baseline years, target years, and reduction percentages may be established for local government operations and community-wide emissions.

Adopted Reduction Targets

Many communities choose to adopt reduction targets that have been established by other organizations or government agencies. The benefit is that these targets have usually been vetted scientifically, they relieve the community of having to develop their own analysis and standard setting, and they create consistency among communities. The downside is that they may not adequately capture local conditions and contexts and may not reflect local values.

International Standards

At this time the most notable international attempt to establish GHG emissions reduction targets has been the Paris Agreement, a protocol of the United Nations Framework Convention on Climate Change (UNF-CCC) that was established in December of 2015 in Paris, France. The Paris Agreement has been signed by 195 countries and ratified or agreed to by 183 countries as well as the European Union. The Paris Agreement set a goal of reducing GHG emissions sufficiently to keep the increase in global temperatures to "well below 2°C above pre-industrial levels, and to pursue efforts to limit the temperature increase to 1.5°C above pre-industrial levels."[14] It allows each country to establish its own GHG reduction target, called a "Nationally Determined Contribution" (NDC), and calls on countries to report on their progress and adopt new, increasingly stringent targets every five years.

The challenge with using the 1.5°–2°C standard is that it does not provide clear guidance or meaning at the local level. In 2009, a group of climate scientists asserted that atmospheric CO_2 should not exceed 350 parts per million (ppm; ~ 450 CO_{2e}) if the 2°C threshold was not to be crossed.[15] As of July 2018, atmospheric CO_2 was 412 ppm.[16] Although it is difficult to translate these standards to a reduction target, research suggests that this would necessitate a 50% to 95% reduction from 1990 levels by 2050.[17] The Under2 Coalition of states and regions around the world have endorsed "reducing greenhouse gas emissions equivalent to 80 to 95 percent below 1990 levels or to less than 2 annual metric tons per capita by 2050" in order to stay below the 2°C threshold.[18]

National and State Standards

There are no official U.S. GHG emissions reduction targets, and states vary as to whether they have adopted standards (see box 4.3).[19] In March

2016, the United States established its NDC under the Paris Agreement at 26% to 28% below 2005 levels by 2025; local governments could use this target, though there is no post-2025 target. Moreover, in 2017 the United States indicated its intent to withdraw from the Paris Agreement, although under the language of the agreement, formal notice of withdrawal cannot occur until at least November 2019 and would take one year to become effective.

Considerations for Adopting Local Reduction Targets

In states with officially adopted GHG emissions reduction targets, cities should consider adopting consistent targets or targets directed by any other guidance. For example, the State of California is recommending that local jurisdictions adopt "targets of no more than six metric tons CO_{2e} per capita by 2030 and no more than two metric tons CO_{2e} per capita by 2050."[20] As of 2018, no state had mandated local targets, but some states have policies and programs that may make consistency beneficial by providing access to grants or by easing other regulatory requirements.

Most communities, recognizing the urgency of the climate crisis and the 1.5°–2°C target established in the Paris Agreement, are choosing to set 2050 goals of reducing GHG emissions by 80%–100%. Interim goals—which also should be established—are then determined based on the local feasibility of bending the emissions curve down toward 2050. For example, Cincinnati, Ohio, has targets of 8% below 2006 levels by 2012 (which they achieved), 40% below 2006 levels by 2028, and 84% below 2006 levels by 2050.

The issue of whether to adopt a percentage reduction of total emissions or a per-capita target is not critical and should be a local preference. Communities should be at least tracking both. For communities that are growing fast, though, per-capita targets may make the most sense. At least over the short- and midterm, reduction of total emissions in a fast-growing community could be daunting and not realistic to the community. Fast-growing communities will likely increase their emissions simply because they are adding people versus slow-growth communities that will see little increase over baseline even if they do nothing.

Box 4.3

National, Regional, and State Greenhouse Gas Reduction Targets

National-Level Targets

- *U.S. Paris Agreement NDC (provisional):* 26–28% below 2005 by 2025
- *Canada:* 17% below 2005 by 2020[1]

U.S. State-Level Targets[2]

- *Arizona:* 2000 levels by 2020 and 50% below 2000 by 2040
- *California:* 1990 levels by 2020, 40% below 1990 by 2030, and 80% below 1990 by 2050
- *Colorado:* 26% below 2005 by 2025
- *Connecticut:* 10% below 1990 by 2020 and 80% below 2001 by 2050
- *Florida:* 2000 levels by 2017, 1990 levels by 2025, and 80% below 1990 by 2050
- *Hawaii:* Carbon-neutral by 2045
- *Illinois:* 1990 levels by 2020 and 60% below 1990 by 2050
- *Maine:* 1990 levels by 2010, 10% below 1990 by 2020, and 75%–80% below 2003 in the long term
- *Maryland:* 40% below 2006 by 2030
- *Massachusetts:* 25% below 1990 by 2020 and 80% below 1990 by 2050
- *Michigan:* 20% below 2005 by 2025 and 80% below 2005 by 2050
- *Minnesota:* 15% below 2005 by 2015, 30% below 2005 by 2025, and 80% below 2005 by 2050
- *New Hampshire:* 20% below 1990 by 2025 and 80% below 1990 by 2050

1. See http://www.climatechange.gc.ca/default.asp?lang=en&n=72f16a84-1.
2. See https://www.c2es.org/document/greenhouse-gas-emissions-targets/.

- *New Jersey:* 1990 levels by 2020 and 80% below 2006 by 2050
- *New Mexico:* 2000 levels by 2012, 10% below 2000 by 2020, and 75% below 2000 by 2050
- *New York:* 40% below 1990 by 2030 and 80% below 1990 by 2050
- *Oregon:* 10% below 1990 by 2020, and 75% below 1990 by 2050
- *Rhode Island:* 10% below 1990 by 2020, 45% below 1990 by 2035, and 80% below 1990 by 2050
- *Vermont:* 40% below 1990 by 2020, and 80–90% below 1990 by 2050
- *Washington:* 1990 levels by 2020, 25% below 1990 by 2035, and 50% below 1990 by 2050

Note: Check with your nation, state, or region for updates.

This does raise the question of whether 80%–100% by 2050 is fast enough (100% essentially being carbon-neutral or zero-carbon). Currently, 2050 is the most common target year for becoming low- or zero-carbon, but a number of cities are pursuing much more aggressive goals. The City of Copenhagen, Denmark, has a goal of carbon neutrality by 2025, and the City of San Luis Obispo, California, has adopted a goal to be carbon-neutral by 2035. Are these realistic? Both cities assert these are achievable goals and are pursuing aggressive action to get there. It is almost certain that waiting until 2050 is waiting too long. The 2018 special report Global Warming of 1.5°C from the Intergovernmental Panel on Climate Change (IPCC) suggests significant global action is needed before 2030:

Estimates of the global emissions outcome of current nationally stated mitigation ambitions as submitted under the Paris Agreement would lead to global greenhouse gas emissions in 2030 of 52–58 $GtCO_{2eq}$ yr–1 (medium confidence). Pathways reflecting these ambitions would not limit global warming to 1.5°C, even if supplemented by very challenging increases in the scale and ambition of emissions reductions after 2030 (high confidence). Avoiding overshoot and reliance on future large-scale deployment of carbon dioxide removal (CDR) can only be achieved if global CO_2 emissions start to decline well before 2030 (high confidence).[21]

The following summarize our recommendations:

1. If your state has a reduction target, consider adopting that target, especially if there are benefits to consistency (such as access to grants or protection from state regulatory action).
2. Consider being consistent with the Paris Agreement and adopting an 80%–100% GHG emissions reduction by 2050 or sooner, with appropriate interim goals.
3. Consider adopting the Under2 Coalition per-capita target of 2 metric tons CO_{2e} per person, especially if in a fast-growing community.
4. Given the urgency of the climate crisis, all communities should aspire to be highly ambitious and consider becoming carbon neutral by 2035 as a goal.

Quantifying Greenhouse Gas Emissions Reductions

Determining the anticipated GHG reductions from each policy or strategy, a process called "quantification," makes it easier to assess whether climate action strategies will achieve the identified reduction targets (see box 4.4). Quantification is therefore one of the most important components of climate action planning and is regarded as the key criterion for evaluating reduction strategies. Unfortunately, there are no standardized GHG emissions reduction estimates that can be assigned to reduction strategies. GHG reductions are estimated based on a variety of measures and assumptions that differ by community or region. For example, electricity in the Midwest is largely produced from coal, whereas in the West it is from natural gas and hydropower, resulting in very different GHG emissions reductions for the same energy efficiency strategies, just as these distinctions result in very different GHG emissions in the inventory.

Successful and useful quantification will clearly show the level of participation needed to achieve the intended reduction. For example, if a strategy to conduct home energy efficiency retrofits is quantified as reducing GHG emissions by 5,000 metric tons of CO_{2e} by 2030, the quantification should clearly say how many houses need to undergo retrofits to reduce emissions by this amount. This level of participation is also called a performance indicator. The quantification should also clearly identify the methods and any assumptions used in determining the GHG reductions. This allows a community to monitor whether it is implementing a strategy at the necessary level to achieve the desired reductions and to make changes to the policy if circumstances change.

Emissions reduction calculations can be detailed quantifications or rough estimates. Most efforts will likely include both depending on the measure type, level of importance, and certainty with which assumptions can be made. In some cases, there will be high levels of uncertainty in estimating strategy effectiveness. This is particularly true for strategies that rely on voluntary community action. Due to high levels of uncertainty, conservative estimates or an estimate range may be enough. Also, strategies that comprise a very small portion of total GHG emissions reduction may not require precise estimates of GHG reductions. For example, an incentive program encouraging drought-tolerant landscaping will reduce GHG emissions associated with the treatment and delivery of water. However, water often represents a very small portion of community emissions, and it is difficult to estimate the level of community participation in this program and the amount of water that will be saved. In this case, a simple set of assumptions that are locally appropriate, such as the percentage of participation and the percentage of water use reduction per participating household, is likely to be enough. If this strategy was a major portion of overall GHG reductions, it may be appropriate for factors such as evapotranspiration rates, wind, and average yard size to be considered in the reduction estimate.

An increasingly popular tool for quantifying the emissions reduction potential of climate action strategies is the World Bank's CURB tool: "CURB is an interactive tool that is designed specifically to help cities take action on climate by allowing them to map out different action plans and evaluate their cost, feasibility, and impact."[22] It can be tailored

Box 4.4

Examples of Greenhouse Gas Emissions Reduction Estimation

The City of Cincinnati, Ohio, adopted the following policy: "Continue to support Red Bike (bike share) as an equitable mobility solution." The following description from their 2018 Green Cincinnati Plan explains the data and assumptions necessary to calculate the annual emissions reductions that would result from implementation of the strategy: "If Red Bike grows by 20,000 rides per year and the average ride is 1.5 miles, and cars emit 4.2 tons of CO_2 per 10,000 miles traveled, this recommendation will avoid 12.6 tons in year 1, and an additional 12.6 tons per year for each subsequent expansion."

The description shows that the source metric is based on assumptions about ridership growth and average ride length. There is also an assumption that these trips will replace car trips. The emissions factor for these displaced car trips is a readily available estimate of CO_2 emissions per mile. From this, the City estimated a 2023 reduction potential of 63 $mtCO_{2e}$.[1]

Contra Costa County, California, adopted the following policy: "Promote installation of alternative energy facilities on homes and businesses." The policy includes numerous specific actions:

1. Amend the County Zoning Code to designate areas and development standards that are appropriate for and supportive of small- and medium-sized alternative energy and energy storage installations not covered by AB 2188
2. Train planning staff to provide guidance and information on the streamlined process and available incentives
3. Create development standards allowing for the ministerial approval of rooftop energy systems on commercial buildings,

---

1. City of Cincinnati, *Green Cincinnati Plan* (2018), https://www.cincinnati-oh.gov/oes/citywide-efforts/climate-protection-green-cincinnati-plan/.

with a focus on warehouses and other structures with large surface area roofs

4. Encourage participation in PG&E's [utility company] green tariff program

In calculating the annual emissions reduction that would result from implementation, the County made assumptions about the specific number of new and existing home and businesses that would be influenced by the various programs and add solar arrays by 2020 and 2035.

They then explained their method:

> Forecasted residential and nonresidential solar installations as a result of the California Solar Initiative and BayREN programs were used to identify solar installations in 2020 and 2035. The county identified a target increase from that number and reductions were estimated based on average kW by installation type. Green tariff reductions are based on expected increases in renewable energy as a result of residential and nonresidential participation in educational and incentive programs. Reductions were applied to forecasted energy usage. These reductions were applied to participating households and businesses, which were identified by applying target participation rates to relevant building types. The sum of these reductions was then converted to $MTCO_{2e}$.

From this, the county estimated that the strategy would reduce 14,840 MT CO_{2e} per year by 2035.[2]

2. Contra Costa County, Climate Action Plan (2015), http://www.co .contra-costa.ca.us/4554/Climate-Action-Plan.

using city-specific data, and it is an Excel-based tool, free, and endorsed by the C40 Cities Climate Leadership Group and the Global Covenant of Mayors. Training and technical support are available. In addition to CURB, the ICLEI ClearPath tool includes modules for GHG emissions reduction quantification and can be useful to communities that conduct their inventories through ClearPath. A challenge with these types of tools is that the default assumptions and parameters may not be representative of any specific community. In addition, software tools inevitably have a level of opaqueness that may make complete understanding, documentation, and additional application more challenging.

Some communities choose to conduct their own GHG emissions reduction calculations. One of the most complete references for quantifying reduction strategies is the August 2010 California Air Pollution Control Officers Association (CAPCOA) guide for local governments, *Quantifying Greenhouse Gas Emissions Measures*, though it is increasingly out of date. The goal of the report is "to provide accurate and reliable quantification methods that can be used throughout California and adapted for use outside of the state as well."[23] The report contains a series of fact sheets on particular types of reduction strategies and accompanying guides on how to use the fact sheets. The quantification methods are based on using readily available data gathered by the planning team. The CAPCOA report describes the basic logic of emissions quantification.[24] It does not include all potential reduction strategies, and some of the methods it includes may not be appropriate for all communities. If a community cannot use the CAPCOA guide or another resource to quantify GHG reductions, planners may create their own method or modify an existing one. These custom methods should be defensible, and as with all quantification, all methods and assumptions should be well documented.

The general equation for emissions quantification is shown here for each GHG:

$$\text{GHG emissions} = [\text{source metric}] \times [\text{emissions factor}] \times [\text{GWP}],$$

where source metric and emissions factor are defined as follows:

- *Source metric:* The "source metric" is the unit of measure of the source of the emissions. For example, for transportation sources, the metric is vehicle miles traveled; for building energy use, it is "energy intensity," that is, the energy demand per home or per square foot of building space. Mitigation measures [reduction strategies] that involve source reduction are measures that reduce the source metric. For example, if a source metric is the number of vehicle miles driven, a reduction in miles will generally lead to a reduction in emissions. Similarly, a reduction in home electricity use by installing energy efficient appliances and lighting will typically reduce the emissions associated with total electricity assigned to dwelling units.
- *Emission factor:* The "emission factor" is the rate at which emissions are generated per unit of source metric (see above). Reductions in the emission factor happen when fewer emissions are generated per unit of source metric—for example, a decrease in the amount of emissions that are released per kilowatt-hour of electricity used or per ton of waste thrown away. Such a decrease may apply if a carbon-neutral electricity source (e.g., from photovoltaics) is used in place of grid electricity, which has higher associated emissions, or if electricity is used instead of combustion fuel, such as with electric cars. Reductions can also occur if a fuel with lower GHG emissions is used in the place of one with higher GHG emissions. From a quantification standpoint, for this type of measure, it is the "emission factor" in the equation that changes.[25]

Including Science in a GHG Emissions Accounting Inventory or Report

The scientific and technical issues in doing GHG accounting raise the issue of whether and how to address the basic science of climate change when documenting or reporting the results. For example, should a community-wide GHG inventory or climate action plan include a section that explains the basics of climate change and GHG emissions? Although this is not necessary, especially given that numerous references on the topic are available, it is common practice to include this information. The *Chicago Climate Action Plan* has a graphically interesting two-page spread that provides a very brief primer on climate change, and the San Francisco climate action plan has 20 pages of climate change science, though mostly on the effects of climate change on the city. Other communities that may not have climate action plans may include web-pages on the topic or staff reports or other public documents.

A primer on the science of climate change, if developed, should answer the following questions for the reader:

1. How do we know the planet is warming?
2. What causes global warming?
3. What are the consequences of global warming?
4. What are the primary sources of anthropogenic greenhouse gases?

The answers to the last two questions should specifically address the local community to the degree possible. For example, it is not expected that global warming will affect all places equally on the globe with respect to heat waves, drought, rainfall, and the like. Nor do all communities produce the same amounts or types of GHGs.

The third question, on the consequences of warming, is difficult to answer for any specific locality given that the science to predict regional changes with confidence is only now emerging. A very useful starting point for understanding the potential local impacts of global warming is the *2017–2018 Fourth National Climate Assessment* produced by the U.S. Global Change Research Program. Volume 1 reviews the science of climate change in the United States, while volume 2 focuses on identifying the impacts and risks of these changes.[26] In addition to this report, many states have also prepared reports on the anticipated impacts of climate change. For example, the State of California produces a biennial climate change assessment report that identifies the impact of climate change on key sectors based on a variety of climate change scenarios.[27] The fourth question, on the source of GHG emissions, can be answered locally through the preparation of a local GHG emissions inventory.

The purpose of explaining the science will vary by community. In some communities, the science simply serves to define the issue. In other communities, the science may be needed to inform a skeptical public of the need for climate action or to explain why the jurisdiction has been motivated to act. Whatever the case, the primer and associated education and outreach should explain to the community the purpose of knowing the science. Thinking this through will help planners focus on what content and what level of detail are actually needed.

Next Steps

Best practice standards for GHG emissions accounting are changing and improving regularly. The choices and assumptions made in GHG emissions inventories, forecasts, and reduction targets influence selection and implementation of climate strategies. Following the process outlined in this chapter is recommended to ensure the effectiveness of the next steps in the climate action planning process.

Chapter 5

Strategies for Creating Low-Carbon Communities

A low-carbon community is one that has eliminated all or nearly all human-generated carbon dioxide and other greenhouse gas (GHG) emissions. In addition, such a community is usually addressing any residual emissions through carbon sequestration and carbon-offset initiatives. Those in the low-carbon community movement go by a number of names, such as zero-carbon, net-zero, carbon-free, carbon-neutral, and climate-friendly communities. These communities also seek not just to reduce emissions but to enhance overall sustainability and livability. A number of cities around the world have made bold announcements (also see figure 5.1):

- Melbourne, Australia, set a target of net-zero emissions by 2020.
- San Luis Obispo (California), U.S.A., adopted a goal of becoming carbon-neutral by 2035.
- Copenhagen, Denmark, is moving quickly to be carbon-neutral by 2025.
- Vancouver (BC), Canada, plans to achieve 80% GHG emissions reduction and 100% renewable energy by 2050.
- Fort Collins (Colorado), U.S.A., aims to reduce emissions 80% by 2030 with the goal of being carbon-neutral by 2050.

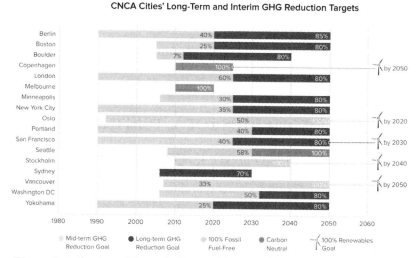

Figure 5-1 Carbon Neutral Cities Alliance (CNCA) long-term and interim GHG reduction targets of member cities

Source: Carbon Neutral Cities Alliance, *Framework for Long-Term Deep Carbon Reduction Planning* (2017), https://carbonneutralcities.org.

To become a low-carbon or carbon-neutral community requires following a path to what has come to be called "deep decarbonization." Deep decarbonization has three pillars:

- *Energy efficiency and conservation:* Lowering the energy consumed per unit of GDP (energy intensity) by technically improving products and processes, including waste reduction and structural and behavioral changes. Examples in transport include improving vehicle technologies, smart urban design, and optimizing logistical chains; in buildings, improving end-use equipment, architectural design, building practices, and construction materials; and in manufacturing, improving equipment, production processes, material efficiency, and the reuse of waste heat.
- *Decarbonizing electricity and fuels:* Reducing the carbon content of all transformed energies: electricity, heat, liquids, and gases. In the power sector, this means replacing uncontrolled fossil fuel-based

generation with renewable energy (e.g., hydro, wind, solar, and geo-thermal) and nuclear power and/or fossil fuels with carbon capture and storage (CCS). For on-site and in-vehicle combustion, this includes decarbonizing liquid and gas fuels through the diffusion of biomass fuel and/or synthetic fuels (e.g., hydrogen) produced through low-carbon processes.

- *Switching energy end-uses to lower-carbon, and eventually zero-carbon, energy carriers (e.g., electricity, hydrogen, and biofuels):* Initially, for example, this entails shifting from coal to natural gas. In the longer run, it means shifting to decarbonized energy carriers such as electrification of space and water heating and cooling; adoption of electric, biofuel, or hydrogen vehicles; and industry directly using biofuels, hydrogen, or synthetic natural gas (syngas).[1]

For communities, these have a number of implications. Energy efficiency and conservation suggests less driving and greater use of transit, bicycling, and walking; green buildings through better codes, incentives, and retrofit programs; and public education about the merits and benefits of conservation. Low-carbon electricity suggests solar rooftops and other renewable energy strategies; municipal or community-based utilities with the ability to develop or purchase carbon-free electricity; and support of state and national efforts to move utilities to renewable energy. Fuel-switching suggests electric vehicles and the supporting infrastructure, especially charging stations; all or mostly electric homes and businesses; and switching from propane and natural gas tools, appliances, and systems to electricity (in careful coordination with the other two pillars). These are not merely technical challenges; they will require changes in behavior and culture around how we build, manage, and live in our communities.

Deep decarbonization requires the adoption of low-carbon strategies (a.k.a. GHG emissions reduction or mitigation strategies) that eliminate or reduce the emissions of GHGs and sequester or offset remaining emissions. The development of these strategies is an iterative process that should balance the GHG reduction potential, up-front and ongoing costs, and social and political feasibility. Most reduction strategies have benefits beyond emissions reduction; these are called "co-benefits." For example, reducing GHG emissions can also lower ground-level ozone concentrations in a community, which will yield public health benefits, especially for those who suffer from asthma or other respiratory conditions. The development of reduction strategies should be seen not only as an opportunity to address climate change but as a chance to position a community to become more economically, environmentally, and socially sustainable.

Because GHG emissions result from a range of urban processes, operations, and behaviors, successful reduction of GHG emissions relies not only on governmental action but also on the commitment of community members and collaboration with business, industry, and community organizations. Many members of a community, including business and industry, have embraced green or sustainability principles and seek to be involved in efforts that show their commitment to a better environment. They bring resources, audiences, and ideas that local governments may not.

GHG emissions reduction is an increasingly common area of policy development. As a result, there are many resources that provide examples of successful reduction strategies. The challenge for communities is identifying those strategies that best meet local needs. This chapter provides guidance for developing such reduction strategies. It does not provide a comprehensive list of emissions reduction best practices; these continually evolve and are available in other resources (see the "Additional Resources" section at the end of the book). Instead, it identifies the key issues and decisions that must be addressed during reduction strategy development. Reduction strategy development builds on data collected through the emissions inventory, policy audit, and public participation process.

Developing Low-Carbon Strategies

One of the first tasks in developing reduction strategies is to organize the community partners and the public to establish a participation process as discussed in chapters 2 and 3. Regardless of how this is done, those teams that will brainstorm, develop, and finalize the reduction strategies must work through the following considerations:

1. What are the key sectors of the community to target for the most effective and efficient reduction of GHG emissions?
2. How will the strategies be specified to ensure effectiveness?

3. What level of analysis will be conducted to estimate the GHG emissions reductions of the proposed strategies, if any?
4. How will the strategies be evaluated?
5. What should a strategy include?

Targeting Key Sectors

One of the first steps in low-carbon strategy development is careful evaluation of the GHG emissions inventory (see chapter 4), policy audit (see
chapter 2), and community characteristics. These provide data necessary
to identify areas of focus for the development of reduction strategies that
will best meet the needs and capabilities of the community.

The sectors shown in the GHG emissions inventory to contribute
most to local emissions should be targeted in the reduction strategies. For
example, in a community where a large percentage of GHG emissions
come from a coal plant that produces electricity used in local buildings, a
strategy should be to reduce electricity use and perhaps explore renewable
energy sources.

The local policy audit, introduced in chapter 2, should be conducted
around the time of the emissions inventory. The audit identifies community policies already in place that may support or be in conflict with
reduction goals. For example, many communities already have programs
to improve energy or water efficiency that also reduce local GHG emissions. Policies such as developing cooling centers or planned low-density
development have the potential to conflict with emissions reduction
goals. Current and pending national, state, and regional policy should also
be included in the policy audit to evaluate changes outside of local control
that may influence local emissions. These policies can include federal
fuel-efficiency standards for passenger automobiles or requirements for
the percentage of renewable energy supplied by energy providers (i.e.,
renewable energy portfolio standards).

Finally, a set of basic community characteristics is important to
complement these resources, including data such as the distribution of
housing stock (age of structures and structure type); recent permit and
building activity; typical commute length; demographic and economic
data such as age, income distribution, and housing affordability; and

environmental data such as topography, temperature profile, wind patterns, and solar exposure. Some of this can be found in the U.S. Census American Community Survey data; some may be available from state or regional agencies, if not available locally. These data provide a strong basis for local strategy development and prioritization. The assumptions used for the business-as-usual forecast in the emissions inventory, such as population, housing, jobs, and transportation growth rates, serve a similar role in the formulation of reduction strategies. For example, slow-growth communities (~ < 1% per year) or communities where the building stock consists primarily of older structures will need to focus more specifically on retrofitting existing buildings to achieve energy efficiency improvements than a rapidly growing region that can more easily achieve efficiency improvements by imposing standards on new construction. Community data can provide additional understanding of the inventory data. For example, a community that has a large incoming daily commute due to housing affordability can address two sources of emissions by focusing on building green, affordable housing. This reduces transportation emissions by reducing commute length and reduces residential energy use through construction of energy-efficient housing.

In summary, a community should answer questions such as the following when beginning development of reduction strategies. These questions can be adjusted and/or supplemented depending on local conditions.

- What are the largest sources of emissions in the community? (GHG emissions inventory)
- What is the community already doing that reduces GHG emissions? (policy audit)
- What are the expected growth/decline rates of population, housing, jobs, and transportation in the community? (GHG emissions inventory)
- Are there community characteristics that influence emissions-generating behaviors? (community characteristics)
- What is the age of the housing stock? (community characteristics)
- What is the typical commute length (and is it more in-commuters or out-commuters)? (GHG emissions inventory and community characteristics)

• What are the topography, temperature profile, wind patterns, and solar exposure of the community? (community characteristics)

Specifying Effective and Appropriate Reduction Strategies

Strategies that serve to reduce GHG emissions take three forms: mandates, incentives or disincentives, and voluntary actions. The choice of strategy type must be made with careful consideration of the local context. The policy audit can be helpful here, since much can be learned from existing community strategies that have proven successful. This helps clarify the full range of policy options, which is important for the process of balancing necessary reduction areas against other community needs.

Mandates may have higher costs or face greater political resistance, but more confidence can be placed in the emissions reductions being realized. For example, a strategy that requires an energy efficiency building retrofit at the point of sale or major renovation is likely to be far more effective in reducing emissions than an incentive program that offers a small rebate to community members willing to voluntarily update household appliances to improve energy efficiency. But requiring such an upgrade may meet some resistance. Mandates should also be evaluated with consideration given to which members of a community are most likely impacted (e.g., bearing the bulk of the cost or excluded due to increased costs). Social justice considerations should be paramount in ensuring that the most vulnerable in a community do not bear a disproportionate or unfair burden.

Incentives and disincentives can take many forms. They may be monetary, such as paying a fee or penalty for an action that increases GHG emissions or a rebate or other incentive payment for an action that decreases them. A common set of examples are rebate programs to incentivize the purchase of LED lightbulbs, energy-efficient appliances, electric vehicles, and other energy-saving actions, though these are usually federal, state, or utility programs. Incentives and disincentives can be nonmonetary as well: for example, a local government could offer expedited permitting for energy efficiency upgrades or solar panel installation, or they could restrict parking or increase parking fees to discourage people from driving to a dense urban core (encouraging them to take other modes of transportation instead).

Voluntary actions can be very attractive politically, but they require more diligence to ensure effectiveness. In general, voluntary measures should be accompanied by strong outreach and education strategies that ensure that those in the community know about the measure and also understand why they should take voluntary action.

Strategy types should also be combined, particularly for strategies that are politically challenging. Successful phasing in of new mandates in the face of political opposition can begin with outreach and education to build community support for the strategy, followed by an incentive program to encourage voluntary compliance, and only then should the proposed changes be required. Many emissions-reducing strategies rely, in part, on voluntary behavior change. As a result, combining incentives and education with strategies such as the provision of new infrastructure bolsters long-term effectiveness.

Evaluating Reduction Strategies

A community may identify many reduction strategies, but only some of them will be appropriate. Therefore, there should be a process to evaluate and prioritize each reduction strategy to ensure that it meets a community's needs and constraints. Identification of local needs and constraints and the establishment of the process necessary for this assessment begin with the formation of the climate action team (CAT; chapter 2) and community outreach (chapter 3). Climate action planning should include disclosure of the analysis of elements that contribute to the selection and prioritization of strategies. This information allows for greater transparency in the planning process and more clearly sets a path for implementation. The questions listed here should be addressed through the work of the CAT and through a public participation process for each reduction strategy considered. Others can be added based on local need. These questions are interrelated. For example, the need for funding may delay strategy implementation, which will subsequently adjust the emissions reduction estimates.

- What is the potential emissions reduction that will result from the strategy's implementation?
- How long will it take to begin implementation of the strategy?

- How long will it take for the strategy to be fully implemented?
- What are the costs (initial and ongoing) of implementing the strategy?
- What is the political and social feasibility of the strategy?
- Are there co-benefits to the strategy's implementation?

WHAT IS THE POTENTIAL EMISSIONS REDUCTION THAT WILL RESULT FROM THE STRATEGY'S IMPLEMENTATION?

The amount of GHG emissions reduction possible from each strategy should be compared to assess the relative value of each. Chapter 4 includes details on the methods for doing quantification. It isn't necessarily the case that strategies with the highest amount of GHG emissions reduction should be prioritized; they may be difficult to implement, expensive, or not widely supported. The emissions reduction is only one factor among many. Once all strategies are identified, the GHG emissions quantification then plays an additional role of allowing those in a community to see what their total reductions will be if all strategies are implemented. This should be an iterative process that gets the community to its overall GHG reduction target.

HOW LONG WILL IT TAKE TO BEGIN IMPLEMENTATION OF THE STRATEGY?

In some cases, a strategy can be universally hailed by staff, the community, and advisory bodies but still require a series of actions to be completed prior to the start of implementation. This can be as simple as the time it takes to update or amend the comprehensive plan or drafting a new ordinance. In other cases, this may involve securing funding through grants or a local fee system to initiate a program. The choice of who will be implementing the strategy will also affect timing, since priorities and capacities will vary. Each measure should be evaluated for how soon it can realistically be implemented.

HOW LONG WILL IT TAKE FOR THE STRATEGY TO BE FULLY IMPLEMENTED?

Full implementation refers to the time it will take to achieve the estimated emissions reduction. For example, a new ordinance can be adopted in the short term. This implements the strategy; however, the experience of the subsequent emissions reductions will be distributed through time.

In some cases, a strategy will identify a change that will take many years to fully achieve. For example, a green building ordinance aimed at new residences in a slow-growing community will likely produce benefits at a much slower rate than a strategy aimed at retrofitting existing residences.

What Are the Costs (Initial and Ongoing) of Implementing the Strategy?

The high up-front cost is one of the biggest limitations of climate-friendly strategies such as building retrofits for energy efficiency, renewable energy, or vehicle upgrades. This is a critical factor for evaluating and planning for strategy implementation. If a funding mechanism is not identified for a strategy, time to raise necessary funds must be planned into the phasing of strategies. The initial costs of a strategy can be a critical consideration when prioritizing it for immediate implementation. Given the limited budgets of local governments, funds must be carefully allocated.

In addition to initial costs, many projects carry ongoing costs of implementation, including materials, maintenance, and administration. Accurate estimation of these costs and a way to budget these funds are both vital to reduction measure formulation. Often these costs can be covered through adjustments in fee structures such as more aggressive tiered pricing for water or the establishment of a fund to hold impact fees from new development. However, adjustments in fees must also be accompanied by an evaluation of which populations or community members will be most impacted. This addresses the issue of who bears the costs and who receives the benefits. This can be difficult politically and raises issues of fairness and social justice. Communities should ensure that the costs of strategy implementation are not unfairly borne by a narrow sector of the community, especially those least well-off.

Cost-effectiveness, or *cost-benefit analysis*, refers to a comparison of the costs and benefits (and possibly co-benefits) of a strategy. Communities can evaluate emissions reduction strategies based on their dollar cost per ton of GHG emissions reduced. They can also compare the cost of the strategy to the monetary return or savings to the local government or to the public. For example, Santa Barbara County, California, estimated the costs and savings of several energy efficiency programs for homeowners, showing how the investments were cost effective.[2] Comparing strategies on cost-effectiveness can allow communities to identify how to get the biggest bang for their buck.

WHAT IS THE POLITICAL AND SOCIAL FEASIBILITY OF THE STRATEGY?

Awareness of potential political challenges is important during strategy formulation. These difficulties can be addressed in a variety of ways, such as direct engagement with concerned stakeholders to devise a more palatable approach, including outreach and education as part of implementation, and careful choice of wording to avoid pitfalls. Strategies to identify community priorities and concerns are discussed in chapter 3.

There should also be consideration given to how responsive the "target" will be to the strategy. For example, an ad campaign to get people to drive less may be fairly simple to create, but it may be a difficult way to successfully realize the emissions reduction, since it requires people to change ingrained behaviors. On the other hand, having a city council raise parking meter rates will assuredly result in a change in parking usage and revenues, although this may meet political opposition. Some communities refer to this issue as "ease of implementation."

Communities are unique. Some climate strategies will fit right in with the current ethos of a community; others might be seen as radical. For example, new bicycle initiatives or public spending on bicycle infrastructure is likely to be easily welcomed in Boulder, Colorado, a city that takes pride in its bike culture. A strategy aimed at creating green jobs is likely to be similarly welcomed in communities with high unemployment rates.

ARE THERE CO-BENEFITS TO THE STRATEGY'S IMPLEMENTATION?

Climate action planning is just one aspect of community planning and can be viewed as an opportunity to meet a variety of local goals. Strategies that carry benefits beyond mitigating climate change are most easily promoted to the public as well as decision-makers. Categories of co-benefits include the following:

- cost savings
- energy conservation
- health benefits

- local business support
- municipal revenue enhancement
- water conservation
- education and awareness
- mobility improvement
- climate adaptation
- smart growth
- water and air quality improvement
- green space and recreation improvement
- quality of life improvement
- job creation
- community development and redevelopment

Of these, cost savings and energy conservation are the most common desired co-benefits. Some communities organize their climate action planning around these as their primary benefits and treat GHG emissions reductions as the co-benefits.

Prioritizing the Strategies

Once the evaluation is complete, there are several methods for using the results to rank the strategies. The most straightforward is to pick a single criterion, then choose the strategies that perform best on that criterion. For example, some communities prioritize cost-effectiveness—they are looking for the greatest emissions reduction for the least cost—whereas others have identified co-benefits as the most important criterion. The challenge arises when multiple criteria are used to rank strategies. In this case, each strategy can be scored on each criterion, then the scores can be added up and strategies ranked based on the best overall scores. The scores can be weighted by adding bonus points or multipliers to the most important criteria.

Contents of a Reduction Strategy

An emissions reduction strategy should contain enough detail that it can be implemented; it should be written as more than a goal. For example, a desired outcome may be "increase transit ridership by 5%." This is a good goal, but it is not a strategy because it does not contain enough information or describe how the goal will be met. Instead, there should be a specific set of actions that, if taken, would result in increasing ridership by 5%, such as a marketing campaign, fare reductions, or routing changes.

The strategy may be relatively brief for inclusion in a planning document if detailed implementation information is provided elsewhere or developed in a follow-up implementation phase. It can also be a fully developed program, ordinance, code, or project. Regardless, best practice suggests that reduction strategies should include five pieces of information: an estimate of GHG reductions, a funding source, a phasing plan (how soon can it be implemented and how long it will take), an entity or department responsible for implementation, and the identification of an indicator that will allow for effectiveness to be monitored. These are discussed in more detail in chapter 8.

Emissions-Reduction Strategy Sectors

Reduction strategies are usually organized in sectors similar to those in the GHG emissions inventory: transportation and land use, energy efficiency, renewable energy, carbon sequestration, agriculture, industry, waste, green living, and offsets. When local governments develop strategies, they should develop both community-wide strategies and local government operations (a.k.a. municipal operations) strategies. Community-wide strategies are those that apply to the broader community, including industry, businesses, residents, visitors, and the public in general. Local government operations strategies are those that directly affect how a local government operates itself, such as facilities construction and management, energy use, vehicle fleets, procurement, and employee commuting and work travel.

Communities often choose to lead by example. This can take the form of adopting more aggressive targets for local government operations or more aggressive implementation plans for reduction strategies that specifically target local government operations and employees. Many communities choose to do this because these are the aspects of the community over which local officials have the most control. A local government can simply transition to more fuel-efficient fleet vehicles as part of standard turnover, which is much easier than devising policy that would result in a community-wide move to improved fuel efficiency. Despite the differences in ease of implementation, the emissions sectors in which strategies can be devised are consistent with those for community-wide reduction strategies. For this reason, the discussion of sectors does not distinctly break out local government operations.

Transportation and Land Use

In the United States, transportation accounts for about 28% of all GHG emissions.[3] These emissions are from the combustion of fossil fuels, including gasoline in personal vehicles, diesel fuel in heavy-duty vehicles, and jet fuel in aircraft. The *Moving Cooler* report prepared by the Urban Land Institute identifies four basic approaches to the reduction of GHG emissions from the transportation sector: vehicle technology, fuel technology, vehicle and system operations, and travel activity.[4] The first of these two areas largely falls outside of the influence of communities, since they are tied to state and federal policy and funding and the evolution of technology, so the focus is on the latter two. The necessary reductions in transportation emissions will require a variety of approaches. *Moving Cooler* states the following:

> The United States cannot reduce carbon dioxide (CO_2) emissions by 60 to 80 percent below 1990 levels—a commonly accepted target for climate stabilization—unless the transportation sector contributes, and the transportation sector cannot do its fair share through vehicle and fuel technology alone. The increase in vehicular travel across the nation's sprawling urban areas needs to be dramatically reduced, reversing trends that go back decades.[5]

To address the issue of vehicular travel—usually measured as the total or average number of vehicle miles traveled (VMT) in a community—the *Moving Cooler* report recommends developing reduction strategies in nine areas:

- *Pricing and taxes:* Raise the costs associated with the use of the transportation system, including the cost of vehicle miles of travel and fuel consumption.
- *Land use and smart growth:* Create more transportation-efficient land use patterns, and, by doing so, reduce the number and length of motor vehicle trips.
- *Nonmotorized transport:* Encourage greater levels of walking and bicycling as alternatives to driving.
- *Public transportation improvements:* Expand public transportation by subsidizing fares, increasing service on existing routes, or building new infrastructure.
- *Ride-sharing, car-sharing, and other commuting strategies:* Expand services and provide incentives to travelers to choose transportation options other than driving alone.
- *Regulatory strategies:* Implement regulations that moderate vehicle travel or reduce speeds to achieve higher fuel efficiency.
- *Operational and intelligent transportation system (ITS) strategies:* Improve the operation of the transportation system to make better use of the existing capacity; encourage more efficient driving.
- *Capacity expansion and bottleneck relief:* Expand highway capacity to reduce congestion and to improve the efficiency of travel.
- *Multimodal freight sector strategies:* Promote more efficient freight movement within and across modes.[6]

These strategies to reduce transportation emissions are aimed at affecting three variables: transportation mode (e.g., the type of vehicle or conveyance), travel distance, and efficiency (see box 5.1 for examples). Changing transportation mode is usually described as "alternative transportation" and involves strategies encouraging community members to change their mode of travel by shifting to walking, bicycling, micromobility options (e.g., electric scooters), or transit instead of private vehicles. Changing travel distance often falls under the concept of smart growth, which recognizes that the distribution of land uses influences travel behavior. Long-term land use planning can aim to shorten the distance between residential areas and common destinations. This reduces the number of miles traveled by vehicle and makes alternative transportation

Box 5.1

*Examples of Transportation Strategies That
Reduce Greenhouse Gas Emissions*

London's Congestion Charge Zone

The City of London, England, designated a portion of the city center as a Congestion Charge Zone. Motorists who want to drive into the Congestion Charge Zone during business hours must pay a fee or risk a fine. The intent of the fee is to reduce congestion and generate funds for improvements to the transportation system, especially alternative transportation modes. This is an example of using a pricing strategy to change motorists' behavior. See https://tfl.gov.uk/modes/driving/congestion-charge.

Portland's 20-Minute Complete Neighborhoods

The City of Portland, Oregon, is implementing a land use planning principle that says people should live in neighborhoods that allow them to walk no more than 20 minutes to access basic daily destinations and services such as grocery stores, restaurants and pubs, laundromats, drug stores, parks, and the like. Using this principle to design neighborhoods would require people to drive less and encourage more walking and biking. This has the co-benefits of increasing the safety and friendliness of the community as well as the health of the residents. See http://www.portlandonline.com/portlandplan/.

Pittsburgh's Martin Luther King Jr. East Busway

The City of Pittsburgh, Pennsylvania, developed a nine-mile bus rapid transit system to link the eastern and downtown areas of the city. The roadway is dedicated to buses only (both local and express), thus decreasing travel times during peak commute hours by offering an alternative to crowded roadways. The City is encouraging infill development and redevelopment along the busway to achieve smart growth principles. The busway has been a success, and the local transit authority is proposing a major expansion. See http://www.portauthority.org/paac/apps/maps/EastBusway.pdf.

San Luis Obispo's South Street Road Diet

The City of San Luis Obispo, California, worked with the state transportation agency to implement a "complete streets" policy on a significant crosstown roadway. South Street was reduced from four lanes to two lanes, bicycle lanes were widened to five feet, transit stops were upgraded, and pedestrian crossings and refuges were added. All of this resulted in no additional vehicle congestion with improved safety, aesthetics, and community connectedness. Building on this success, the City is moving ahead with additional projects as part of its Vision Zero program. See https://www.slocity.org/government/department-directory/public-works/programs-and-services-/transportation-planning-and-engineering/traffic-safety.

more feasible. Changing efficiency includes a move to more fuel-efficient vehicles, alternative fuels, or hybrid or electric vehicles or an increase in the average number of passengers in a vehicle (carpooling). The various ways to address transportation emissions can be taken together to guide urban design principles for accessible services and streets that accommodate all forms of transportation and all members of society, referred to as "complete streets."[7]

Many strategies that reduce transportation-related emissions also provide the co-benefits of improvements to air quality and human health and safety. Many lower the costs of transportation, since transit, bicycling, micromobility options (scooters, skateboards, etc.), and walking are less expensive than driving. In addition, strategies that improve the safety of pedestrian travel, such as vegetated medians, also promote carbon sequestration, improve stormwater management, and enhance overall aesthetics. Land use strategies that place residents and services (school, employment, grocery, etc.) in close proximity have the potential to promote community cohesion and quality of life.

Shifting to Alternative Transportation Modes

Because the choice to replace a vehicular trip with walking, biking, micromobility, or public transit is voluntary, education, outreach, and other programs to encourage behavior change are often critical to emissions reduction. In parallel with improving the availability of travel options, many cities conduct extensive outreach and incentive programs. These strategies can include bicycle safety education programs, the provision of bicycle and transit maps, and discount transit passes. Another way to influence travel mode is by working with employers to develop incentives for employees who choose to commute using an alternative to a private vehicle.

Encouraging a shift to alternative travel modes requires that walking, bicycling, public transit, or other travel options are convenient and accessible to all community members. Evaluating the opportunity for and constraints of alternative travel modes as well as the factors that influence community willingness to utilize them contributes to the development of effective policies.

Alternative transportation strategies yield emissions reductions only when they replace a trip that would have yielded higher emissions. Therefore, the types of trips that can be replaced dictate which types of alternative transportation options to emphasize. Walking, biking, and micromobility strategies are most effective for reducing VMT from the portion of vehicular trips that begin and end within the community, especially at the neighborhood or downtown scale. Walking and bicycling reduction strategies may include an expansion or improvement of infrastructure (bike routes and sidewalks) to ensure that walking and biking can be safely enjoyed by all community members. Micromobility is relatively new, and most communities are still working out how to best plan for and manage this option.

The emissions associated with trips that originate or end outside the community are best addressed through public transit or ride-sharing programs in the short term and by land use that reduces the need for longer trips in the long term. The choice of where to focus efforts can be made through careful evaluation of existing alternative transportation networks and by soliciting community input regarding needed improvements and identified barriers (e.g., perceptions of danger, convenience, and weather patterns). Bus or train travel can be encouraged through expanded routes, hours of operation, or stops.

In some cases, it may be necessary to combine strategies because emissions reductions cannot be separated. For example, if a community increases the number of bike paths, improves lighting, and adds bicycle storage, it is difficult to assign particular reductions to any one of these strategies individually. In this case, an overall increase in bicycle mode share could be assumed. However, assumptions about eventual shifts in the mode share of bicycling must be supported through demonstration that the community may be able to achieve this level of ridership. A more detailed manner of quantifying transportation shifts can be made by assuming that a portion of the community will increase their reliance on alternative travel options (this can be done separately for walking, biking, and public transit). The next question is to decide what portion of the population will change their travel behavior and what portion of their vehicle trips will be replaced. For example, improved bicycle infrastructure with accompanying education and incentive programs may result in 5% more community members riding their bikes. Of these 5%, it could be assumed that they reduce their average daily VMT by 50%. In addition, an average fuel efficiency must be identified that provides a GHG per VMT constant. A GHG reduction would then be calculated via the following equation:

$$\text{Estimated GHG reduction} = [\text{community population} \times 5\%] \times [\text{average daily VMT per capita} \times 50\%] \times \text{GHG per VMT}$$

Growing Smarter to Reduce Travel Distance

Reduced distance between residential areas, employment centers, and services such as grocery stores not only shortens the distance traveled by car but also makes alternative travel modes more convenient. Specific populations and those with the longest commutes should be targeted. Low-income residents may be forced to commute longer distances due to the availability of less-expensive housing in outlying areas. An inclusive housing policy in areas closer to jobs and amenities (often referred to as jobs–housing balance) may help reduce daily miles traveled. Reduced travel distances can be encouraged by altering land use policy to encourage smart growth and by providing incentives to developers for infill or mixed-use development (see box 5.2).

The emissions consequences from mixed-use and infill development are difficult to quantify. These changes in land use patterns alter VMT and improve the feasibility of alternative transportation options. Quantifying these changes can be completed as a rough estimate through a reduction in per-capita VMT from the business-as-usual forecast in the emissions inventory.

Box 5.2

Smart Growth Principles

- Mix land uses.
- Take advantage of compact building design.
- Create a range of housing opportunities and choices.
- Create walkable neighborhoods.
- Foster distinctive, attractive communities with a strong sense of place.
- Preserve open space, farmland, natural beauty, and critical environmental areas.
- Strengthen and direct development towards existing communities.
- Provide a variety of transportation choices.
- Make development decisions predictable, fair, and cost effective.
- Encourage community and stakeholder collaboration in development decisions.

Source: Maryland Department of Planning, Smart Growth Online, https://smartgrowth.org/smart-growth-principles/.

INCREASING TRAVEL EFFICIENCY

Encouraging community members to carpool or utilize higher-efficiency vehicles such as hybrids, electric vehicles, or high-fuel-efficiency vehicles can be achieved by making these options more convenient than the alternative. Designated lanes or parking for carpool, hybrid, and electric vehicles provide incentives for use, and increased parking or driving fees (such as congestion pricing) are disincentives for driving. Providing electric vehicle charging at workplaces and retail destinations is an increasingly common incentive.

There are several emerging vehicle technologies that are raising considerable uncertainties regarding future travel behavior, especially VMT. These are transportation network companies (TNCs, also called "ride-sharing") such as Uber and Lyft, micromobility options such as electric scooter services from Lime and Bird, and autonomous vehicles, most notably from Waymo (Google), Uber, and Tesla. These technologies have been touted for their potential to reduce VMT and GHG emissions, especially when they are powered by electricity. But early evidence suggests that they may mostly be replacing trips that were previously taken by foot, bike, or transit[8] and that they may be increasing VMT.[9] It is still too early to know for certain how these technologies will affect our communities, so it is best to exercise caution when considering these technologies in climate action planning.

Energy Efficiency

GHG emissions are produced in the generation of electricity using fossil fuels and through the direct use of other fuels, such as natural gas or propane. These energy sources are used primarily in buildings for lighting, appliances and devices, heating, and cooling. Measures that improve energy efficiency reduce GHG emissions. Greater efficiency can be achieved in a variety of ways, from energy-efficient appliances and fixtures and building materials such as insulation or high-efficiency windows to solar orientation and use of trees for shade (see box 5.3). There is a well-established knowledge base for improved energy efficiency in buildings broadly referred to as "green building." Energy efficiency, which includes reduced heating, cooling, and water demand, can be achieved

Box 5.3

*Examples of Innovative Energy Efficiency
Strategies to Reduce Emissions*

City of Chicago Retrofit Chicago Energy Challenge

In 2012, the City of Chicago launched the Retrofit Chicago Energy Challenge to support the City's goals for energy efficiency and climate action. This is a voluntary program in which the owners and managers of large municipal, commercial, institutional, and multifamily residential buildings commit to do the following:

- reduce energy use by at least 20% within five years of joining the program
- track and share energy efficiency progress through ENERGY STAR Portfolio Manager
- serve as ambassadors to other buildings interested in saving energy

The challenge is a partnership among the City and numerous private and nonprofit organizations who provide technical advising and networking opportunities to support the retrofits. Key aspects of the program include the following:

- peer-to-peer learning roundtable for building engineers
- production of a Best Practices Report that serves as a resource for participants and others
- a mayor's awards program to recognize the accomplishments of participants

There are more than 70 buildings participating, and as of 2016, they had reduced electricity consumption by 90 million kWh and reduced GHG emissions by 70,000 metric tons. The program has won numerous awards for its innovation and success. See https://www.chicago.gov/city/en/sites/retrofitchicago/home.html.

California Youth Energy Services

In California, the nonprofit Rising Sun Energy Center has part-nered with the investor-owned utility Pacific Gas & Electric and numerous communities to offer Green House Calls through the California Youth Energy Services (CYES) program. CYES is

> a unique program that addresses youth unemployment, reduces local greenhouse gas emissions, and prepares the next generation of climate leaders. CYES employs youth as Energy Specialists, training them to be environmental leaders in their own communities by providing local resi-dents with our Green House Call service.

The Green House Call is a service free to residents that "includes an energy efficiency and water conservation assessment of the home, the installation of efficient devices such as LED light bulbs and shower heads, and education on ways to save even more." Since its inception, the program has trained almost 2,500 youth and adults, served 43,000 households, saved residents over $20 million, and reduced GHG emissions by 105,000 metric tons. This is an excel-lent example of not only how to achieve community-wide energy efficiency but also how to build partnerships and achieve broader community benefits in job training. See https://risingsunopp.org.

through a variety of complementary strategies. There are many resources from which to draw strategies, including the U.S. Environmental Protection Agency (EPA), the U.S. Green Building Council, and Build It Green.

In addition to building design, energy use in buildings is associated with the behaviors of occupants. The choice of indoor temperature and the act of turning off lights and other energy-using appliances, includ-ing computers when they are not in use, are examples of how occupant behavior influences energy demand. Community members may not be aware of the energy demand resulting from various choices. The first step in changing energy use choices is increasing awareness through extensive outreach and education. Altering the pricing structure of energy can also yield changes in behavior, but the effectiveness of this measure will likely be higher when paired with outreach. Increasingly, builders and homeowners are choosing "smart" lighting and thermostats that make conservation easier. Programs that support the purchasing and use of these devices should be supported.

Programs that target behavior change are often implemented in combination with other strategies such as incentive programs or pricing adjustments. If a program that seeks to alter user behavior is used to support another strategy, there should not be a separate estimate of emissions reduction. Instead, the outreach should be viewed as part of the implementation plan for the strategy it supports.

The other area in which energy efficiency can be improved is in governmental services and infrastructure, such as the treatment and conveyance of water and the regulation of streets. The energy required to treat and deliver water throughout a community can be reduced in two ways: (1) improve the energy efficiency of pumps and treatment plant operations and (2) reduce demand for water, which lowers the volume of water requiring treatment and delivery. Streetlights and traffic signals require a considerable amount of energy in dense urban settings. Many communities are now switching to LED lighting and using smart systems to control the lighting.

Energy efficiency strategies have many co-benefits. Retrofitting existing buildings and constructing new energy-efficient buildings contribute to a community's resilience in the face of climate impacts. For example, green roofs have the potential to sequester carbon, reduce energy use, and provide protection to inhabitants facing heat-related climate impacts. In addition, a local requirement for energy-efficient construction creates a demand for specific construction expertise that has the potential to promote an area of economic growth. Finally, reduced energy demand lowers the monthly costs for residents, making housing more affordable.

Three areas in which to target energy efficiency strategies—existing buildings, new structures, and water treatment and delivery—are discussed in the following sections.

EXISTING BUILDINGS

Community-wide improvement in energy efficiency must address the structures already in place. In many cases, considerable energy savings can be achieved through retrofitting existing buildings, particularly those that predate modern building codes. The efficiency of these structures can be upgraded in a variety of ways. Buyers of existing buildings or homes can be required to upgrade fixtures such as lightbulbs or appliances at the point of sale. Rebate or microloan programs are also commonly used to offset the up-front cost for more expensive building retrofits such as insulation or windows.

Many of these strategies not only reduce energy needs but also remove GHGs from the atmosphere. For example, installing a green roof can improve insulation and natural shading as well as introduce plants that can sequester carbon. Similarly, planting street trees along the sides of buildings with the highest solar exposure reduces energy demand by regulating indoor air temperature, improves the quality of the streetscape, and sequesters carbon.

If a strategy supports or requires retrofitting a particular aspect of building operation, the required information for quantifying the strategy is best obtained from the manufacturer of the item (e.g., appliances or windows) or from the agency that regulates appliance efficiency (e.g., the Energy Star Program or the Department of Energy Home Energy Saver). The other necessary information is an estimate of existing energy use (from the emissions inventory) and participation rates.

NEW STRUCTURES

New building requirements are more easily implemented because energy-saving strategies can be included in the design and budgeting of a project and can be a requirement for permitting. The manner in which new development is regulated varies, meaning the opportunities for promoting or mandating green building are similarly varied. Specific green building policies can specify actions such as requiring energy efficiency as a condition of permit approval, which is often referred to as a green building ordinance. Such requirements can also be part of a larger green building program where minimum building standards are set and incentives such as expedited processing are provided for more advanced green building techniques.

WATER TREATMENT AND DELIVERY

Reducing the energy required to treat and convey water and wastewater can be achieved through upgrading the pumps and other equipment required for treatment and delivery or reducing community water demand. Decreasing water demand can be achieved by upgrading water fixtures (such as toilets, sinks, and showers). It can also be achieved through increased participation of households in rainwater capture or graywater systems or citywide water recycling. These strategies can be implemented to serve nonpotable uses such as irrigation of yards and landscaped areas.

Water use can also be limited through landscaping and yard vegetation choices. Outdoor water use is one of the largest consumers of potable water in the United States. Vegetation choices that require less water can result in substantial reductions in water use for residential yards and irrigated park areas. Communities can promote these changes through educational materials such as planting guides, incentives such as cash-for-grass programs that compensate for the removal of residential lawns, or mandates such as vegetation and irrigation requirements on building permits. Quantification of these measures draws heavily on data in the emissions inventory, including a conversion factor of carbon dioxide equivalents (CO_{2e}) per gallon of treated water and the average water use per household. Using these constants, the estimated gallons of water saved can be converted to CO_{2e} based on the anticipated effectiveness of and participation in a program. Energy use by existing pumps can be directly measured, and new pumps are rated, so assessing the efficiency of water conveyance pumps and lifts is relatively straightforward.

Renewable Energy

Renewable energy—such as solar, wind, or biomass—provides electricity and heat without the same level of GHG emissions associated with traditional energy sources. The addition of local renewable energy generation lowers GHG intensity (GHG per unit energy). The largest deterrent for renewable energy is the initial cost of installation. The most appropriate type of renewable energy varies regionally based on factors such as solar exposure, available surface or land area, wind speed, biomass sources, coastal conditions, geothermal resources, and social acceptance of the proposed technology. Once a renewable energy technology or suite of technologies has been selected, implementation requires a series of actions, including a funding mechanism, the choice between distributed and centralized generation, and the phasing of implementation. Funding renewable energy has been an area of considerable innovation and creativity (see box 5.4). Traditional funding mechanisms include allocation of local funds, external investment by the private sector, or grant dollars procured from an outside entity. In addition to these funding sources, there are increasingly creative means of funding renewable energy, including providing investment opportunities for local residents, developing a microgrant or loan program, and funding renewable energy through impact fees for environmentally damaging actions.

Quantifying reductions in GHG emissions from renewable energy requires that assumptions be made about the efficiency of energy technology (e.g., wind and solar energy capture rates), the local availability of these sources, and the potential locations for installation. National maps of solar and wind potential are now available, and in many regions, maps have been generated that have higher resolution. Implementing renewable energy strategies has the potential to complicate the quantification of energy efficiency measures. Because renewable energy changes the energy intensity (GHG per kWh), it also influences the reductions experienced as part of improved efficiency. As the percentage of the electricity supplied from renewable sources increases, the GHG reduction from efficiency measures decreases. It can also influence phasing of energy strategies where efficiency makes the most sense as a short-term goal.

One of the important co-benefits of renewable energy programs is that they foster local economic growth by employing the workforce needed to install the systems and, if materials are manufactured locally, the employees of the manufacturer. In addition, renewable energy increases human and ecosystem health due to removal of air pollution associated with energy generation from fossil fuels.

Box 5.4

*Examples of Innovative Renewable Energy
Strategies to Reduce Emissions*

City of Miami Beach Solar Power Initiatives

In 2017, the City passed an ordinance to require that more than 75% of all new residential developments over 1,100 square feet and any existing residence that is being rebuilt must include a rooftop solar photovoltaic (PV) system. In addition, the City has acted to make it easier to add rooftop solar systems to existing homes by doing the following:

- waiving permits fees for solar PV installations
- creating height exceptions to allow for solar panels
- launching the EnergySage Solar Market to inform homeowners about financing options and selecting solar contractors
- adopting a PACE (Property Assessed Clean Energy) program that allows property owners to pay off green energy investments through an assessment on their property tax bill

Because of these actions, the City has been recognized as a bronze-level SolSmart by the U.S. Department of Energy. See http://www.mbrisingabove.com/climate-mitigation/renewable-energy/.

Marin County's Marin Clean Energy Program

In Marin County, California, communities have worked together to establish Marin Clean Energy (MCE), an example of community choice aggregation (CCA). *CCA* is the aggregation of electricity demand among various community users (residents, businesses, etc.) to facilitate the purchase of electrical energy, especially from renewable energy sources. The MCE program automatically subscribes electricity customers in the participating communities to the program. MCE then purchases renewable energy in cooperation with the franchised commercial energy provider. MCE has a number of notable successes:

- over 910 MW of new renewable energy installed and under development
- choice of rate plan, including percentage renewable and solar
- reinvestment of rate premiums into new renewable energy projects
- numerous rebates to customers, especially those with low incomes
- about 300 metric tons of GHGs eliminated as of 2017

See https://www.mcecleanenergy.org.

Carbon Sequestration

In addition to trying to reduce emissions, climate strategies may take the approach of capturing some of the carbon and sequestering it in terrestrial vegetation (e.g., trees) and soil. Terrestrial vegetation, such as forests, sequesters carbon through increasing the volume of woody mass. Trees can be used as a shade crop in agricultural practices, as street trees in cities, and for larger-scale reforestation projects. Particularly in urban areas, trees provide shade for structures, which improves energy efficiency and the pedestrian environment, making alternative transportation more appealing. The type of vegetation should be considered carefully to ensure consistency with the local climate and soil conditions, as well as the intended role of the vegetation in addition to carbon capture.

Soil carbon sequestration refers to the organic content of soils such as leaf litter and other biomass. Strategies to increase soil carbon content directly address widespread soil degradation. To sequester carbon, the soil carbon must be stored long term and not released back into the atmosphere. Successful implementation of soil sequestration strategies also improves soil and agricultural productivity. A variety of methods can be used to increase soil carbon levels that should be chosen based on local conditions, including no-till or conservation tillage farming practices, use of cover crops, management of the nutrient input to soils, agroforestry, woodland regeneration, crop rotation, and improved grazing practices.[10]

Quantification of GHG reductions due to sequestration relies on improvements in vegetative uptake or change in conditions from the baseline established in the emissions inventory. Newly planted vegetation such as street trees or wind breaks and newly introduced soil management practices are quantified, whereas contributions from existing green spaces that predate the climate planning effort are not because they are assumed to be included in the baseline. The estimated sequestration possible for vegetation such as street trees varies by climate region, tree species, and age. Many state forestry departments and universities provide lists that estimate sequestration potential that is regionally accurate. Similarly, soil carbon content varies by climate, soil type, and land activity.

Agriculture Management

Agriculture, which accounts for 9% of U.S. GHG emissions,[11] has been identified as an area with significant emissions reduction potential through carbon sequestration and alternative management practices. Thus far, climate planning has been largely focused on cities, but the more recent emergence of regional efforts and county plans has required agriculture to be addressed directly.

Including rural areas in climate planning will require the measurement of annual variability in emissions associated with agriculture. The fluctuations in agricultural emissions result from variations in climate, soil type, and agricultural practice. In addition, the longevity and permanence of sequestration efforts can vary. Carbon sequestration in agricultural lands is effective for a specific duration of time (e.g., 15–30 years). Shifts in management practices can reverse the benefits resulting from a reduction strategy. Many argue that this results in agriculture being best pursued in the short term, providing time for more expensive or time-intensive strategies such as large-scale renewable energy or land use change to be implemented.

Agricultural practice is vulnerable to potential shifts in temperature and precipitation that are projected to result from climate change. It is possible to devise reduction strategies that have the co-benefit of bolstering adaptive capacity, but not all strategies meet both reduction and adaptation goals. For example, increased food production intended to bolster local food security can be achieved through converting additional land to agriculture and/or increasing the application of fertilizers. Both of these actions have the potential to increase emissions. Conversely, some reduction strategies have the potential to reduce production, placing them in conflict with adaptation needs. As a result, agricultural emissions reduction strategies must be carefully identified and constructed to ensure the best balance among reduction, adaptation, and local needs such as food supply, ecosystem protection, and local employment. Reduction strategy development must be conducted in close collaboration with local agricultural communities to ensure feasibility and regionally appropriate strategies.

A wide variety of strategies can reduce agricultural GHG emissions (see box 5.5). The choice of action will depend on factors such as the local environmental condition, type of agriculture, current management practices, soil properties, local climate, economics, and local workforce. Reduction strategies can be broken down into a set of broad categories: carbon sequestration (discussed in the prior section), livestock management, and rice paddy and wetland strategies (not addressed in this book).

Livestock has climate and other environmental impacts associated with soil degradation, methane output, biodiversity loss, water usage, and land use change. The strategies discussed earlier as part of the sequestration section also apply to grazing lands. This section focuses on two sources of emissions associated directly with animals: ruminant digestion and manure management. Ruminants (cows, goats, sheep, llamas, etc.) release methane, which has 28 times the global warming potential of CO_2, as part of the digestive process. Methane emissions are higher when an animal's diet is poor.[12] One way to curb these emissions is through

Box 5.5

*Carbon Sequestration and Agriculture
Strategy Summary*

- *urban land:* tree planting, waste management, wood product management
- *agroforestry:* better management of trees on cropland, conversion from unproductive cropland and grassland
- *cropland:* reduced tillage, rotations and cover crops, nutrient management, erosion control and irrigation management, organic farming
- *forestland:* forest regeneration, fertilization, choice of species, reduced forest degradation
- *restoring degraded land:* conversion to cropland, grassland, or forestland
- *rice paddies:* irrigation, fertilizer management, plant residue management
- *grassland:* conversion from cropland
- *livestock:* use of more easily digested feed, more monogastric animals, herd health programs, anaerobic manure digesters that produce biogas

Sources: Adapted from Intergovernmental Panel on Climate Change, *Land Use, Land Use Change and Forestry, Summary for Policymakers*, ed. Robert T. Watson et al. (Cambridge: Cambridge University Press, 2000); Food and Agriculture Organization of the United Nations, *Soil Carbon Sequestration for Improved Land Management* (Rome: Author, 2001); N. V. Nguyen, *Global Climate Changes and Rice Food Security* (Rome: International Rice Commission, Food and Agriculture Organization of the United Nations, 2004); P. Smith, D. Martino, Z. Cai, D. Gwary, H. Janzen, P. Kumar, B. McCarl, et al. "Policy and Technological Constraints to Implementation of Greenhouse Gas Mitigation Options in Agriculture," *Agriculture, Ecosystems and Environment* 118 (2007): 6–28; H. Steinfeld, P. Gerber, T. Wassenaar, V. Castel, M. Rosales, and C. de Haan, *Livestock's Long Shadow: Environmental Issues and Options* (Rome: Food and Agriculture Organization of the United Nations, 2006).

improved nutrition. There are feedstuffs with increased digestibility that can take the form of feed additives. Another strategy is a move to more efficient animals that are monogastric, such as poultry.[13] The expense of changing animal feed is partially offset by findings that animals grow larger and milk production increases with more easily digested feed. Other strategies that reduce methane production are herd health programs.

The other source of GHGs associated with livestock animals is derived from manure, which also results in methane production. Similar to the direct emissions, a shift in livestock feed can limit some of the methane production. A low carbon-to-nitrogen ratio results in increased emissions from manure. If the collected manure can be stored at a warmer temperature or outdoors in temperate climates, emissions will be lower. The manure can also be handled in a digester, a closed vessel with controlled conditions. Technology already exists not only to reduce the emissions but to generate energy from the biogas produced in the digester.[14]

Quantification of agricultural measures should be tied directly to assumptions in the emissions inventory. If the inventory includes agriculture, an emissions rate per head of livestock for manure disposal will have been established. Reductions based on changes in feed, land management, or manure handling should be calculated based on improvements from baseline. In the case where manure is used to generate methane, the production of energy can be gathered from the information provided by the manufacturer or supplier of the digester.

Industrial Facilities and Operations

Industrial sector emissions present a special challenge for communities. Since most aspects of industrial operations are regulated at the regional, state, and federal levels, local governments have little ability to mandate industrial changes. The approach with the industrial sector should focus on outreach and partnership. Not only should awareness of climate change and reduction strategy development process be promoted, but the concerns and goals of the industrial sector should be solicited and considered in strategy development. Reduction strategies that focus specifically on this sector should be developed in a manner that seeks to ensure that long-term emissions reduction goals are compatible with long-term local economic viability.

Many GHG reductions in the industrial sector can be achieved through the energy efficiency strategies included in the building and renewable energy sections above. Industrial structures can be upgraded for efficiency, and the large roof surfaces of many industrial structures are ideal for installation of photovoltaic panels or a green roof. Emissions reductions can also be achieved through changes in operational procedures and in the relationship between industries in the same community. *Operations* can refer to a variety of factors, from the efficiency of machinery to the vehicles used on-site. Strategies regarding the relationship between industrial entities are captured in the principles that govern eco-industrial parks. An eco-industrial park is an industrial complex that seeks to collectively manage resource use, energy, and material flows for enhanced efficiency and improved environmental performance. For example, this would include pairing companies where the waste product from one industrial process can serve as the input for another.

Quantification of industrial measures draws on those methods described for energy efficiency in buildings and renewable energy. In the case of eco-industrial parks, the reductions can be determined by calculating the reduced miles traveled by trucks hauling waste off-site and input materials on-site. The local values for GHG per heavy-duty-truck mile can be obtained from the emissions inventory. Additional reductions can be calculated on a case-by-case basis using the baseline assumptions defined in the inventory.

Waste

Waste deals with the treatment or disposal of postconsumer solid waste and waste resulting from the treatment of wastewater that generates methane during decomposition. Reducing emissions from waste treatment can be achieved in two ways: by reducing the amount of waste produced and by reducing the emissions associated with waste disposal. This twofold approach is necessary because waste disposed in a landfill will emit methane for decades following the initial disposal of the waste. As a result, reduction of waste will not lower landfill emissions in the near future, although some methods for assessing the emissions reduction from landfill diversion account for this by annualizing emissions. What will decrease immediately with reduced waste production are GHG emissions associated with the collection, delivery, and handling of waste.

Co-benefits of waste strategies include environmental benefits from reduced consumption of land for disposal and improved air quality that will result from reduced collection and delivery vehicle emissions. Consumption and disposal behaviors also contribute to overall community sustainability.

Waste Production

Reduced waste production can occur through both government action and community behavior change; long-term success will rely on both. Recycling programs are some of the most well-established means of solid waste reduction. A city can increase the local diversion rate (percentage of waste stream recycled) by increasing the number of products that can be recycled, increasing the convenience of recycling through provision of bins and pickup services, making recycling mandatory or providing incentives for it, and conducting outreach to increase the participation rate of the community. An emerging area of emphasis in recycling is disposal of e-waste such as computers. Programs can be developed to safely disassemble e-waste to recover resources. Waste reduction can also be achieved through strategies to reduce packaging and other materials that accompany products.

Organic waste from food or outdoor vegetation is another opportunity for waste diversion that directly addresses the organic matter that generates methane. Strategies for addressing organic matter include composting and converting vegetative material to mulch. These strategies can be implemented on a city scale or on an individual scale depending on housing type. A city-scale program will require a facility designed to accept the waste, a means for waste to reach the facility, and a program to encourage participation. The challenge of individual composting or yard waste programs is getting participation to a level that impacts

GHG emissions. Some cities have begun residential curbside composting programs.

WASTE DISPOSAL

Landfills and wastewater sludge both generate methane that can be captured and converted to electricity. This requires that waste be covered and the landfill or collection point be retrofit for technology to allow methane capture. This produces an immediate reduction in methane generation associated with waste disposed of in the past.

Other disposal methods pose their own sets of challenges. Incineration or waste-to-energy plants primarily emit carbon dioxide instead of methane. While carbon dioxide is a less-powerful GHG than methane, waste-to-energy plants also emit a variety of other air pollutants that contribute to acid rain and may pose a threat to human health. The benefit of these plants is that they do not consume the land area of a landfill.

Green Living

Green living refers to reduction strategies aimed at daily behaviors in the home and workplace that may not be covered by other sectors. These may include strategies to motivate people to eat more locally and sustainably, grow their own food, or purchase more environmentally friendly products (see figure 5.2). These are usually implemented through public education and outreach campaigns. Some communities have implemented challenges or competition campaigns intended to increase the profile of green living activities and accelerate behavior change. Green living strategies are difficult to quantify and are usually favored more for their co-benefits than for their potential GHG emissions reductions.

WHICH ACTIONS WILL YOU TRY TAKING?

Reduce my garbage

- ☐ Reduce the amount of food my household wastes.
- ☐ Compost organic waste in my backyard or purchase compost pick-up.
- ☐ Fix things that are broken instead of buying new.
- ☐ Use the Hazardous Products Center and bulky item pick-up programs to properly dispose of old refrigerators, e-waste, and air-conditioning units.
- ☐ Talk with my contractor about alternatives to traditional building demolition, such as relocation, deconstruction, and salvage.
- ☐ Shop locally and support local businesses.
- ☐ Support efforts to reduce and limit single-use disposable plastics.
- ☐ Eat more low-carbon foods, such as minimally processed foods, fruits, grains, and vegetables.
- ☐ Encourage the creation of community gardens on public and private lands including school campuses, City lands, and church properties.
- ☐ Start a tool lending library in my community.

Reduce my energy use

- ☐ Get an energy audit to find ways to increase energy efficiency at home and at work.
- ☐ Install energy conserving appliances and fixtures, such as on-demand tankless water heaters, Energy Star appliances, and LED lightbulbs.
- ☐ Install electric furnaces, water heaters, dryers, stoves, and more.
- ☐ Voice my support for City policies that reduce greenhouse gas emissions.
- ☐ Install solar PV and storage at my home—or sign up for the APS Solar Communities program to use my roof for solar.
- ☐ Replace a wood-burning fireplace with gas or electric.
- ☐ Install alternatives to air conditioning when renovating my home.

Embrace non-car travel

- ☐ Increase the number of trips I make by transit, carpooling, walking, or biking.
- ☐ Try out an electric bike for my commute.
- ☐ Organize a "walking school-bus" to walk a group of kids to school.
- ☐ Delay my next purchase of a new vehicle, if it's possible to get more life out of my current car. When I decide to make a purchase, I'll investigate electric vehicles and hybrids.
- ☐ Use alternatives to air travel when possible.
- ☐ Support development that creates vibrant, higher density, mixed-use areas to reduce the need for driving in Flagstaff.

Conserve water

- ☐ Conduct a water audit at my home, and replace inefficient toilets and fixtures.
- ☐ Set a goal of reducing my household's hot water use by 15%.
- ☐ Consider efficient alternatives to traditional water heaters, like tankless water heaters, electric heat pump water heaters, or solar thermal hot water heaters.
- ☐ Install a rain barrel to harvest rainwater for outdoor use.
- ☐ Replace turf grass with drought tolerant landscaping or native plants; install smart technology on existing irrigation systems.

City of Flagstaff
Community Climate Action Guide

Figure 5-2 City of Flagstaff Community Climate Action Guide for the public

Source: City of Flagstaff, Climate Action and Adaptation Plan (2018), https://www.flagstaff.az.gov/ClimatePlan.

Carbon Offsets

Offset (or carbon-offset) programs are designed to deal with difficult-to-reduce GHG emissions occurring in one sector or community by taking action to lower emissions elsewhere. For example, if a city cannot control GHG emissions from its electric utility provider, it may choose to offset those emissions by planting trees in a forest in the region (to act as a carbon sink). Offsets can be managed through compensatory or reciprocal strategies, or they can be structured financially through purchase arrangements. The purchase of offsets is accomplished by setting up a financial system where individuals, businesses, or communities that create GHG emissions offset those emissions by purchasing credits or paying into a fund. The credits or fund is then used to finance other emissions-reduction strategies. Offset programs are very popular at the international level, in states with cap-and-trade programs, and in colleges and universities (particularly for air travel). Many industrialized nations are participating in programs that offset some of their emissions by investing in energy efficiency and renewable energy programs in developing countries; thus the programs provide economic development and social justice benefits as well.

Several important issues must be addressed when considering offset programs. First, if the offset program works through purchases, then a mechanism must be in place to manage and track financial transactions. This could be done by the local government, a local nonprofit, or an established international program such as MyClimate or TerraPass. Second, the location of the offset project is important. Most communities have developed policies that require offset funds to be spent in the community. This promotes local investment and benefits but may limit the number or quality of opportunities. The last issue is a set of related questions about who pays, how much, for what strategies, and whether it is voluntary.

Local examples of offset programs are few. The City of San Francisco, California, set up the San Francisco Carbon Fund to invest in local sustainability projects.[15] A nonprofit based in northeast Iowa—the Winneshiek Energy District—has created a local offset program called Oneota Tags that will subsidize home energy retrofits.[16] Depending on the program, GHG reduction as a result of carbon offset can be quantified on a dollar basis (GHG per dollar) or directly if funds are used for projects such as reforestation where GHG reduction can be estimated based on setting, number, type, and age of trees planted.

Chapter 6

Climate Change Vulnerability Assessment

The 2018 Fourth National Climate Assessment[1] and the 2014 Intergovernmental Panel on Climate Change (IPCC) Fifth Assessment Reports[2] describe the dramatic changes projected to result from climate change, highlighting the need not only to reduce greenhouse gas (GHG) emissions but also to adapt to the consequences of climate change. Adaptation strategies prepare a community to be resilient in the face of unavoidable climate change impacts. Climate impacts—such as extreme heat events, sea-level rise, changes in precipitation patterns, ocean acidification, and altered wind and storm patterns—can have a variety of secondary impacts on community conditions ranging from human health and safety to economics to ecosystem integrity. Developing strategies to address these impacts relies on the development of a vulnerability assessment that not only provides an assessment of the projected impacts for a specific community but also includes an evaluation of how the impacts may affect the community and how ready a community is to address them. This information is critical to the identification and prioritization of adaptation strategies (see chapter 7).

Evaluating the threat posed by climate change begins with an assessment of the changes to which a community is exposed (including the rate and magnitude of change), the sensitivity of the local community to these changes, their potential impacts, and the local capacity to adapt. This chapter describes the steps of the vulnerability assessment process, which is part of a broader climate adaptation strategy development process (see figure 6.1). The vulnerability assessment is similar to GHG accounting in that it provides the basis for climate adaptation planning and strategy development.

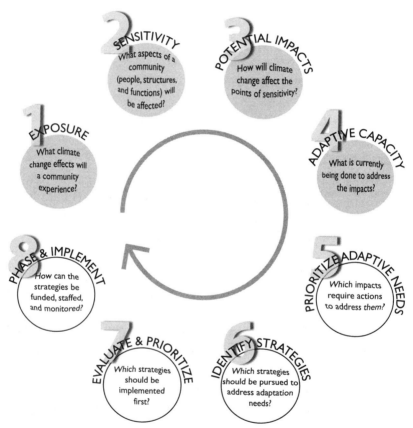

Figure 6-1 Climate change adaptation strategy development process. The process has two phases: vulnerability assessment (shaded in gray) and strategy development.

Source: Adapted from California Office of Emergency Services and California Natural Resources Agency, *California Adaptation Planning Guide* (Sacramento, CA: Author, 2012), http://resources.ca.gov/climate/safeguarding/adaptation_policy_guide/.

Climate Change Impact Sectors

The impacts of climate change can set off a cascade of consequences in a community, including altering biophysical conditions, public safety, human health, structural viability, and social, economic, and cultural stability. Not only that, but these consequences interact by either escalating disruption or moderating the impacts. A vulnerability assessment is a systematic way to identify these consequences and evaluate the level of risk presented to a community. For each potential impact, such as flooding, fire, or changes in water supply, the potential risks to the community must be assessed.

These impacts can generally be broken down into broad sectors: built environment, including infrastructure and physical damage; social justice; economic systems; and ecosystem health (see box 6.1). These sectors often interact. For example, sea-level rise may endanger critical transportation infrastructure in coastal areas, which has the potential to disrupt evacuation routes, posing a threat to public safety. The chance of an impact occurring in any one sector will vary by community. As a result, the second step of the vulnerability assessment, following an assessment of climate exposure, is identifying the potential points of sensitivity from all sectors.

Built Environment

INFRASTRUCTURE

Transportation and other linear infrastructure serve a community by providing connections between homes, workplaces, and basic services (e.g., transportation, electrical, communication, water, and wastewater), allowing the provision of goods and services. Disruption of transportation networks, including roadways, marine ports, airports, and train lines, must be carefully evaluated. Damage to or the loss of these networks due to a fire, flood, or landslide can drastically impact the local economy, isolate populations, and endanger community members. A community should evaluate threats to critical links and nodes in its infrastructure. For example, transportation networks can be affected by changing conditions such as seasonal climate alterations. Temperature extremes or repeated

Box 6.1

Sectors to Be Evaluated for Vulnerability

Built Environment

Infrastructure

- transportation (roadways, airports, marine ports, trains)
- water and wastewater
- energy
- communication

Buildings and Planned Development

- businesses
- residences
- community services (hospitals, schools, fire, police)

Social Justice

- public health
- public safety
- vulnerable populations (factors include medical conditions, linguistic isolation, residential and work locations, and poverty)
- food security

Economic Systems

- economic health
- import/export of goods
- employment level and security
- flexibility

Ecosystem Health

- terrestrial ecosystems
- freshwater aquatic ecosystems
- marine ecosystems and coastal environments
- agriculture and rangeland

---

freeze-thaw cycles can cause roadways to wear more quickly and, in some cases, result in roadways and railroad tracks buckling. These impacts not only reduce safety but also require heightened diligence regarding maintenance. There are points in any infrastructure network where disruption will affect large swaths of a community or various community functions. These nodes should be prioritized when evaluating areas in need of strategy development.

Components of a community's infrastructure located in coastal or floodplain areas—including transportation, water infrastructure, and energy plants—are potentially vulnerable to the impacts associated with sea-level rise and increased flooding. Because it is more efficient for wastewater to be conveyed via gravity flow, many water reclamation facilities are located in low-lying areas. Sea-level rise or increased flood severity may necessitate the implementation of protective measures or, in some cases, relocation of the facility. Identification of critical infrastructure with careful assessment of climate science and local conditions allows communities to take early steps to prepare for these impacts. Such preparation can lighten the eventual financial burden and lower community risk.

Similar to water reclamation facilities, energy plants are frequently located near marine or freshwater sources for cooling water necessary to control plant temperatures. The widespread impact of operations disruption at an energy plant may be a high enough risk to demand action regardless of probability and/or uncertainty. In addition to the possible threats to the structural integrity of energy plants, climate change can impact the efficiency of energy transmission and energy demand. Hot weather or prolonged periods of extreme heat result in not only increased energy demand due to air conditioning use but also lower transmission efficiency.[3] Increased demand and reduced efficiency may have a range of other outcomes such as brownouts that will impact nearly all aspects of a community. The trickle-down consequences of climate impacts on energy supply and demand must be carefully evaluated, with particular attention paid to those populations, services, and business that may be most affected.

Communication nodes such as cell phone towers also must be assessed for the potential effects climate change will have on them. Loss or disruption of communication is particularly problematic when a community is responding to hazards or events exacerbated by climate change, such as extreme heat. Communicating with a community about current conditions, supportive resources, and emergency facilities is critical to effectively managing responses to extreme conditions.

Buildings and Planned Development

In addition to infrastructure, homes, businesses, and structures that hold critical community services can also be vulnerable to climate impacts. These impacts can be flood related, due to rapid snowmelt or extreme rainfall, wildfire, storm events, sea-level rise, or extreme wind. A community must evaluate the presence of vulnerable structures in areas at risk of climate change impacts, including proximity to structures such as dams or levees. The structures that may be subject to physical damage due to climate impacts should be identified and mapped. The structures can hold important economic (including employment), cultural, or safety (e.g., hospitals) roles in the community, which can result in loss well beyond that of the structures themselves.

A vulnerability assessment must consider not only existing buildings but also future planned development. Comprehensive plans and zoning codes designate undeveloped areas for future growth. If future development is planned in areas that may be vulnerable to fire, flood, landslide, or other climate impacts, these are local vulnerabilities until the plans are adjusted. Clearly defining the risks posed to planned future development allows communities the opportunity to preemptively develop measures to address climate change through adjusted building standards or by changing the planned location of future growth.

Social Justice

Climate change vulnerability assessment should include consideration of particular populations that are disproportionately vulnerable to impacts due to personal characteristics, characteristics of residences, workplace location or characteristics, income levels, and other factors that limit adaptive capacity. Coastal counties constitute less than 20% of U.S. land, yet over half of the population lives in these areas.[4] As a result, sea-level rise and the associated impacts have the potential to threaten the safety of large numbers of people. The vulnerability of these residents should be assessed based on proximity to projected flood impacts, their ability to evacuate, and their capacity to make changes to their homes. For example, Hermosa Beach, California, conducted a vulnerability assessment and discovered that a coastal section of their city was disproportionately inhabited by renters paying more than 50% of their income to rent. These residents are less likely to make improvements to their homes to address hazards related to climate change, such as sea-level rise or heat, making them more vulnerable than others.[5] This is also true for other hazards, such as flooding, landslide, and fire. The characteristics of community members and their proximity to areas prone to these hazards must be part of a vulnerability assessment.

For many impacts, it is not just the location of structures that may place populations at risk but the quality of those structures. Some portions of a community's housing stock may increase occupant exposure to climate impacts. Housing units can be poorly ventilated or have high sun exposure without having access to cooling such as air conditioning. These living quarters, often serving low-income communities, have the potential to amplify the health consequences of heat exposure. Similarly, some structures are more vulnerable to fire, high wind, or other impacts. If a community is projected to experience an impact more frequently, an evaluation of roofing materials, landscaping, and other building practices that reduce risk should be conducted. A community's building stock should be evaluated to identify structures that place inhabitants' safety or health at risk.

Public health can also be impacted by climate change. A change in climate can alter water quality, cause septic system overflows, and foster increased pest populations. In each case, it is an additional source and transmitter of infection, illness, and disease. The potential physical locations and causes of these vectors should be identified. In addition, the populations most likely to be vulnerable to these threats should be identified and their potential exposure evaluated. Extended periods of high temperatures such as heat waves can result in a variety of health impacts, including severe sunburn, physical weakness and decreased energy, heat stroke, and even death. Heat is particularly dangerous for vulnerable populations such as the young, old, or immunocompromised. Globally, heat waves have resulted in a large number of deaths in the last several years, such as those in Japan,[6] the United Kingdom,[7] and Canada.[8] These instances highlight the need to identify vulnerable populations when evaluating the risk presented by heat. In addition to those populations that may have compromised health, those community members who do not have a means to moderate temperature at home through air conditioning or those who work outside, such as construction or agriculture workers, are also disproportionately vulnerable to heat. High temperatures also increase the rate at which ground-level ozone is formed, a priority air pollutant that requires nitrogen oxides, volatile organic compounds, and sunlight to be produced. Ozone has been associated with a wide range of respiratory ailments[9] and should be of particular concern for urban areas due to the combination of increased ozone precursors, the urban-heat-island effect, and increased heat due to climate change.

Economic Setting

Economic setting refers to the manner in which climate impacts affect public health, safety, disadvantaged communities, and economic stability. Vulnerability in this sector can be produced directly or as a consequence of impacts in other sectors, such as infrastructure. When assessing the vulnerability of the built environment, particular interest should be paid to structures that serve critical community functions, such as hospitals, schools, cultural centers, emergency services, and critical business hubs. Effects on local economic stability can result from the disruption of transportation networks, changes in resource availability, and changes in the employment base. A community should first evaluate the local business sector to understand the impact of climate change on the viability of these businesses for both local employment and the provision of local goods and services. A business community dominated by a specific sector such as agriculture or trade may be particularly vulnerable. Any number of climate change impacts can have detrimental impacts on a local economy, such as disruption of transportation networks that allow for the flow of goods necessary for business. Climate impacts can also affect the financial viability of business through changes like reduced availability of water, increased temperatures that alter crop productivity, or coastal erosion that reduces the recreational value of a tourist beach.

Ecosystem Health

Projected climate impacts have the potential to drastically change the functioning of ecosystems, including the services on which communities depend, such as moderation of flood waters. The shift in seasonal patterns may alter the location and quality of available habitats. It may also alter the frequency of ecosystem disruptions such as fire, flood, or pest outbreaks. With altered precipitation patterns and increased temperature, the annual hydrograph and water quality of rivers and streams will be impacted by climate change. Alterations in flow levels can affect both instream habitats and riparian areas. Lower flows and longer low-flow periods can influence fish passage, the viability of water-dependent flora and fauna, and the availability of water supply for community use. Changes in water temperature can also influence habitat conditions. Increased temperature may result in cold-water fish losing habitat and warm-water species expanding their range. Temperature can impact disease vectors and provide an improved habitat for insects. Upstream flooding and higher tides may result in more frequent or permanent inundation of coastal habitats. This can alter coastal estuaries and wetlands, dune habitat, and nearshore stream and riparian habitats. Species such as migratory birds, shellfish, anadromous fish, and native plants can all be impacted by shifts in habitat. These changes can also impact commercial fishing and shellfish operations. Another economic role of coastal ecosystems is tourism. For example, the erosion and/or loss of coastal habitats can damage beach recreation and tourism. As sea level slowly rises, the first impact may be increased maintenance costs for these areas, particularly those that serve tourism or coastal industries and harbors.

Climate change can leave forests more vulnerable to threats such as insects and fire. The overall impact of climate change on forest productivity varies by location. In some fortunate places, forest productivity may increase, but it will decline in many others. A decline in forest health can be tied to changes in precipitation patterns and temperature that may alter the timing of rain events, the duration of drought events, and the timing of spring snowmelt. These changes can result in increased tree mortality, species migration, invasive species, pest outbreaks, and changes in interactions between competitive species. Forests stressed by high temperature and limited water are more vulnerable to fire. Large wildfires are projected to increase, and areas with a historically low probability of experiencing fire may be more vulnerable in the future. Damage to forest ecosystems can have economic as well as human health and safety risks. Communities must pay particular attention to the wildland–urban interface.

Agricultural growers must match their management practices, including crop choice, tillage practices, planting, harvest, and grazing density, to local climatic conditions. Changes in these conditions, such as amount and timing of precipitation, temperature, and the timing of seasons, can have detrimental effects on crops and livestock operations. Changes can cause crop damage or failure, new weeds, expanded ranges for existing weeds, new diseases and pests, and damage from extreme rain events or flooding of agricultural areas. These impacts all have the potential to result in reduced yield, which has consequences for the grower, agricultural employees such as field-workers, related industries, and the community at large. Climate change will also impact livestock operations from the stress on animals that results from extended periods of high temperatures or limited water supply. These stressors can result in increased vulnerability to disease and can limit the productivity of livestock operations.

The Vulnerability Assessment Process

This chapter focuses on the first four steps in the climate change adaptation strategy development process, which cover the vulnerability assessment (see also figure 6.1):

1. *Exposure:* an assessment of the ways in which climate change may impact a community
2. *Sensitivity:* identification of the aspects of a community potentially affected by the climate change impacts to which they would be exposed
3. *Potential impacts:* an examination of the extent to which an impact will affect a community
4. *Adaptive capacity:* an assessment of the degree to which a community is prepared for the projected impacts of climate change

Step 1: Exposure

Climate change will not impact all communities in the same manner or to the same degree. The first step for a community vulnerability assessment is to identify the consequences of climate change most likely to occur locally. To conduct the identification and assessment process, other information must be gathered, such as which climate change effects should be assessed, which scientific projections should be used, and which local experts can aid in an evaluation of degree of impact.

Projected climate change impacts are most often reported at global, national, state, or regional scales and not at local ones. The challenge for local jurisdictions is to identify the climate impacts and the magnitude of change to expect. International and national entities may have projections specific to the region in which a community is located, but it is often best to first seek climate science reports supplied by state and regional entities such as emergency management and natural resources agencies. For example, the State of California has developed an interactive website to explore state-generated, down-scaled climate change projections to support local jurisdictions seeking to develop adaptation strategies.[10] As of early 2018, 21 states had adaptation plans completed or in progress. In the absence of or to complement these reports, national and international data sources can be examined. From these reports, a community should seek to gain an understanding of the impacts that will be experienced locally. These data may be uncertain, particularly at smaller spatial scales. To account for this uncertainty, a community should identify a range of possible outcomes defined for various future dates, such as 2030, 2050, and 2100. In each case, the data and identified thresholds must be tailored for local contexts.

Primary climate change impacts include changes in temperature; changes in precipitation; sea-level rise; changes in the frequency, severity, and location of storm events; and ocean acidification. Together, the primary climate change impacts can result in a suite of other landscape-scale biophysical outcomes, including wildfire, landslide, and inland flooding (see table 6.1). Accurate estimates of these factors can be supported through collaboration with scientific organizations. Projections at various scales for temperature, precipitation, and sea-level rise are commonly available. The other two, regarding storms and ocean acidification, have fewer readily available projections but should also be considered.

Characteristics of projected impacts are critical for developing and prioritizing adaptation strategies. The critical questions to ask to assess each climate change impact are as follows:

- What is the difference between current conditions and those projected for 2050 and at the end of the century?
- How quickly are these changes projected to occur?
- Where are the changes projected to occur?

A critical aspect in answering the above questions is choosing the appropriate scenario from available science. In this early step, communities would be best served by choosing both the most optimistic projection (based on aggressive GHG emissions reductions) and the worst-case scenario (little or slow progress on GHG emissions reductions). These two set the ends of the spectrum of potential climate change outcomes for each impact. Based on who or what is at risk or the expected duration of adaptation strategy implementation, a determination of where on this spectrum the science used to inform strategies ought to come. For this first step, the range of potential outcomes is the critical information.

The other two informational goals are determining how quickly these changes are projected to occur and designating a narrowed spatial extent for where impacts may occur. Some aspects of climate change are progressing more slowly than others. The projected pace of impact onset is critical to the eventual strategy development process, as it provides context

Table 6.1. Secondary impacts associated with primary impacts alone or in combination

Primary impact	Associated secondary impact
Sea-level rise	Inundation or long-term waterline change
	Extreme high tide
	Coastal erosion
	Saltwater intrusion
Changes to precipitation and temperature patterns	Seasonal pattern shifts
Increased temperatures	Heat wave
Increased precipitation	Intense rainstorms
	Flooding
	Landslide
Increased temperatures and/or reduced precipitation	Wildfire
	Reduced snowpack
	Drought
Ocean acidification	
Changed frequency, severity, and location of storm events	

Sources: Adapted from Intergovernmental Panel on Climate Change, *Climate Change 2013: The Physical Science Basis. Contribution of Working Group I to the Fifth Assessment Report of the Intergovernmental Panel on Climate Change*, ed. T. F. Stocker et al. (Cambridge: Cambridge University Press, 2013), 1535; Intergovernmental Panel on Climate Change, *Climate Change 2014: Impacts, Adaptation, and Vulnerability. Part A: Global and Sectoral Aspects. Contribution of Working Group II to the Fifth Assessment Report of the Intergovernmental Panel on Climate Change*, ed. C. B. Field et al. (Cambridge: Cambridge University Press, 2014), 1132; U.S. Global Change Research Program, *Impacts, Risks, and Adaptation in the United States: Fourth National Climate Assessment*, vol. 2, ed. D. R. Reidmiller et al. (Washington, DC: Author, 2018), 1515, doi: 10.7930/NCA4.2018; California Office of Emergency Services and California Natural Resources Agency, *California Adaptation Planning Guide* (Sacramento, CA: Author, 2012), http://resources.ca.gov/climate/safeguarding/adaptation_policy_guide/.

for how quickly implementation should progress. Location also serves to narrow subsequent steps in the vulnerability assessment. Impacts may be focused on areas that hold either particularly important or particularly vulnerable assets or people. Knowing the locations of potential impacts supports several other steps in the vulnerability assessment.

Step 2: Sensitivity

For each of the climate change impacts profiled in the Exposure step, an assessment of what or who may be affected is conducted (see box 6.2). This step does not ask a community to assess the extent to which a community function, structure, or subcommunity may be affected; it just asks whether they are potentially affected or not. This step includes considering not only physical assets (e.g., buildings or infrastructure) but also populations of community members and aspects of community function. While many communities will recognize the process of assessing the sensitivity of physical assets due to its similarity to a Local Hazard Mitigation Plan (LHMP) development process, the identification of subpopulations that may be sensitive to the impacts identified in step 1 may be less familiar.

Subpopulations include individuals who may be less able to cope with climate impacts like increased costs for basic services or those who may be more vulnerable due to factors such as linguistic isolation. The subpopulations that can be identified include low-income individuals, individuals who are homeless, communities of color, women, and the lesbian, gay, bisexual, and transgender (LGBT) community. This should also include populations that are physically at risk due to the location or characteristics

---

Box 6.2

Potential Points of Sensitivity

- *essential facilities,* such as hospitals and other medical facilities, police and fire stations, emergency operations centers and evacuation shelters, and schools

- *transportation systems,* such as airways (airports, heliports, highways), bridges, tunnels, overpasses, transfer centers, railways (tracks, tunnels, bridges, rail yards, depots), and waterways (canals, locks, seaports, ferries, harbors, dry docks, piers)
- *lifeline utility systems,* such as those related to potable water, wastewater, fuel, natural gas, electric power, and communication
- *high potential loss facilities,* where damage would have large environmental, economic, or public safety consequences, such as nuclear power plants, dams, and military installations
- *hazardous material facilities,* including those housing industrial/ hazardous materials like corrosives, explosives, flammable materials, radioactive materials, and toxins
- *vulnerable populations,* such as non-English-speaking people or elderly people who may require special response assistance or special medical care after a climate-influenced disaster
- *economic elements* that could affect the local or regional economy if disrupted, such as major employers and financial centers
- *areas of special consideration,* where damage could result in high death tolls and injury rates, such as areas of high-density residential or commercial development
- *historic and cultural resource areas,* such as areas that may be identified and protected under state or federal law
- *natural resource and biophysical systems,* such as areas that are protected as rare and critical under state and national law as well as areas that serve as buffers to impacts (e.g., wetlands) or hold special local cultural and social meaning
- *other important facilities* that help ensure a full recovery from or adjustment to changed climate conditions, such as those that serve government functions or major employers, banks, and certain commercial establishments like grocery stores, hardware stores, and gas stations

of their residences or workplaces. For example, extreme heat may be more likely to affect individuals who work outside (e.g., construction or agriculture) or live in a home that does not have access to air conditioning and/or has poor insulation. There are also populations that are less able to cope or adapt to climate change impacts due to medical conditions that limit mobility or their ability to function in atypical conditions (in terms of temperature, precipitation, etc.). These could include respiratory ailments or any number of other medical conditions. They may require close collaboration with local public health departments.

Step 3: Potential Impact

This step asks a community to assess the degree of potential impact that may be felt at each point of sensitivity. It relies heavily on the climate action team assembled for development of climate-related planning strategies. The data gathered in step 1—impact location and speed of onset—should be used in this assessment, as they allow assessment of whether the impact is likely to have permanent or reversible consequences on a point of sensitivity. These data also can help in determining the extent to which an impact endangers the health or safety of an identified local population. In combination with the assessment of impacts on populations, the community's ability to provide critical services and maintain regular community function should be evaluated.

When completing this step, communities should be able to determine the level of specificity desired given the local support for the process. It can be handled qualitatively, quantitatively, or using some combination of the two methods. For example, a community with few resources to dedicate to a vulnerability assessment can define criteria for ranking impact severity and then use the assembled local and technical knowledge on the climate action team to rank the potential impact for each point of sensitivity. For example, when the City of Los Angeles developed its *Climate Action and Adaptation Plan for the Metropolitan Transit Authority*, as part of the impact assessment, it included a criterion of "criticality" for determining if points of sensitivity had high potential impact. The evaluation of criticality focused on the potential impact on bus users in the city, who rely on the service, and found over one million weekday boardings, an annual budget over \$300 million, and project costs over \$10 billion for the 2005–2040 period.[11] Criteria like this one must be determined by local staff who know the best indicators of a given impact to a point of sensitivity.

Some climate change impacts could be deemed critical enough for a given community that a subset of the impacts and points of sensitivity requires a more-specific, quantitative assessment, including a determination of specific environmental thresholds (e.g., air quality, local flooding), numeric estimation of exposed populations, values of assets potentially impacted, or other community resources. These data often require detailed assessment by local staff or consultants with specific knowledge or skills.

Regardless of the approach chosen, the climate action team will need to use the information from steps 1 and 2 to define the scenarios in order to assess the physical integrity and impact of the disruption of associated services. For example, the potential impact on a community-serving facility is not just on the physical asset but also on all residents relying on the provided service. All residents should be considered potentially impacted along with the physical resource. For each point of sensitivity, the following questions should be answered either qualitatively or quantitatively:

1. How long is the impact likely to last?
2. What is the extent of the impact (size of area, number of people)?
3. What is the level of disruption to normal community function?

Step 4: Adaptive Capacity

The complement to the inventory of local potential impacts due to climate change is an inventory of the resources and barriers for reducing vulnerability and adapting to those projected changes. These resources include existing policy, local expertise, the capacity for technological innovation, flexibility in the economic base, and high levels of community cohesion. It is important for communities to begin their adaptation strategy development with resources available locally. Actions that draw directly on local resources are more likely to be implemented quickly and supported in the long term because they rely less on outside help.

The vast majority of communities have existing plans or strategies in place to address some of the potential impacts of climate change.

The methods used to develop these existing plans are likely appropriate for some of the impacts that have not yet been addressed, which will build on local expertise. As a result, the first step in evaluating a community's capability for dealing with local impacts is conducting a policy audit (described in chapter 2). Local hazard mitigation plans and comprehensive plan safety elements are the best starting points. In some cases, communities may also have policies that address hazards such as forest management plans or building codes for homes at the wildland–urban interface. Existing plans should be evaluated regarding the extent to which they address the impacts identified as part of step 3 (see box 6.3). This evaluation acts as a gap analysis that identifies areas of need in existing adaptation strategies. The other benefit of building on existing policy is that strategies that have proven locally effective can be identified. The final piece of assessment in the

---

Box 6.3

Evaluating Adaptive Capacity

For each impact assessed in step 3, the following evaluation should be completed:

- Identify an action in progress, planned, or readily implemented to address the potential climate change impact.
- Evaluate the time and resources needed for implementation if a policy or program has not yet been implemented.
- Assess the extent to which an existing policy or program addresses potential impacts (e.g., "Is it enough?").
- Note the degree to which an existing policy or program could be strengthened.

Source: Adapted from California Emergency Management Agency and California Natural Resources Agency, *California Adaptation Planning Guide—Planning for Adaptive Communities* (Sacramento, CA: Author, 2012), http://resources.ca.gov/docs/climate/01APG_Planning_for_Adaptive_Communities.pdf.

evaluation of existing policy is whether simply strengthening policy is enough in the face of the projected climate impacts. In some cases, climate impacts will be enough of a deviation from current conditions to require new strategies.

Addressing climate change impacts requires updating existing policy and developing new strategies and programs. Devising and implementing these strategies requires knowledge, funding, collective community action, and in many cases, innovation. It is important for communities to clearly understand the local resources for addressing the needs identified through impact assessment and existing policy evaluation. In order to prioritize strategies, the ease or difficulty of taking adaptive action should be clearly understood. Elements contributing to local capability can include scientific expertise that can aid in the local interpretation of climate science over time and community organizations that can aid in outreach. Infrastructure concerns can benefit from the capability of local utility providers to make facility adjustments given changing climatic conditions.

Another critical part of a comprehensive adaptive capacity assessment is a realistic review of the community's existing ability to address impacts and disruptions to community function and service provision. It is easy to view the future in a manner that obscures current deficiencies in community continuity and resilience. Recognition of current needs for improvement or points that could quickly become areas of escalating risk is a critical part of adaptive capacity assessment. This assessment should identify areas in need of bolstering simply to ensure ongoing community function when faced with new and escalating disruptions.

Using the Vulnerability Assessment

At the completion of the vulnerability assessment, a community should have an understanding of both the potential impacts they are facing and how prepared they are to address them. These two pieces of information allow adaptation needs to be prioritized by the process of adaptation strategy development discussed in chapter 7. The same climate action team that developed the vulnerability assessment will be integral to the design of strategies to address the profiled impacts.

Chapter 7

Strategies for Creating Resilient Communities

Resilient communities are those that can function economically, socially, and environmentally in the face of disruptive impacts associated with climate change. Resilience does not imply a particular approach to address impacts; rather, it allows for context, impact, and situation to dictate the best approach. The term *resilience* has been used in an engineering context to describe structural performance or a system property. In the case of local planning, the system is the community, defined by the interacting elements of the biophysical setting, built environment, and sociopolitical conditions. The resilience concept can be most clearly understood by considering three broad forms:

1. The direct strength of structures or institutions when placed under pressure
2. The ability of systems to absorb the impact of disruptive events without fundamental changes in function or structure
3. The ability of systems to adjust to provide similar functions achieved in new ways

Climate adaptation refers broadly to measures that increase the ability of a community to withstand, recover from, and adapt to climate impacts. Adaptation planning strives for resilience (see box 7.1). The engineering or structural resilience can be seen as a component of system resilience. Resilience allows for strategies to be viewed in a larger context and can be freeing for the process of policy development. For example, the strengthening of levees in flood-prone areas such as New Orleans improves short-term structural resilience in the face of sea-level rise and increased hurricane intensity. But this measure alone does not address citywide or systematic resilience. Addressing adaptation on a local scale may result in policy that does not act directly on a projected impact. Strategies aimed at system resilience may include those that improve the flexibility of the economic sector so that it may adjust more quickly to changes brought about by climate change, or policy measures may aim to improve conditions for populations that are disproportionately vulnerable to impacts.

Resilience efforts can be categorized in three ways: (1) resistance, often structural barriers like a sea wall; (2) retreat, meaning actions such as moving back from coasts, floodplains, or fire-prone areas; or (3) accommodation that speaks to actions that bolster local ability to accept and adapt to changes, often through dynamic self-organization. Accommodating the effects of climate change may include actions as diverse as wetland restoration to limit flood severity or economic diversification to limit the extent to which disruption of a particular economic sector harms an overall community's economic vitality.

Getting Started on Climate Adaptation Strategy Development

Before starting climate adaptation strategy development, there are several issues that should be considered because they affect vulnerability assessment and strategy development. These include addressing how the greenhouse gas (GHG) emissions reduction and adaptation strategies relate to each other, how adaptation planning will be coordinated with local hazard mitigation planning and other local plans, and how to accommodate uncertainty. The White House Council on Environmental Quality, in its Progress Report of the Interagency Climate Change Adaptation Task Force: Recommended Actions in Support of

Box 7.1

Attributes of Resilient Communities

- diversification of livelihood activities, assets, and financial resources particularly into activities that have low levels of sensitivity to climatic variability or extreme events
- mobility and communication, particularly the ability of goods, people, information, and services to flow between regions in ways that enable local populations to access markets, assets, the media, and other resources beyond the likely impacts of specific climatic events
- ecosystem maintenance, particularly maintenance of the basic ecosystems services (such as drinking water) without which local populations cannot survive
- organization, particularly the social networks, organizations, and institutional systems that enable people to organize responses as constraints or opportunities emerge
- adapted infrastructure, particularly the design of physical structures (for water, transport, communication, etc.) in ways that can maintain their basic structure and function regardless of changes in climatic systems
- skills and knowledge, in particular the ability to learn and the basic educational skills required to shift livelihood strategies as required
- asset convertibility, the development of assets or markets that enable populations to transform the nature of assets and their uses as conditions evolve
- hazard-specific risk reduction, the development of early warning, spatial planning, implementation of building codes, establishment of community DRR [disaster risk reduction] organization, and other systems to reduce exposure and vulnerability to know climate-related hazards

Source: Marcus Moench, "Adapting to Climate Change and the Risks Associated with Other Natural Hazards: Methods for Moving from Concepts to Action," in *Adaptation to Climate Change*, ed. E. Lisa F. Schipper and Ian Burton (London: Earthscan, 2009), 273.

a National Climate Change Adaptation Strategy, provides a useful set of principles to keep in mind when pursuing adaptation planning (see box 7.2).

Relationship to GHG Emissions Reduction

GHG emissions reduction and adaptation goals are complementary in many ways (see figure 7.1) but do have the potential to conflict. It is also important to recognize that the considerations that contribute to strategy development differ, even if some of the measures are ultimately similar. A particular adaptation need, such as protection against extreme heat, can be addressed in a variety of ways. GHG reduction should be considered a potential co-benefit for adaptation measures, but this is secondary to the requirement that measures adequately address the scale and severity of the climate change impacts. For example, tree planting both sequesters carbon and helps alleviate the impacts of extreme heat, while strategies such as cooling centers that offer protection from heat may rely on air conditioning, which can be associated with the release of GHGs due to energy use. The trees address both emissions reduction and adaptation, but they may not offer protection from heat for the most vulnerable populations in a community, making the cooling centers a short-term necessity. Of course, the cooling center could be retrofitted with rooftop solar to mitigate the GHG emissions.

There is disagreement among climate policy experts regarding the relative importance of these goals. Some believe that reduction goals

---

Box 7.2

Guiding Principles for Adaptation

- *Adopt integrated approaches:* Adaptation should be incorporated into core policies, planning, practices, and programs whenever possible.
- *Prioritize the most vulnerable:* Adaptation plans should prioritize helping people, places, and infrastructure that are most

vulnerable to climate impacts and be designed and implemented with meaningful involvement from all parts of society.

- *Use best available science:* Adaptation should be grounded in the best available scientific understanding of climate change risks, impacts, and vulnerabilities.
- *Build strong partnerships:* Adaptation requires coordination across multiple sectors and scales and should build on the existing efforts and knowledge of a wide range of public and private stakeholders.
- *Apply risk management methods and tools:* Adaptation planning should incorporate risk management methods and tools to help identify, assess, and prioritize options to reduce vulnerability to potential environmental, social, and economic implications of climate change.
- *Apply ecosystem-based approaches:* Adaptation should, where relevant, take into account strategies to increase ecosystem resilience and protect critical ecosystem services on which humans depend to reduce vulnerability of human and natural systems to climate change.
- *Maximize mutual benefits:* Adaptation should, where possible, use strategies that complement or directly support other related climate or environmental initiatives, such as efforts to improve disaster preparedness, promote sustainable resource management, and reduce greenhouse gas emissions, including the development of cost-effective technologies.
- *Continuously evaluate performance:* Adaptation plans should include measurable goals and performance metrics to continuously assess whether adaptive actions are achieving desired outcomes.

Source: The White House Council on Environmental Quality, *Progress Report of the Interagency Climate Change Adaptation Task Force: Recommended Actions in Support of a National Climate Change Adaptation Strategy* (Washington, DC: Author, October 5, 2010), 10.

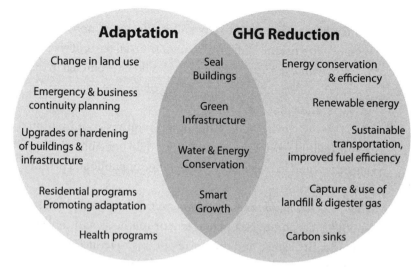

Figure 7-1 Overlap between greenhouse gas emissions reduction and climate adaptation measures

Source: "What Does Climate Resilience Look Like?," Center for Clean Air Policy, https://ccap.org/what-does-climate-resilience-look-like/.

should always be prioritized over adaptation goals, but adaptation has been the focus of increasing attention in many recent guidelines. We firmly believe that the two overarching goals of emissions reduction and adaptation should be treated as equal, with the relative priority of emissions reduction versus adaptation made on a strategy-by-strategy basis and consideration given to local needs. Figure 7.2 is an example of the manner in which Cleveland included and weighed adaptation measures and GHG reduction strategies. This evaluation includes how the measures achieve the primary goals of adaptation and/or GHG reduction but also examines the outcomes for vulnerable populations.

Relationship to Local Hazard Mitigation Planning

Hazard mitigation is a policy area with a significant amount of overlap with climate adaptation; climate change often exacerbates hazards by changing their frequency, severity, and location. Natural hazards have a longer history of being addressed through planning than climate change

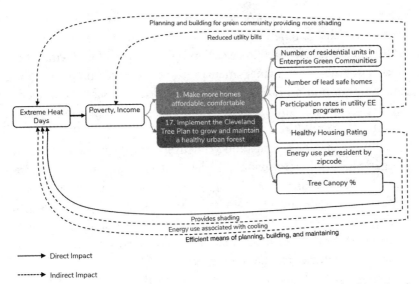

Figure 7-2 Evaluation of two climate planning strategies in Cleveland, Ohio, and the roles of GHG reduction and adaptation in each measure, including the social vulnerability assessment

Source: City of Cleveland, *Cleveland Climate Action Plan: Climate and Social Vulnerability Assessment Appendix C* (Cleveland, OH: Author, 2018), 56.

and provide lessons for climate adaptation. To incorporate climate change into the natural hazards planning process, one must recognize that historic patterns of natural hazard occurrence alone are no longer appropriate predictors for future occurrences. This change does not invalidate natural hazard planning tools, but it does mean that these tools require adjustment and updating to accommodate the evolving nature of the hazards being addressed.

Communities may engage in some form of local hazard mitigation planning. This could be through safety or hazard mitigation elements of a comprehensive plan, or it may be through preparation of a plan under the federal Disaster Mitigation Act of 2000 (DMA 2000). The DMA 2000 Local Hazard Mitigation Program provides communities with a financial incentive through grant eligibility to prepare a Local Hazard Mitigation Plan (LHMP). Hazard mitigation is defined by FEMA as "sustained action taken to reduce or eliminate long-term risk to people and their property from hazards."[1] This should not be confused with "climate mitigation," which refers to the reduction of GHG emissions. Nor should hazard mitigation be confused with other aspects of emergency management, such as pre-event preparation or emergency response. Hazard mitigation includes actions such as floodplain regulation, seismic retrofit of buildings, and reduced structural ignitability for wildfire.

The well-established steps and logic that define the process of hazard mitigation are similar to adaptation planning. It is based around the core idea of risk assessment (risk being the likelihood that a hazard event causes harm), which includes identifying hazards, profiling hazard events, inventorying community assets, and estimating the potential losses from disasters. This risk assessment then informs the development of hazard mitigation strategies for the community.

Since climate change has the potential to alter the type, frequency, and severity of natural hazards, it will affect a community's risk assessment. Any work on adaptation planning should be coordinated through a revised risk assessment that accounts for the incremental impact of climate change on natural hazards in the community. This revised risk assessment would then inform adaptation planning, local hazard mitigation planning, and community land use planning. The strategies in these various planning documents should then be coordinated or integrated to comprehensively address risks that currently exist and future risks that will be influenced by climate change.

The Climate Adaptation Strategy Development Process

Once a community conducts a climate change vulnerability assessment (as described in chapter 6), they must devise ways to address the identified points of community vulnerability, finding the strategies that position them to be resilient to projected climate change impacts. This process relies heavily on the climate action team (CAT, discussed in chapter 2), as it requires an understanding of not only the identified impacts but also the current state of the community, its capabilities, and the obstacles that must be addressed. The four steps in the adaptation strategy development process (introduced in chapter 6) are displayed in figure 7.3: step 5, prioritize

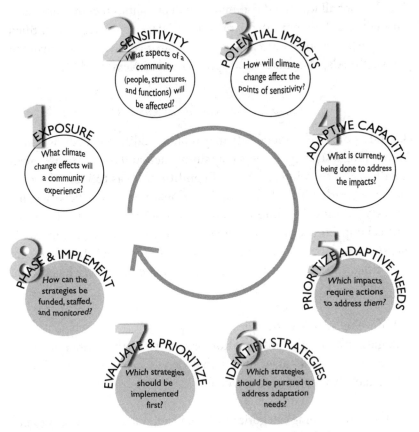

Figure 7-3 Climate change adaptation strategy development process (shaded in gray)

Source: Adapted from California Emergency Management Agency and California Natural Resources Agency, *California Adaptation Planning Guide—Planning for Adaptive Communities* (Sacramento, CA: Author, 2012), http://resources.ca.gov/docs/climate/01APG_Planning_for_Adaptive_Communities.pdf.

adaptive needs; step 6, identify strategies; step 7, evaluate and prioritize; and step 8, phase and implement. These steps include two prioritization steps (5 and 7). Step 5 prioritizes the impacts to be addressed, recognizing that not all identified community vulnerabilities require immediate strategy development. Step 7 prioritizes adaptive strategies identified in step 6 based on characteristics of the strategies themselves. Finally, in step 8, the adaptive strategies are phased and implemented.

Step 5: Prioritize Adaptive Needs

Certain points of vulnerability may require additional analysis before developing a strategy. Others may simply demand that steps are taken to allow the ongoing tracking of conditions so as to identify when action is needed. This differentiation of adaptive needs allows a community to prioritize funding, staff, and other resources for the most critical impacts because not all identified impacts will require immediate strategy development. When faced with a potential climate impact identified in the vulnerability assessment, a community has several options:

1. develop adaptive strategies,
2. gather additional information or data to further understand the impact and risks associated with it, or
3. establish a monitoring protocol.

These overarching categories are based on the adaptive capacity evaluation in the vulnerability assessment (step 4), the length of time estimated for the impact to be observable, the severity of the impact, the potential cost of addressing the impact, or any number of other factors. The factors used to define which community vulnerabilities should be addressed in strategy development should be defined by the CAT.

Develop Adaptive Strategies
There are a few factors that should be considered when deciding which community vulnerabilities should be prioritized for action. Communities should prioritize developing adaptive strategies when implementation

is relatively easy, the impact is severe, the time of onset is soon (or now), or the length of implementation is long.

- *Ease of implementation:* Those vulnerabilities for which a community already has measures in place (as identified in step 4) that could be easily bolstered may only require continuation or strengthening of an existing measure. Ease of implementation also refers to vulnerabilities where addressing the adaptive need is projected to be low-cost, meaning it can easily be handled in a community's annual budget. Opportunities such as having an existing policy and low-cost implementation must be identified to demonstrate short-term effectiveness. This may be critical for building the social capital required for long-term implementation of other measures that require a greater investment of time and resources.
- *Severity of impact:* In some cases, a climate impact may be unlikely, but the potential consequences are so severe that immediate action or initiation of strategy development is required. For example, sea-level rise or catastrophic flooding may endanger not only industry and infrastructure (such as airports or water reclamation facilities) but also residential communities near coasts or rivers. These events may be identified as so severe that even if the likelihood is low, action should be taken due to how disruptive the consequences would be.
- *Time of onset or length of implementation:* The time until onset and time required for effective policy implementation should also be factors considered when prioritizing adaptive needs. Impacts where the effects are likely to be experienced more quickly (within 5 to 10 years) should be prioritized for strategy development. This is particularly true for impacts that exacerbate existing areas of vulnerability. For example, a community may already be struggling to address existing flooding, fires, or other hazards that are likely to be exacerbated by climate change. These impacts demand action. Similarly, the anticipated time it will take to develop and implement strategies should be considered. Some adaptation measures require a long implementation period because they will require adjustments in land use patterns, realignments of major infrastructure, or other changes that take time to implement. These changes should be prioritized.

GATHER ADDITIONAL INFORMATION

In some communities, the potential impact has a longer causal chain, meaning the extent of impact is dependent on several factors about which a community may not have much information or uncertainty is high. In this case, the community should delay developing specific adaptive strategies while they gather additional information. They also may want to bring in new members to the CAT or hire an external consultant so that the needed information may be gathered. For example, if the levels of uncertainty for changes in precipitation amount or timing have the potential to adversely impact a community, additional scientific assessment may be needed either to refine the climate change projections or to better understand the local water system (surface water, groundwater, infiltration rates, current soil conditions, etc.) to gain greater specificity in identifying impacts. This approach may also be appropriate in cases where local impact must be contextualized regionally, such as sea-level rise or fire risk. The actions of neighboring communities may influence potential impacts locally. Looking at a different scale, such as taking a regional perspective on potential impacts and preparedness, also may require additional data collection.

ESTABLISH A MONITORING PROTOCOL

Climate change is progressive, and the science that projects potential impacts is constantly evolving based on changes in global GHG emissions or advances in climate science. If a climate impact is forecasted to take a long time to be experienced or if the change from current conditions is not as large as other impacts, immediate action may not be required. However, communities should establish a monitoring program so that the need or lack of need for strategy development can be tracked and periodically evaluated based on updated climate change projections or community development. For example, a community may not be vulnerable to some impacts due to a lack of development in locations vulnerable to impacts. Through time, this may change, meaning a community should be monitoring local vulnerability to ensure that adaptive strategies continue to be unnecessary and to be aware when an impact deserves strategy development.

For each community vulnerability, the various factors evaluated for deciding which approach is best must be balanced against each other. The data used is generated in steps 3 and 4, Potential Impact and Adaptive

Capacity, of the adaptation strategy development process. The information used by the CAT to categorize adaptive needs can be evaluated using decision matrices. These matrices provide an effective tool for balancing the various considerations and narrowing the list of impacts that require strategy development (see figure 7.4).

Step 6. Identify Strategies

Each of the community vulnerabilities identified as needing to go through the strategy development process are addressed in step 6. In addition, a program for additional data acquisition and monitoring networks for the vulnerabilities to be tracked through time also should be established. The development of adaptation strategies has the potential to provide long-term fiscal benefits to a community in addition to benefiting other aspects of community function, such as public safety or community cohesion. In most cases, communities can save three to four dollars in avoided future losses for every one dollar spent to preemptively implement measures to address vulnerabilities when compared to actions reactively addressing impacts as they occur.[2]

ADAPTATION STRATEGY CHARACTERISTICS
Developing strategies that anticipate climate change impacts with the intention of reducing future risk is inherently uncertain. Adaptation

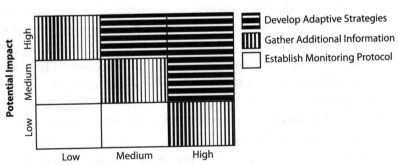

Figure 7-4 Example decision matrix balancing some of the factors that contribute to impact prioritization

strategies vary widely because in contrast to GHG emissions reduction strategies, which are more likely to provide equal benefits to all stakeholders, the benefits of adaptation tend to be more spatially explicit. As a result, effective strategies are as varied as the settings and communities for which the measures are developed. For example, adaptation strategies focused on sea-level rise disproportionately benefit coastal residents and will likely reflect the needs and values of this subpopulation. Step 2 of the strategy development process, Sensitivity, identifies the community structures, functions, and populations potentially impacted. Adaptation strategies should address these points of sensitivity, with particular attention paid to whether a strategy in one area of focus, such as infrastructure, creates a disproportionate impact (like a fee or other cost burden) on another, such as a specific subpopulation of a community.

The following list covers some key characteristics of effective adaptation strategies:

- *Flexible:* Because climate science is evolving and uncertain, adaptive policy should be robust—that is, applicable under a wide range of conditions. This also implies that policy should be enacted with the assumption that implementation and/or direction will be adjusted over time. Taken to an extreme, the idea of flexibility can be seen as the reversibility of a policy if conditions change or implementation produces unexpected outcomes.
- *Cost-effective:* The benefits of adaptive strategies may not be realized for many years, if not decades. In an economic modeling sense, the further out the benefit, the lower the current value. One way of avoiding this potential conflict between current cost and future benefit is to seek adaptive strategies that have both long-term and short-term benefits or serve as both GHG emissions reduction and adaptation strategies.
- *Specific:* Uncertainty is most easily evaluated in the context of a narrow issue in need of resolution. Climate impacts that require adaptive policy have a projected speed of onset, rate of change, and scale. Policy will be more effective if tailored to address these impact characteristics.
- *Integrative:* Climate impacts have the potential to initiate outcomes in a community across many sectors. Strategy development will be most effective if the interrelated nature of climate impacts is

recognized. Climate change acts directly on things like temperature and precipitation, but adaptive policy may focus on secondary impacts, such as how the change in temperature and precipitation affects crop yield. This policy may be a change in agricultural regulation that will facilitate adaptive change.[3]

The other critical aspect of strategy development is the identification of multiple strategies that address the same impact. Because climate change is progressive, most strategies will not be effective indefinitely. It is likely that multiple adaptation measures will need to be used in combination or in sequence. Organizing strategies into a sequence triggered by identified thresholds (environmental, social, or other local factors) indicating that a strategy is no longer effective is commonly termed a "pathways approach" to adaptation.[4] As a threshold or trigger is reached, a set of strategy options appropriate for that trigger can be evaluated, with a path ultimately being chosen. The sequence of strategies and identification of triggers occurs as part of the prioritization of strategies (step 7). However, in step 6, multiple approaches to a single impact that address various phases of impact occurrence (e.g., near-, mid-, and long-term) should be identified. This allows for a pathway to be defined in step 7. The identification of multiple strategies for each impact frees communities to consider approaches to adaptation that may not typically garner attention, such as ecosystem-based measures, those that may take a long time to implement, or those that the current community is resistant to. In association with strategy development, the local conditions that might signal (trigger) the need for an approach to be considered should also be identified. The specific sequencing can be defined in step 7.

In addition to triggers and considering multiple ways to address a potential climate impact, the CAT should also evaluate the way strategies affect social equity so that these outcomes can be addressed as part of implementation. For example, some strategies may create or exacerbate social inequities by creating burdens on a particular population in a community due to either physical location or individual characteristics. Strategies such as those that seek to address climate change may include alteration of major infrastructure such as roadways or water lines. These alterations may create a burden on particular subpopulations in a community. Acknowledgment of the secondary outcomes of a strategy allows them to be preemptively addressed. Such evaluation is critical in climate adaptation planning because, in many cases, the most vulnerable are often those who are least able to adapt due to factors such as income, workplace, or health characteristics. The City of Flagstaff (drawing lessons from the City of Portland) developed a social equity checklist to evaluate all measures developed for their climate action and adaptation plan (see box 7.3).

Box 7.3

City of Flagstaff, Arizona, Climate Action and Adaptation Plan

Flagstaff's 2018 Climate Action and Adaptation Plan is a strong, implementable climate plan that integrates both GHG emissions and climate change adaptation. Among the things that stand out is the integration of social equity into the plan. Each of the strategies from seven sectors was evaluated using nine equity considerations. The seven sectors in the plan are natural environment, water, energy, transportation and land use, waste and consumption, public health and safety, and prosperity and recreation.

The key equity considerations, taking lessons from the City of Portland, are as follows:

- *Disproportionate impacts:* Does the proposed action generate burdens (including costs), either directly or indirectly, to communities of color or low-income populations? If yes, are there opportunities to mitigate these impacts?

- *Shared benefits:* Can the benefits of the proposed action be targeted in progressive ways to reduce historical or current disparities? Are the benefits dispersed not only equally but equitably?
- *Accessibility:* Are the benefits of the proposed action broadly accessible to households and businesses throughout the community—particularly communities of color, low-income populations, and minority-owned, women-owned, and emerging small businesses?
- *Engagement:* Does the proposed action engage and empower communities of color and low-income populations in a meaningful, authentic, and culturally appropriate manner? Are community stakeholders involved and engaged in implementation?
- *Capacity:* Does the proposed action help build community capacity through funding, an expanded knowledge base, or other resources?
- *Alignment and partnership:* Does the proposed action align with and support existing communities of color and low-income population priorities, creating an opportunity to leverage resources and build collaborative partnerships?
- *Relationship building:* Does the proposed action help foster the building of effective, long-term relationships and trust between diverse communities and local government?
- *Economic opportunity and staff diversity:* Does the proposed action support communities of color and low-income populations through workforce development, contracting opportunities, or the increased diversity of City and County staff?
- *Accountability:* Does the proposed action have appropriate accountability mechanisms to ensure that communities of color, low-income populations, or other vulnerable communities will equitably benefit and not be disproportionately harmed?

Source: City of Flagstaff, *City of Flagstaff Climate Action and Adaptation Plan* (Flagstaff, AZ: Author, 2018), 156, https://www.flagstaff.az.gov/DocumentCenter/View/59411/Flagstaff-Climate-Action-and-Adaptation-Plan_Nov-2018.

TOPICAL AREAS FOR ADAPTATION STRATEGIES

Dividing adaptation strategies into categories is a convenience that most adaptation guidance documents and plans use, but it often masks the interrelated nature of adaptation measures. Strategies can be divided and organized in various ways, from the impacts listed in step 1, Exposure, to those listed in box 6.1 in the prior chapter. This section offers another organizing structure based on climate change's consequences: sea-level rise, extreme heat, wildfire, changes to air quality and public health, flooding, reduced water quality and supply, altered ecosystem health, hazards and emergency preparedness, and impacts on vulnerable populations. Similar to other categorizations of climate adaptation sectors, there are issues or topics that crop up across multiple categories, such as infrastructure. This section summarizes the common types of adaptation strategies in each category.

SEA-LEVEL RISE

Sea-level rise results in a wide range of hazards in most coastal areas: coastal erosion, including bluff and dune retreat; coastal inundation increased flooding at the outlet of rivers; back-flooding of stormwater infrastructure; and disruption of coastal industrial and infrastructure facilities. Communities should assess who and what are at risk of coastal climate change impacts. Box 7.4 shows the approach of the City of Del Mar, California, in identifying multiple strategies for creating an adaptation pathway for sea-level rise. Strategies that adapt to near-term sea-level rise are often things that coastal communities already have implemented, such as beach nourishment or sea wall reinforcement. Long-term strategies are likely to directly address the projections for the distant future, requiring actions such as strategic retreat, living sea walls or berms, ground raising, or the restoration of natural coastal barriers (e.g., mangroves, estuaries, or tidal wetlands).

The other sea-level rise impacts, back-flooding of stormwater infrastructure and disruption of industrial and infrastructure facilities, may require measures that include realignment. Coastal facilities can be armored in the short term, but many of these facilities discharge to marine environments and increasingly must rely on pumps rather than gravity. In addition, they may be vulnerable to disruption due to higher

high tides such as king tides or coastal storms. This can result in tempo-
rary closure of a plant or coastal roadway. Solutions to such disruption
are often relocation of the facility once short-term protective measures
are no longer adequate. For infrastructure, particularly water and power,
relocation of a water reclamation facility, roadway, or power plant requires
the realignment of related linear infrastructure such as sewer lines, con-
necting roadways, and power lines. Stormwater infrastructure is a similar
challenge because rainwater will not drain from low-lying areas of a
community, causing inundation. Communities can install subsurface
storage vaults to hold stormwater to limit flooding, and this solution

---

Box 7.4

Del Mar Sea-Level Rise Adaptation Plan

The specific impacts of sea-level rise—including river flooding,
bluff erosion, and beach erosion—were assessed and the various
strategies for addressing the impacts were evaluated. Benefits and
constraints were considered for each group of strategies. The summary of benefits and constraints for the identified options for sand
retention are in table A below:[1]

Table A. Sand retention measures, benefits, and constraints summary

Type of sand-retention structure	Benefits	Constraints
All	Retains sand	Requires mitigation
Groins	Maintains wider beach	Affects horizontal access along beach
Breakwater	Maximizes wave reduction and sand retention	Destroys surfing resources
Artificial reefs	Creates rocky reef habitat Has potential to enhance surfing resources	Is experimental

1. ES-59.

Each of the strategies to address the many sea-level rise impacts to the city was similarly assessed. These assessments, when combined with the scientific projections for the onset of impact, were used to establish adaptation pathways. The adaptation pathway for beach erosion combines beach nourishment, strengthened sea walls, sand retention, elevation, and relocation of structures with the needed lead times[2] (see table B).

Table B. Possible lead times for planning beach erosion adaptation options

Risk	Actions	Lead times	Adaptation options
Beach erosion	Protect	5–10 years	Beach and dune nourishment
		10–15 years	Raising and improving sea walls
		15–20 years	Sand retention strategies
	Accommodate	5–10 years	Elevating structures
	Retreat	15–20 years	Relocating public infrastructure

Source: City of Del Mar, *City of Del Mar Sea-Level Rise Adaptation Plan* (Del Mar, CA: Author, 2018), 96, accessed on December 15, 2018, http://www.delmar.ca.us/DocumentCenter/View/3487/Adaptation-Plan-clean_4102018-with-Appendices?bidId=.

2. ES-59.

may work for a period of time, but it may not be a long-term solution. Communities also can raise the base height in their building code, but that still leaves the roads to these structures regularly inundated. Raising the elevation of major facilities and supporting infrastructure is an option, but having development move away from coastal areas is likely the long-term option best pursued.

Extreme Heat

Extreme heat can itself be a hazard resulting in public health consequences and the need for increased maintenance of infrastructure such as roads. It also can contribute to the frequency and severity of other impacts, like fire, drought, or agricultural yield reduction. Public health is most often the first impact identified with extreme heat. This impact is also frequently associated with climate justice assessments. Communities least able to afford air conditioning and most likely to have homes with poor insulation and ventilation are often the most likely to experience extreme heat. Youth and those who are elderly, poor, and health compromised are the most vulnerable. In many locations, this is an immediate need. In the short term, measures such as cooling centers can be established; however, cooling centers can increase GHG emissions unless powered by renewable energy. Another component of establishing cooling centers is instituting a notification system so that those most vulnerable know of its availability and having a transport system so that those who need to can reach the center. Other strategies that seek to establish more shade and vegetative elements often take time to be implemented before there is an observable impact on extreme heat. In this case, a cooling center can be a short-term solution with reflective pavement and street trees (shade and evapotranspiration) the long-term one. The local building codes can also be adjusted to foster measures such as natural ventilation and passive heating and cooling in designs. Measures encouraging the retrofit of existing buildings to be more resilient during heat events must include a component that lifts the financial burden from those most vulnerable.

Heat can also stress systems, both built and natural. Roadways may require more frequent maintenance, and alternative materials should be considered for future paving and repaving projects. Similar to roads, extreme heat can stress existing conditions by making a landscape more flammable or a drought more severe. Heat is one factor that contributes to fire and drought, which may threaten many aspects of community function and safety. One measure to address the risks of drought is water supply diversification, and from an ecosystem perspective, there are many management strategies that can increase system resiliency. Fire-specific measures are summarized in the next section.

Wildfire

Climate change has the potential to increase wildfire frequency and severity by altering several factors that contribute to wildfire exposure, including the species serving as fuel in a fire, the moisture level in vegetation, wind events, and pest outbreaks that result in large numbers of dead trees. Together these factors result in longer fire seasons and larger, more severe fires. Response to this climate-exacerbated hazard can take two basic approaches: management of the forest, including controlled burns, and management of human development, particularly the wildland–urban interface (WUI). Management of forests or wildland areas can include thinning, understory fuel load reduction, controlled burns, and many other forest management strategies.

Communities at risk of wildfire should have several components included in their local plans, from building codes that require fire-resistant design and materials, to defensible space around each residential home, to bolstered emergency response capabilities. *Defensible space* refers to landscaped areas near structures (such as residential homes) designed to reduce fire risk. Roadways need to allow both for the evacuation of residents out of a neighborhood and for emergency vehicles traveling in. The communication of evacuation and emergency response should be well developed, with outreach to all community members prior to wildfire events. The community should also ensure that all necessary resources are available, from water to shelters. Long-term land use should be evaluated to limit the extent to which communities are exposed to fire risk, particularly regarding the WUI.

CHANGES TO AIR QUALITY AND PUBLIC HEALTH

Several aspects of air quality can be exacerbated by climate change, including increased production of ozone and pollutants such as black carbon (associated with fuel combustion and fire). With higher average temperatures, areas with high levels of ozone precursors (nitrogen oxides and volatile organic compounds) only require higher temperatures to produce ground-level ozone. Ozone places community members at risk, particularly children, older adults, those with asthma, and those whose livelihoods require spending long hours outside, such as construction or agricultural workers. Ozone can cause respiratory ailments and may alter the body's ability to intake some nutrients.[5] This is particularly true in dense urban settings and places specific subpopulations at risk. Black carbon is a component of fine particulate matter (PM2.5) and is associated with a wide range of health impacts, from asthma to respiratory hospital visits.

FLOODING

Climate change increases the variance of weather events, which results in an increase in the severity and frequency of climate extremes, including flooding. This means that the FEMA FIRM maps, which show the 100-year storm floodplain, may begin to underestimate the size of recurring storms. This can affect any structure—homes, roads, or other facilities—located in expanding floodplains, and the solutions are often similar to the choices available to address sea-level rise. Protective structures, such as river-retaining walls, can be built or fortified. As floods continue to grow, migration away from waterways can become an option. Ecological solutions can also be pursued, including wetland and floodplain restoration or reestablishment.

In addition to inundation due to flooding, intense rainfall and floodwater can result in increased erosion and overwhelm stormwater systems. Stormwater systems should be analyzed to identify pinch points or areas where the system backs up or the volume of water cannot be accommodated. Once the analysis has occurred, the points can be prioritized for action based on how quickly they are projected to become recurring problems for the community. Actions may include replacing drainage infrastructure with higher-capacity pipes or installing vaults or retention basins to limit the amount of water that the stormwater system must deliver.

Reduced Water Quality and Supply

Increased temperature lowers the ability of water to carry oxygen and changes the rate of aquatic reactions. This can affect the viability of waterways for aquatic biota and result in increased algal blooms. The extremes of the water levels can also affect water quality, where periods of low rainfall and water levels serve to concentrate existing water quality issues, particularly in areas where waterways are receiving urban runoff. Extremely high water levels can overwhelm drainage systems and, in many areas, result in combined sewer overflow.

This is a critical consideration for ecosystem function and increasingly can affect water used by communities for drinking. Varying water levels in aquatic systems can result in more uncertainty in the water systems, often resulting in highest demand in the summer when there is the least supply. Further challenging water supplies is the decrease in snowfall. Even if the total precipitation is unchanged, rain instead of snow means that less of the water supply remains local. Solutions to these challenges include increased water storage to replace what would have been held as snow until a spring melt. Other adaptive strategies include soils and forestland management that retains more of the water where it falls.

Altered Ecosystem Health

Ecosystems refer to natural systems, sensitive landscapes, plants, soils, and wildlife with an eye toward restoration and preservation. What is important for communities to keep in mind is that intact ecosystems often moderate climate impacts, whether they are wetlands limiting floods or coastal ecosystems moderating coastal storms. Climate change impacts include reduced forest health, fire, flood, insect outbreaks, and habitat shifts due to new seasonal patterns of precipitation and temperature or sea-level rise. The specific needs for ecosystems will vary widely with context. Different ecosystems are vulnerable to different impacts and will be stressed in different ways. A few key strategies useful in multiple contexts include the acquisition of open space to develop migration corridors (including designation of funds to acquire lands), the establishment of regional partnerships to foster collaboration with neighboring jurisdictions, restoration programs, and ongoing ecosystem management programs.

HAZARDS AND EMERGENCY PREPAREDNESS

Chapter 6 discussed the overlap between local hazard planning and climate change adaptation. Climate change will influence both the hazards that must be prepared for and the emergency response that will be needed when a hazard occurs. One of the most important considerations to be included in adaptation planning is identification, assessment, and strategy development for critical nodes. Such evaluation is of vital importance in ensuring that no climate-exacerbated hazard will be disruptive to community function. Another aspect of adaptation and hazard planning, which includes both predisaster strategies and disaster response, is to ensure that emergency response has the resources (facilities, staff, and funding) to continue to be able to respond to hazard events when their severity and frequency are escalating through time due to climate change. These measures should evaluate local plans for hazards and assess them for deficiencies in the context of progressive climate change. This may mean additional staff or emergency shelters. It can also mean an assessment of notification procedures and current response procedures, including evacuation routes. These should also be evaluated for vulnerability to progressive (nonhazard) climate change impacts that may hamper local ability to respond to hazards (climate exacerbated or otherwise).

IMPACTS ON VULNERABLE POPULATIONS

Climate justice demands that climate impacts are viewed through an ethical lens that understands that the very populations least able to adapt are often those that are most at risk. Identification and engagement of vulnerable populations is a way for climate action planning efforts to explicitly address climate justice. One primary task in ensuring that vulnerable populations are addressed in adaptation strategies is to develop a network of representatives from local advocacy organizations and establish a dialogue, allowing community members who are not typically engaged to be heard. Facilitation of this dialogue should utilize diverse forms of communication. Through this dialogue, education of both residents and the local staff should take place, allowing each to better understand the other's needs. From here, communities can identify specific actions such as the provision of supportive services like emergency response or cooling centers during a heat wave. Other potential measures include incentives or programs that reduce costs to vulnerable populations for particular adaptive actions. These individual strategies are specific to the local biophysical, social, and economic context.

Step 7. Evaluate and Prioritize

This step relies on the data gathered in earlier steps but adds factors critical to local implementation, such as projected costs, duration of implementation, social acceptance, and community co-benefits. A pathways approach can be particularly helpful in building public understanding and support by providing a transparent adaptation decision-making sequence. Conducting outreach early in the adaptation strategy development process allows the community to understand likely climate change impacts, community vulnerabilities, and associated thresholds that have been defined. Associated with awareness of the defined thresholds, outreach can raise awareness of the strategies that may be triggered, reducing public outcry when the strategies are eventually implemented. Many times, the strategies that communities must face involve relocation of homes and infrastructure or alteration of local land use, programs, and codes. These changes can be difficult to implement without community collaboration.

A first step in the evaluation conducted by the CAT is a systematic assessment of each strategy defined in step 6. Organization and development of these data again rely on the CAT, which knows the local community best. Each potential strategy should be evaluated systematically, creating an adaptation portfolio for each impact for which strategies are being developed.[6] These points of evaluation can include the following, but the CAT should define the list of evaluations relevant to the community. In this process, community understanding and support for the strategies are critical for ongoing implementation.[7]

- *Costs:* Cost estimates include the initial costs as well as any ongoing funding requirements, including personnel.
- *Available funding:* Potential sources for the funding should also be identified for each strategy. This can include the relative ease or difficulty of obtaining the funding. Can it be supported through the existing municipal budget? Does it require reallocation of funds from elsewhere or necessitate a new source of funding (fees, grants, etc.)?
- *Duration of implementation:* This requires two time periods to be assessed: the time necessary to initiate strategy implementation and the length of the implementation period. Initiation of a strategy can be delayed by reliance on technological advancements or policy change prior to implementation. Implementation duration can vary widely, from weeks to years. Updating local codes such as a coastal grading code or building codes to reduce fire vulnerability takes much less time than the eventual relocation of a water reclamation facility.
- *Social acceptance:* Adaptation policies are often housed in plans that require community feedback, advisory board approval, and adoption by elected officials. To successfully navigate this process, a strategy's level of acceptance should be assessed. This does not mean that less-popular strategies should not be pursued, but rather it is intended to highlight those strategies requiring additional time or outreach efforts prior to adoption and implementation.
- *Community co-benefits:* Most communities have many immediate needs or aspirations for the near future. The other benefits that may be experienced when a strategy is implemented should be identified. These can include economic improvement, better public safety, greenhouse gas reduction, improved public health, and many other community goals.

The data gathered in this step provide a detailed portfolio of strategies that, together with some of the vulnerability assessment, can be used to prioritize the measures for implementation. Each community vulnerability has a set of strategies identified to address it. These strategies are prioritized based on factors such as the speed and cost of implementation.

Some strategies may address immediate needs, whereas others may focus on long-term impacts. For example, some measures may address immediate needs for protecting local resources from impacts such as increased flood risk or sea-level rise by fortifying protective structures, whereas long-term measures may focus on land use change and migration away from rivers and coasts.

Strategy prioritization is also a critical step in developing pathways. Each strategy should have an envisioned trigger, such as beach width or disruption recurrence for a roadway or other piece of infrastructure. Strategies can be clustered and tied to triggers; when a trigger is set off, the strategies associated with it are considered. With triggers identified, the strategies can be arranged sequentially. In many cases, the strategies that are pursued first are those that are easily implemented and have limited costs. The data and assessments of each strategy should be used to determine the sequence of strategies. These data can be evaluated using a decision matrix similar to step 5, but this matrix may balance speed or severity of impact with duration of implementation or cost. Balancing the various strategies so that they are appropriately sequenced ensures that a community is prepared for even the most severe of potential impacts. The City of Del Mar adopted a sea-level rise adaptation plan in 2018 that uses the pathways approach. It includes measures that can be difficult for communities to support, such as migration from the coast, but it makes transparent to the community how much sea levels must rise before this action is pursued (see box 7.4).

Step 8. Phase and Implement

Long-term effectiveness for climate change adaptation relies on strong political leadership. Adaptation strategies address impacts projected to occur years to decades in the future and are less likely to yield observable benefits in the short term. Strong political leadership provides consistent and sustained support, which is critical to successful implementation. Strong leadership also is needed due to the diversity of adaptation strategies and the need for ongoing evaluation and updates. Actions being pursued by many departments or entities must be coordinated, and this too requires strong leadership.

Once the strategies have been prioritized and sequenced into pathways (step 7), effective implementation of individual strategies depends on several factors. A department, staff member, or entity should be defined as responsible for implementation, leading the team working on the measure. The steps necessary for effective implementation should be established in a phasing program that provides a clear time frame as well as a budget. The sources of funding to support implementation should be identified and obtained, whether this is done through the reallocation of current funds or the acquisition of additional funds through fees, taxes, or a grant. Finally, a means to track implementation progress and effectiveness should be developed so that strategies can be updated as new information is revealed, such as updated science or local risk.

The following list details some key aspects of implementation that should be defined for each adaptation strategy:

1. *Identify the responsible person, department, or entity:* Having adaptation strategies detailed in a plan does not ensure implementation. Implementation often relies on the designation of a specific person, department, or entity as responsible for implementation. Having a single person or entity tasked with implementation also allows the CAT to coordinate the responsible parties, provide a forum to share progress, identify points of overlap, and discuss solutions to unexpected challenges.

2. *Identify and obtain funding:* Often the most difficult and important component of ensuring implementation is identifying a funding source to support identified strategies. Each strategy should have an estimated cost for initial and ongoing materials, staff time, administrative support, outreach, and long-term monitoring. One way to smooth the funding justification and acquisition process is to identify ways in which a strategy meets multiple current community needs in addition to climate adaptation. Positioning strategies as compatible with other planning goals rather than competition can help a community justify the pursuit of adaptation goals. There are a variety of ways adaptation strategies can be funded, including government grants, general funds, taxes, fees (including impact fees), bonds, and more.

3. *Establish systems for monitoring implementation progress and effectiveness:* Climate change is dynamic, and both the climate change impacts, which are dependent on global GHG emissions, and the community's structure and function will continue to evolve. As a result, monitoring is required to track not only progress toward implementation but also strategy effectiveness. In the case where strategies have been arranged into pathways with identified triggers, the monitoring program should specifically be designed to track these identified triggers, signaling the community when effective adaptation requires a shift to a new measure. Comprehensive adaptation programs track scientific updates as well as the tools and technology available to address the impact projections. Many states as well as national and international entities provide climate science updates. Communities should track these updates to remain aware of projects that may result in greater or changed local impacts.

4. *Establish feedback loops:* Monitoring strategy effectiveness and scientific advancements is only useful if an organizational structure is established to allow communities to evaluate and adjust adaptation strategies when necessary. More than just checking for shifts and identified triggers, periodic reviews and updates that evaluate the potential effectiveness of entire adaptation pathways should be integrated into implementation plans. Given the uncertainty inherent in climate projections and impact assessment, an iterative approach that is unafraid of adjustment is critical to long-term policy effectiveness and efficient use of resources.[8]

Strategy implementation may in some cases only require updating code. This is often a shorter process for a city to complete when compared to land use or structural adjustments, but the achievement of adaptive action on the ground may take a longer time period. If, for example, a building code is adjusted, the adaptation outcomes will not be achieved for some time unless a community pursues a program to update existing buildings to meet the new standards in tandem with the updated code. A good example is New York City's building code, which designates design flood elevations (DFE) based on structural occupancy category and building orientation with respect to potential waves by adding height to the base flood elevation. This code update balances buildings of particular importance, such as schools, hospitals, and those housing critical equipment, with a building's exposure to flood waters or storm events.[9] The intended outcome of this building code is bolstered by *PlaNYC*, which has measures intended to update existing structures damaged in past events (e.g., Hurricane Sandy) and those that are vulnerable to future impacts.[10] Together, *PlaNYC* and the building code should bolster the resilience of the city to climate-change-exacerbated flood events due to increased rainfall, bigger storms, and/or sea-level rise.

Chapter 8

Pathways to Successful Implementation

A plan is only as good as its implementation. Too often communities invest considerable effort in preparing quality plans, policies, and programs only to see little happen because of failure to implement. Climate action planning presents an implementation challenge, since the field is rapidly evolving, issues often cut across organizational boundaries, and there is often a lack of dedicated funding. These are all challenges that can be addressed during the planning process. This chapter addresses phase 3, "Implementation and Monitoring," of the climate action planning process presented in chapter 2. All climate action planning should address how implementation will be ensured and the following questions:

- Who will be responsible for the oversight and management of implementation?
- Who will actually implement each strategy?
- What will be the timeline or phasing (programming) for the implementation of the strategies?
- How will the implementation of the strategies be funded?
- How will the implementation be monitored and evaluated?

Keys to Successful Implementation of Local Climate Action Plans, Policies, and Programs

A study of successful implementation completed by the book authors over a seven-year period revealed several keys to successful implementation. These are common principles that emerged from communities all over the U.S. that completed a climate action planning process and showed early success at getting their plans, policies, and programs implemented:

1. Broaden action
2. Empower staff
3. Organize an implementation team
4. Allocate funding
5. Support climate champions
6. Engage the public
7. Communicate co-benefits
8. Cultivate partnerships
9. Lead by example

Broaden Action

Given the scope of the climate crisis and the need for "all hands on deck," the responsibility for climate action cannot be limited to a single individual, agency, or organization. Local governments must broaden action by making climate action a regular and important part of business rather than isolating climate action responsibilities in the planning or public works departments, for example. All departments and agencies should establish procedures and policies that ensure the objectives of climate action are being pursued when it is most effective and efficient to do so. This may include standardized reporting of greenhouse gas (GHG) emissions in the same way that most agencies have to report budget tracking. Most departments wouldn't think twice about being asked about the fiscal implications of a new program or project or for a report of their year-end budget balance. Climate action should be the same way—it should be a regular and expected part of business. During the climate action planning process, each department should identify how it will broaden action.

All departments should be tracking GHG emissions from their own operations and ensuring that data are collected to support community-wide emissions inventories. For example, a transportation agency should track the emissions attributable to their road maintenance operations to both support the local government operations inventory and provide better knowledge about how they might reduce their emissions. Also, they should be tracking VMT and vehicle type (if possible) to support periodic community-wide emissions inventories.

For climate adaptation, all agencies should be reviewing projects and programs to understand how climate change may present a risk. For example, the housing agency can evaluate whether increased future heat waves may necessitate retrofitting existing housing and building new housing to be more thermally efficient.

Perhaps most importantly for broadening action, climate goals and strategies need to be in the municipal budget. When climate action is in the budget, it signals its importance, motivates administrators, provides resources for planning and implementation, and creates a clear mechanism for accountability; more details on this are provided in subsequent sections.

Empower Staff

As interest in climate change and sustainability has grown, many local governments are establishing specific offices or departments and creating a sustainability or climate program coordinator position to organize implementation across city agencies. The increasing sophistication and comprehensiveness of climate action planning is generating a need for this new profession. Examples include King County, Washington, which has senior climate change specialist and climate engagement specialist positions, and the City of San Luis Obispo, which has a sustainability manager in the city manager's office (see box 8.1 for the job description).

In 2013, the Rockefeller Foundation created the 100 Resilient Cities program.[1] Part of that program funded city chief resiliency officers (CROs) who would work directly for the chief executive of the city in developing and implementing resiliency programs. There are now about 90 CROs around the globe supported through this program, and this type of position is increasingly seen as valuable and necessary.

Box 8.1

Job Description for the City of San Luis Obispo,
California, Sustainability Manager

Job Summary

Performs a variety of project management and policy analysis assignments related to the City's sustainability efforts. Responsible for the overall administration, development, and management of environmental sustainability and climate action policies and programs. Leads citywide efforts and assists departments with planning, developing, implementing, and managing program initiatives and special projects within approved work plans and as directed.

Examples of Duties and Responsibilities

- plans, develops, implements, coordinates, monitors and updates the City's climate action plan and other related policies and projects
- coordinates and leads the personnel involved in the implementation of the climate action plan and other related policies and projects
- serves as a leader and champion for sustainability in the organization and community
- develops the operating budget for program-specific sustainability projects
- performs departmental and citywide program-specific organizational, operational, financial, and policy analysis; prepares narrative and statistical reports to support recommendations; implements policy and procedural changes after approval
- monitors and reports to city management and city council on the progress of the climate action plan

- conducts complex studies and prepares a variety of reports, correspondence, policies, procedures, ordinances, agreements, and other written materials
- applies for and manages grant applications and funding
- meets with community groups; neighborhood, civic, and business organizations; and members of the public
- communicates regularly with the public and organizations on sustainability policies and projects
- represents the City as a member of regional climate initiatives
- represents the department or City at public hearings and makes public presentations; will represent the department or City in contacts with the media
- analyzes and summarizes initiatives, legislation, and actions for reducing climate change that the council may choose to support

Education and Experience

- graduation from an accredited college or university with a bachelor's degree in sustainability, environmental science, urban planning, public or business administration, or related field
- three years of progressively responsible professional experience in environmental program development, sustainability, resource conservation, waste reduction, recycling, climate change, or related area; public sector experience is highly desirable

Source: City of San Luis Obispo, http://agency.governmentjobs.com/slobispo/job_bulletin.cfm?JobID=1906802 (edited for brevity).

Most communities have chosen to house climate offices and staff in environmental, planning, or public works departments to take advantage of the specialized expertise and similarity of mandates. The risk here is that these offices may be seen as operating in a limited domain and may not be able to achieve the institutionalization of action as described above. It is recommended that communities locate these offices and staff in the mayor's or city manager's office to take advantage of the authority and visibility of those offices and ensure broad action.

Communities unable to establish new offices or hire for new staff positions can rely on the existing organization for implementation. The benefits of this approach are that it requires little or no new resources, does not disrupt the existing institutional culture, and empowers those closest to actual implementation to act. The potential problems are that existing mandates and programs may overshadow the new climate strategies, implementation may be uneven across parts of the organization, and accountability may be diffuse. Part of this limitation can be addressed through institutionalizing action as discussed above and creating an implementation (a.k.a. "green") team. Regardless of which choice a community makes, all should consider following the City of Fort Lauderdale's lead; in 2015, it had all 2,600 city employees go through a training on how they can support and contribute to the City's climate action goals.[2]

Organize an Implementation Team

Implementation teams can be a very effective approach for ensuring the implementation of climate programs and strategies. If a community decides not to have a dedicated team, then the plan should clearly designate a responsible entity for ensuring the implementation of each greenhouse gas reduction and climate adaptation strategy.

Decisions about how to structure an implementation team should be based on the nature of the emissions reduction and adaptation strategies in the plan (see box 8.2). Communities with plans prepared by citizen committees or task forces may want to continue or modify those groups so that they are directly involved in implementation or serve in an oversight or watchdog capacity over those who will implement the plan.

Box 8.2

Ohio's Green Cincinnati Plan Steering Committee

There are two important aspects of the *Green Cincinnati Plan* (formerly called the *Climate Protection Action Plan*) that affect implementation. First, the original preparation and 2018 update of the plan was led by the mayor-appointed Green Cincinnati Plan Steering Committee and assisted by task teams composed of hundreds of community members. Due to its success, the committee was also empowered to lead the effort on implementation. Second, climate action strategies were adopted that required action from businesses and nonprofits in addition to the municipal government. The plan empowers the committee to monitor and provide oversight of plan implementation. In Cincinnati, the plan is best described as belonging to the community as a whole; thus implementation is thought of as the responsibility of the community rather than just the municipal government, although the municipal government is an important responsible party. The committee, which is made up of community leaders, plays a critical role in ensuring that the community responds to its responsibility for implementation. The committee must also prepare an annual report and regularly update the city council on progress.

Communities that adopt emissions reduction and adaptation strategies dependent primarily on government action may want to transition their climate action team (see chapter 2) into an implementation team.

Key Questions for Implementation Teams
- Who will serve on the team and how will they be chosen?
- What will be the role of the team? Will it be mostly oversight, or will the team take direct responsibility for implementation?
- What authority will the team have to ensure implementation? Will the team control funding associated with implementation?
- How will the team be held accountable?

- Will the team have responsibility for outreach and communication?
- Will the team have responsibility for monitoring, evaluation, and progress reporting?
- Are team members subject to state or local "sunshine" or open government laws for monitoring conflicts of interest, financial disclosures, ex parte communications, and the like?

Allocate Funding

Finding money for implementing climate action strategies can be the most challenging aspect of implementation. Climate action must compete against all the other needs in a community, which in difficult economic times can be a problem. Communities that are successful in implementation allocate funds that are ensured rather than dependent on uncertain potential funding sources. Often communities will prepare plans, policies, and programs where implementation is dependent on competing for public or private grants or where funding simply isn't identified. This can mean that well-intentioned plans sit on a shelf collecting dust. Local governments should allocate funds under their control through the budgeting process to support their key climate actions. Brent Toderian, former chief of planning for the City of Vancouver, says, "The truth about a city's aspirations isn't found in its vision. It's found in its budget."[3] Communities that go through the effort of developing visions and strategies for addressing climate change should follow through with specific funding allocations.

Emissions reduction and climate adaptation strategies should have estimated costs for implementation attached to them. These costs can then be assembled into a budget based on the prioritization and timeline that have been established. In addition to the costs for each strategy, there should be a budget for overall program administration that includes staffing, education and outreach, plan monitoring and updating, and so forth. The following are potential sources of funding for climate action (e.g., see box 8.3).

General Funds
A community may choose to allocate a portion of the local government's general funds to implementation. The general fund is the local

Box 8.3

Example of Funding Source Identification: Homer, Alaska

The City of Homer included the following in the "Implementation" section of their climate action plan:

> The City of Homer will establish and promote a "Sustainability Fund" which will be used to help cover the costs of implementing the Climate Action Plan.
>
> Possible sources of revenue for the Sustainability Fund include:

- Grant funding from state and federal programs and private foundations
- A Climate Action Plan tax modeled after Boulder, Colorado's innovative program. The CAP tax in Boulder, approved by voters, involves an agreement with the local investor-owned electric utility to assess a tax for residential, commercial, and industrial customers based on electricity usage. The tax is collected as part of the utility's normal billing process.
- A per-gallon tax on all fuel transferred within the City of Homer
- Voluntary "offsets" contributed by individuals and businesses who wish to reduce their carbon footprint by supporting projects aimed at reducing greenhouse gas emissions in the community at large
- Funds contributed by the City of Homer to offset employee travel (calculated as \$X per ton of travel-related CO_2)
- Savings resulting from increased energy efficiency/conservation as CAP measures impacting City operations are implemented
- Homer Spit parking fees
- General funds

- Bonds
- Taxes and fees (impact fees)
- Government grants
- Carbon offset programs
- Self-funding and revolving fund programs
- Volunteer and pro bono resources
- Private grants
- Private investment

Source: City of Homer, Alaska, Climate Action Plan (December 2007), 40.

government's primary operating account with revenues that are usually generated from property taxes, local sales taxes, and other local taxes and fees. Assigning general funds can be challenging because it usually means shifting them from another community program. Most local governments have tight operating budgets that make assigning them to climate action a challenging proposition, yet this is the most consistent source of funding available.

BONDS

Local governments may issue bonds, essentially borrowing money from the bond holder to finance climate strategies. Bonds are usually used for capital projects (e.g., public buildings, roads, sewer and water infrastructure) or for projects that generate revenue to pay off the bond (pay-parking garages are a typical example). If an emissions reduction strategy fits one of these project types, then issuing a bond may be a viable approach.

TAXES AND FEES

Local governments can initiate new taxes or fees to fund climate programs. Taxes and fees can be broadly applied, such as a sales tax, or they could be tailored to link certain behaviors. For example, in the City of Boulder, Colorado, voters approved Initiative 202 in November 2006, which established the climate action plan tax (also known as the carbon tax or CAP tax). The local utility provider, Xcel Energy, collects a tax on electricity for the City, and the City uses it to fund implementation. Not only does the tax raise funds, but it also increases the cost of electricity, which should lower its use, thus providing a direct emissions reduction benefit.

GOVERNMENT GRANTS
Federal and state governments offer a variety of grants to assist local governments in implementing emissions reduction and climate adaptation strategies. The types of grants will need to be monitored year to year, since they change frequently. Some grants require matching funds, some are competitive, and some require certain conditions to be met. Communities should investigate these and prepare to satisfy these types of conditions in advance so that they can quickly take advantage of new rounds of funding.

PRIVATE GRANTS
There are numerous for-profit and nonprofit organizations that offer grants to support programs that have climate action benefits or co-benefits. These may not be obvious because they may not directly fund climate action but support things like biking and walking, energy efficiency, public safety, or public health. Communities should look to their nonprofit partners, who likely have expertise and experience in finding and securing grants.

PRIVATE INVESTMENT
Some climate strategies may attract private investment. Two common examples are micromobility services (such as bike and scooter sharing services) and solar power purchase agreements (SPPAs). Public–private partnerships or cooperative agreements can leverage public funding to provide a greater benefit.

CARBON-OFFSET PROGRAMS
Certain activities can be linked to the required or voluntary payment of an additional fee in relation to the amount of GHGs the activity would create. Activities could be driving, flying, disposing of waste, using water, and the like. The idea is to offset the GHGs the activity creates by funding

strategies that compensate with an equivalent reduction. This is usually done when reducing the emissions of the original activity itself is very difficult, or perhaps impossible, at the local level. For example, the City of San Francisco has the San Francisco Carbon Fund, which is voluntarily funded by conferences and conventions in the city looking to offset associated GHG emissions, especially from air travel. The fund then supports community-based projects such as urban gardens and forests, open-space conservation, and environmental education. Communities should look to develop carbon-offset programs that fund local projects rather than paying them into global carbon-offset programs. While offset programs are generally seen as a last-resort option for emissions reduction, they can be a good source of funding for programs.

SELF-FUNDING AND REVOLVING FUND PROGRAMS

These are programs established to generate their own revenue and are similar to municipal enterprise funds. Usually the revenue generated is directly from the recipient of the benefits of the program; thus they are often seen as fair and equitable programs. The City of Berkeley, California, created the Berkeley FIRST program to finance the cost of solar energy installations through an annual special tax on a homeowner's property tax bill that is repaid over 20 years. The key innovation is that since the installation is an improvement to the property, the loan stays with the house. If the house is sold, the new owner would take over the payments for the improvement, since they would reap the benefits of the lower utility costs. The Berkeley FIRST program requires little up-front cost to the property owner and thus creates a strong incentive to install solar. The City of Phoenix, Arizona, created the Phoenix Energy Conservation Savings Reinvestment Fund to provide capital for energy efficiency projects. As the City invests in energy efficiency measures, such as installing high-efficiency lighting, it reinvests half of all documented annual energy savings, up to a limit of $750,000, into a revolving fund.

VOLUNTEER AND PRO BONO RESOURCES

In many communities, nonprofit and service organizations, businesses, and individuals are willing to donate money and services to important causes. The City of San Luis Obispo, California, has bicycle valet parking year-round at its Thursday-night farmer's market. The bike valet is provided at no charge to the community by a local nonprofit and is staffed by volunteers.

Support Climate Champions

Communities that successfully implement climate strategies usually have a climate champion. The climate champion educates, inspires, demands accountability, and mediates. Often, the climate champion is a mayor or elected official. In 2005, Mayor Greg Nickels of the City of Seattle began the U.S. Mayor's Climate Protection Agreement, and by 2018, 1,060 mayors had signed the agreement. These visionary mayors committed to inventorying GHG emissions in their communities and developing climate action plans. These mayors championed climate action in their communities and began the movement for local action.

Not all climate champions are mayors; they can also be prominent or respected members of a community who have leadership skills, a strong network, and the willingness to take risks and push hard for climate action. Occasionally, climate champions are staff members of the local government who are able to drive climate action because of their knowledge of the bureaucracy and ability to motivate others. The City of San Luis Obispo, California, included "climate champion" as a responsibility in the job description for its sustainability manager (see box 8.1). And of course, communities may have multiple climate champions, sometimes organized as coalitions. Regardless of who the climate champion is, they need support.

The City of Cincinnati, Ohio, included an explicit role for climate champions in their Green Cincinnati Plan (2018); the plan states, "Cincinnati is full of businesses, nonprofits, and other institutions that play a key role in moving Cincinnati toward sustainability. Many times, these entities can help accomplish sustainability measures that are not well suited for City implementation. The City will partner with these entities and promote their initiatives. Each recommendation in the Plan identifies one or more 'Champions' who will lead the implementation of that recommendation. The City will monitor and support the efforts of these champions to ensure that implementation is progressing."[4]

Engage the Public

Often public participation will end once a plan or policy is adopted, but this should not be the case (see chapter 3 for a detailed description of public participation in climate action planning). Many climate action plans, policies, and programs require significant cooperation from community stakeholders and the general public. For example, increasing bicycling in a community isn't just about adding bicycle infrastructure. It also requires that the public make the choice to leave their cars at home and begin bicycling. This behavioral and cultural change will not occur with just a public education campaign. It requires a more fundamental level of ongoing engagement with the public.

The public wants to be kept informed on progress in implementing strategies, achieving GHG emissions reductions, and increasing community resilience. Moreover, successes should be celebrated, including the achievement of co-benefits such as saving money or improving public health. The salience of public policy issues can wax and wane; therefore, it is important that the community come to see the importance of climate action and view it as a regular and indispensable part of the community, such as having running water or fire protection services.

Communities that develop citizen advisory bodies or task forces during the planning phase should consider extending or reconstituting similar groups for the implementation phase. These groups can be tasked with evaluating progress and adjusting strategies to optimize success. They can support outreach and information campaigns, and they can provide continuity for climate action that could be lost through election cycles or municipal staff turnover.

Communicate Co-benefits

As mentioned in chapter 1, co-benefits are community benefits that occur from climate action in addition to the GHG emissions reduction or climate adaptation benefits. For example, urban street trees that provide both carbon sequestrations and urban heat mitigation also provide aesthetic benefits and can be shown to increase shopping activity in downtowns. Some members of a community may be more interested in these kinds of benefits, especially if they are skeptical or uninterested in the issue of climate change. Co-benefits also can broaden the base of support for climate actions. For example, climate actions that have public health benefits can attract the interest and support of public health agencies and the medical community.

For implementation, it is important both to communicate the co-benefits of action and to track and demonstrate its success and impact. Implementation often requires sustained effort. An important consideration when developing a communications strategy is whether to lead with the co-benefits or the direct climate benefits, so it is important to understand how receptive the community may be to different messages (see chapter 3 for more information on this).

Cultivate Partnerships

Most climate actions are sufficiently complex and cross-cutting that they are best implemented by developing robust, committed community partnerships among government agencies, businesses, and community groups. Many climate actions cannot be accomplished by local government action alone, which may lack the formal or moral authority, resources, or expertise.

Take, for example, a community with a goal to increase bicycling. They usually need to increase the amount of bicycle infrastructure. This requires the action of municipal transportation agencies to create bike paths and lanes, but it also may require the participation of businesses and developers to provide bicycle parking at destinations. Although local governments could take on the role of bicycle education, this might better be provided by school boards for K–12 students and by bicycle advocacy groups for adults. Local bike shops can provide education and services that make it easier to choose to bike. And employers can provide bicycle commute incentives and provide showers and changing facilities. The best way to increase bicycle ridership is to work collaboratively with a variety of community partners to address all facets of the issue.

One of the most important local partners is the utility provider. Most actions aimed at energy conservation, renewable energy, and electrification will be more successful with their active cooperation and partnership.

Moreover, actions may only be possible with the cooperation of the utility. Utilities can provide funding or rebates, help with outreach and communications, and provide technical expertise on energy issues. In some communities, the utility providers have become fully committed partners in addressing local climate and energy issues.

Lead by Example

Communities that have shown success in climate action have local governments that are leading by example. The classic case is putting solar panels on city hall. The public and potential partners and champions are more motivated to act when they see the City taking the issue of climate change seriously. This approach is valuable in two ways. First, by demonstrating a commitment to climate action, it positions the city for moral leadership and messaging on the issue. It is easier and more compelling to ask people to do things you yourself are willing to do or have already done. Second, these actions may be able to serve as demonstration projects. Putting solar panels on city hall can serve to show payback periods to local businesses that may be considering solar.

Local governments can take many climate actions, including the following:

- shifting municipal vehicle fleets to low- or zero-carbon fuels
- supporting municipal employee transportation demand management programs
- increasing the efficiency of municipal buildings through lighting and other upgrades
- building green and hazard-resistant buildings
- using low-water landscaping
- moving infrastructure and resources out of areas susceptible to climate hazards

Perhaps one of the most notable actions by local governments has been the commitment to carbon-free or net-zero-GHG-emissions energy for municipal operations. The City of Atlanta, Georgia, has developed a plan to achieve 100% clean energy for municipal operations by 2025 and community-wide by 2035: "The Plan provides different models for how the City of Atlanta's municipal operations and the entire community can transition to 100 percent clean energy using different policies and programs."[5]

Entities Responsible for Implementing Strategies

The implementation team or climate program coordinator must identify a specific individual, agency, department, or partner organization responsible for implementing each strategy. For example, a strategy to replace lightbulbs in traffic lights with high-efficiency LEDs would likely be assigned to a municipal transportation or public works department. Assigning this responsibility may be met with some resistance from local staff. Local government agencies and departments may feel this is another burden on their already busy staff. Community partners may not feel they have the knowledge or capacity to implement strategies. This is why chapter 2 suggests that local government and community partners be involved in preparation of the plan from the beginning. They need to buy in to the process and contribute to the development of strategies knowing they may be assigned some responsibility for implementation.

One consideration in implementation is how to hold these entities accountable. This is where having an implementation team with the right people can be critical to success. If it is staffed by the people who have decision-making authority in their respective agencies and partner organizations, then it is much easier to ensure implementation. This is usually easier to accomplish with strategies that are to be implemented by local government agencies and departments, since they usually have clear lines of authority compared to those delegated to community organizations such as nonprofits, which may have unclear hierarchies or little organizational capacity. In this case, the implementation committee may have to take a stronger role in ensuring accountability.

Programming of Strategies for Implementation

Previous chapters on GHG emissions reduction and climate adaptation strategies discussed strategy evaluation and prioritization. This information should be used by the implementation team or climate program coordinator to program the priority and timing of strategy implementation (see box 8.4). Typically, priority and timing are driven by access to funding or the capacity/capability of the implementing organization. For funding, budget cycles, grant-funding cycles, and fund-raising programs may drive when a strategy can be implemented or how quickly it can be fully implemented. For capacity and capability, issues of staffing levels, staff expertise, workload, consistency with current mission, and timing will be important. Other projects may need to be completed first, staff may need additional training to support the program, or some level of reorganization may be needed; each of these can delay action.

Priority and timing may also be driven by external events or circumstances, strategy synergy, and outreach considerations. Sometimes a

---

Box 8.4

Example of Evaluation Criteria from the City of Oakland, California, Energy and Climate Action Plan

Evaluative criteria	Issues to consider
GHG reduction potential	• magnitude of GHG reductions • measurability of reductions
Implementation cost and access to funding	• cost to City budget • cost to other stakeholders • access to funding
Financial rate of return	• return on investment to City and/or stakeholders implementing the action • protection from future costs
GHG reduction cost-effectiveness	• relative cost-benefit assessment in terms of estimated GHG reductions
Reduction of local vulnerability and risk	• potential for improved safety • risk for damage or loss of critical assets • cost savings for preemptive action (vs. reactive)

(*Continued*)

Evaluative criteria	Issues to consider
Economic development potential	• job creation potential • business development and retention potential • workforce development potential • cost savings to community • education benefits for community
Creation of significant social equity benefit	• benefits to disadvantaged residents in the form of jobs, cost savings, and other opportunities • reduction of pollution in heavily impacted neighborhoods • equity in protection from impacts of climate change
Feasibility and speed of implementation	• degree of City control to implement the action • level of staff effort required • resources required • degree of stakeholder support • amount of time needed to complete implementation • amount of time before an impact is expected to be experienced • time period during which implementation can begin
Leverage of partnerships	• leverage of partnerships with community stakeholders • leverage of partnerships on a regional, state, or national level • facilitation of replication in other communities
Longevity of benefits	• persistence of benefits over time • opportunity to support future additional benefit

Source: City of Oakland, Energy and Climate Action Plan (updated March 2018), http://www2.oaklandnet.com/oakca1/groups/pwa/documents/policy/oak069942.pdf.

higher-priority strategy may partially depend on or be synergistic with a lower-priority strategy or other community action. In this case, it may make sense to deviate from a strict prioritization scheme. Communities should consider which strategies can be piggybacked on existing actions—for example, taking advantage of a road repaving to add bicycle lanes. They should also consider strategies that have high public visibility that can serve to educate or motivate the public. Regardless of the rationale, all strategies should be assigned a priority and timing for implementation.

Monitoring and Evaluation

Climate action strategies should contain a program for monitoring progress on implementation and achieving GHG emissions reduction or adaptation targets as well as a program for reporting and publicizing these achievements and a process for evaluating and updating the plan:

1. *Basic monitoring:* This includes determining whether the strategy was in fact implemented, met its budget, and was implemented on schedule.
2. *Monitoring the success of desired direct action:* If the strategy was implemented, did it produce the desired effect or outcome? For example, with GHG emissions reduction, did the number of people expected to install solar panels through a solar incentive program do so, or did the expected increase in transit ridership from an employee rider discount program in fact occur? And for adaptation, how much more flood resistant is a building, or how many more people are prepared for a wildfire evacuation?
3. *Monitoring the level of GHG emissions reductions:* How much did GHG emissions change, and does the change meet the adopted GHG emissions reduction target? (There isn't an agreed upon singular metric for resilience.)

Each of these levels of monitoring can be linked to performance indicators that show how well the community is doing in achieving expected levels of performance for each strategy (see box 8.5). For

Box 8.5

Examples of Progress Indicators

Climate action strategy	Progress indicator
Develop an energy efficiency financing program (through PACE, Energy Upgrade, or other mechanisms) allowing property owners to invest in energy efficiency upgrades and renewable energy installations for their buildings.	Percentage of households and businesses participating Average electricity savings Average natural gas savings
Revise policies and regulations as needed to eliminate barriers to or unreasonable restrictions on the use of renewable energy.	Megawatts of renewable energy systems installed
Implement curbside compost pickup in combination with existing green waste pickup.	Tons of food waste diverted and tons of green waste diverted
Amend applicable ordinances and policies to direct most new residential development away from rural areas and to concentrate new residential development in higher-density residential areas located near major transportation corridors and transit routes, where resources and services are locally available.	Percentage of residents within half a mile of a transit stop
Incorporate "complete streets" policies into the circulation element and implement complete streets policies on all future roadway projects.	Miles of bike lanes and sidewalks installed
Implement tiered water rate structures to incentivize water conservation.	Gallons of water saved Per-capita water use reduction
Develop and disseminate appropriate best management practices for the application of pesticides and fertilizers, tillage practices, cover crops, and other techniques to reduce nitrous oxide emissions, maximize carbon sequestration, reduce water use and runoff, and reduce fuel use.	Crop fertilization rates per acre

example, if a community identified that it needed energy efficiency retrofits on 10% of its houses and businesses to achieve the desired GHG emissions reduction in that sector, then the performance indicator would track and report the number or percentage of retrofits led by the implementing organization and partners. These performance indicators can be tracked regularly and reported as a scorecard for implementation. This allows progress to be easily communicated so that decision-makers can adjust program implementation. For an example, see the City of Fort Collins' Climate Dashboard (https://ftcollinscap .clearpointstrategy.com).

Communities should consider annual or biannual reporting of progress on implementation, GHG emissions reductions, and enhanced resilience. An annual report can be used to inform those who participated in creating and adopting the plan of the progress of their work. In addition, the annual report can serve as an important component of educating and motivating the public about what needs to be done to address the climate change problem and helps ensure that the climate action isn't ignored, holding accountable those responsible for implementation. For example, the sustainability coordinator for the City of San Mateo (California) provides an annual climate action implementation and monitoring report, including a summary of progress and key metrics, to the City's sustainability commission and city council, and it maintains all annual reports on the City's website for transparency.[6]

It would not be reasonable to expect a GHG emissions inventory, climate vulnerability assessment, and planning update to occur annually or biannually; instead, communities should consider a five-year evaluation and update schedule. In between the major updates, the community can use the annual report as an opportunity to modify strategies and include interim updates as needed. Press releases can accompany the releases of annual reports and updates, which can be made available on websites and in public places such as libraries.

Including Climate Action within the Comprehensive Plan

More communities are considering integrating their climate action policies and strategies into their comprehensive land use plan. There are several reasons for this: the comprehensive plan is an existing, recognized legal instrument for implementing and enforcing policies and strategies; comprehensive plan implementation is usually linked to specific departments, thus providing ownership and accountability; and there will often be overlap in issue areas where synergies can be captured and potential conflicts resolved. In the long term, complete integration of climate action strategies in community planning documents may become standard. Integration with comprehensive plans requires consideration of how they are structured and where climate action may best fit.

Plan Content and Structure

The content and structure of comprehensive plans will vary based on state law or local preferences. An accepted hierarchy has evolved to include a vision, planning principles, goals, objectives, policies, actions or implementation measures, and indicators or performance measures. Comprehensive plans include multiple components or elements to address key issues such as land use, transportation/mobility, public utilities and infrastructure, safety and hazards, noise, housing, agriculture, open space, energy, air quality, water resources, biological resources, historic preservation, cultural resources, public health, parks and recreation, and economic development. Comprehensive plans often balance land use and social, environmental, and economic objectives.

Plan Integration

Communities should identify their key goals related to climate action and then develop, update, or amend their comprehensive plans to reflect those goals accordingly. The integration of climate action into a local comprehensive plan is most straightforward when the plan is being updated or developed concurrently with or following a climate action planning process. Climate action goals, policies, and actions should be incorporated across the various elements of the comprehensive plan rather than into a single element.

- *Land use:* With regard to land use, the most important actions to reduce GHG emissions discourage auto-dependent, low-density development and promote complete communities that provide mixed land uses, higher densities in core areas and transit nodes, affordable housing, compact form, smart growth, and bicycle- and pedestrian-friendly infrastructure.
- *Transportation, circulation, or mobility:* Transportation-related policies should discourage vehicle miles traveled, specifically travel by single-occupant motor vehicles, and encourage the use of mass transit, bicycling, walking, and telecommuting. Local governments should accommodate all modes of transportation and make them attractive and convenient. Local streets should be "complete streets," which accommodate users of all transportation modes throughout the community. Communities should incentivize the use of and fund the necessary infrastructure for transit, plan for complete networks of bikeways, ensure that streets have safe and inviting sidewalks and street crossings, provide park-and-ride facilities, and plan shared parking where appropriate.
- *Housing:* The key connection between the housing element and GHG emissions is the community's jobs–housing balance. The housing element should include policies and actions to ensure a balance between job and housing availability as a means to reduce vehicle miles traveled. In addition, housing elements can include policies on energy conservation or green building, resilience to projected impacts, and renovation.
- *Conservation, environmental, or natural resources:* Policies in this element should promote energy, water, and other resource efficiency and conservation and also identify opportunities for expanding the resilience of natural resources and systems.
- *Open space and agriculture:* Policies in this element should address the protection of agriculture, forests, and woodlands and the expansion of urban parks and street tree programs, as these resources serve as carbon sinks or sequestration opportunities as well as provide potential moderation of impacts such as flood or heat.
- *Natural hazards or safety:* Climate change may increase the frequency and severity of natural disasters such as wildfires, flooding, droughts,

and heat emergencies. This element can direct adaptation to these changes—for example, by incorporating policies that restrict development in the wildland–urban interface, along shorelines, and in floodplains.

In the long term, it is possible that the goals of reduced GHG emissions and resilience in the face of unavoidable climate impacts will become ubiquitous and a standard component of comprehensive plans.

Chapter 9

Communities Leading the Way

This chapter presents seven cases of communities that have engaged in climate action planning and are now in the process of implementing their plans, strategies, and actions. The cases are chosen for their diversity of experiences and lessons learned. They illustrate many of the principles outlined in this book and demonstrate that climate action planning is possible in all types of communities. There are enough communities around the world now acting on climate change that there is much to be learned and shared. The experiences of these communities should prove useful to other communities that are early in the planning process or struggling to achieve implementation success. Global knowledge sharing and cooperation have become the rallying cry of many mayors and city leaders.

The City of Portland and Multnomah County, Oregon, have been in the business of developing and implementing climate strategies since the early 1990s and show how to construct a successful program over the long term.

The City of Evanston, Illinois, confirms the benefits of building "social capital" in the community that creates a grassroots capability for doing community-based climate action planning.

The City of Boulder, Colorado, leads on climate action funding with their unique carbon tax on electricity and demonstrated sustained climate action in the 15 years before its adoption.

The City of Pittsburgh, Pennsylvania, demonstrates the power of local partnerships among public, private, and nonprofit entities to develop and implement plans.

The City of San Mateo, California, proves that when a dedicated council and staff work together with stakeholders and citizens, they can achieve significant change.

Miami-Dade County and the Southeast Florida Regional Climate Change Compact show that counties can do climate action planning and that it can be integrated into a larger regional effort for achieving sustainability.

And finally, the City of Copenhagen, Denmark, leads the world on climate action by proving that their goal of being carbon-neutral by 2025 is possible.

Communities engaging in climate action planning can look to these communities for best practices and lessons learned.

City of Portland and Multnomah County, Oregon: Integrating Equity with Climate Action[1]

The City of Portland, Oregon, has been a leader in climate change policy development for 25 years (see box 9.1). The City adopted the first carbon-reduction plan in the United States in 1993. Since that time, Portland has forged a collaborative relationship with Multnomah County and has revised this original plan three times (2001, 2009, and 2015). These revised plans had the benefit of learning from the successes and

---

Box 9.1

City of Portland and Multnomah County, Oregon, Summary

Population (Portland): 647,805 (2017)
Population (Multnomah County): 807,555 (2017)

Key Climate Action Initiatives

- Carbon Dioxide Reduction Strategy (1993)
- Carbon Dioxide Reduction Strategy: Success and Setbacks (2000)
- Local Action Plan on Global Warming (2001)
- Climate Action Plan (2009, 2015)
- Climate Action through Equity: The Integration of Equity in the Portland / Multnomah County 2015 Climate Action Plan (2016)

GHG Emissions

- 8,989,460 metric tons (MT) CO_2 equivalents (CO_{2e}) in 1990
- 7,695,000 MT CO_{2e} in 2013

GHG Emissions Profile (2017)

- transportation (37%)
- commercial (24%)
- residential (20%)
- industrial (18%)
- waste (1%)

GHG Emissions Reduction Targets

- 40% below 1990 levels by 2030
- 80% below 1990 levels by 2050

Climate Impacts

- increase in temperatures (both day and night) and frequency of high-heat days
- increase in incidence of drought
- increase in wildfire frequency and intensity
- increase in incidence and magnitude of damaging floods
- increase in incidence of landslides

challenges of earlier efforts. Over the 25 years since the first plan, the city and county's population has grown by 30% and the economy by 40%, simultaneous with a 40% reduction in GHG emissions since 1990.[2] The sustained and gradual effort by Portland to reduce greenhouse gas (GHG) emissions provides critical lessons for cities that are much earlier in the climate planning and implementation process.

Portland and Multnomah County's plans were developed through collaboration among multiple departments, local organizations, and the public. The success of Portland and Multnomah County's efforts can be tied to the development of strong community partnerships, a commitment to the idea that climate action plans should meet a variety of community goals in addition to GHG reductions, and long-term monitoring that has allowed strategy effectiveness to be assessed.

The first plan adopted by the City of Portland in 1993 was motivated by the City's participation in the World Conference on the Changing Atmosphere held in Toronto, Canada, in 1988 and the United Nations' development of the Kyoto Protocol in 1992. The plan was titled *Carbon Dioxide Reduction Strategy*. The target established in this plan went beyond that of the Kyoto Protocol; the City aimed to reduce emissions to 20% below 1988 levels by 2010. The reductions required to reach this target were divided among five local action sectors: transportation, energy efficiency, renewable resources and cogeneration, recycling, and tree planting. The breadth, level of detail, and ease of implementation of the strategies included in this 1993 plan set the stage for the success of future plans and actions.

Monitoring and evaluation of strategy effectiveness allowed the City to identify areas of success as well as confounding factors for overall emissions reduction. The 2000 status report, *Carbon Dioxide Reduction Strategy: Success and Setbacks*, individually evaluated the action items in the 1993 plan. Overall, this report showed a reduction in per-capita emissions, but increases in the community-wide total indicated that the City was falling well short of the 2010 target. Evaluation of individual strategies revealed several useful lessons, particularly regarding the role of greater-than-expected growth in the population and the economy on total emissions. This information was critical to future policy development, as it indicated areas that needed policy intervention.

The 2001 plan, *Local Action Plan on Global Warming*, made some minor adjustments, such as changing the baseline from 1988 to 1990 and revising the goal to a 10% reduction by 2010, closer to the 7% target for the United States under the Kyoto Protocol. Overall, the plan's organization and target areas remained the same. The biggest change was the addition of a close partnership with Multnomah County for development and implementation of the plan. Inclusion of the County allowed for explicit recognition of the regional context and formulation of direct action to address regional issues.

The 2001 plan, *City of Portland/Multnomah County Local Action Plan on Global Warming*, included a review of implementation success in each sector addressed in the prior plan, *Global Warming Reduction Strategy* (1993). The strategies included in the plans are detailed and designed to yield GHG reductions quickly. Each action has a specific, measurable outcome, which makes implementation and tracking progress possible. The 2001 plan also contained one new section focused on education and outreach that included strategies intended to ensure that community members as well as decision-makers have a clear understanding of climate science, the challenges posed by climate change, and the options for addressing these challenges. During the period following the 2001 plan, Portland and Multnomah County exhibited not only continued per-capita GHG reductions but also reductions in overall GHG emissions. By 2005, emissions in the county had been reduced to 1990 levels, and they were several percentage points below 1990 levels by 2008. As a result, the City and County were nearly on track to reach the targets set in 2001, though they are still unlikely to meet the original 1993 goal.

Implementation highlights for the City and County plan during the period between 2001 and 2009 include the following:

- Transit ridership has increased by 75%.
- Bicycling has quintupled, with mode share over 10% in many parts of the city.
- Recycling rates reached 64%.
- The City saves $4.2 million annually due to reductions in energy use (~20% of total energy costs and $38 million since 1990).

- Thirty-five thousand housing units have been improved in partnership with utilities and the Energy Trust of Oregon.
- Reductions in vehicle miles traveled have resulted in $2.6 billion in annual savings.[3]

The *Climate Action Plan 2009* maintained the earlier versions' sectors of focus, with energy efficiency and renewable energy combined into one and two additional focus areas added: preparing for climate change (e.g., climate change adaptation) and food and agriculture.

The major difference is that the 2009 plan established emissions reduction targets for the combined city and county of 40% below 1990 levels by 2030 and 80% by 2050. The 2050 target requires dramatic emissions reduction and shows the City's commitment as a member of the Carbon Neutral Cities Alliance. The plan included both short-term actions that were to yield immediate reductions in GHGs and those that will lay the foundation for the vision for 2050. One example of the long-term focus is the goal of twenty-minute neighborhoods, "meaning that they [residents] can comfortably fulfill their daily needs within a 20-minute walk from home."[4] Strategies such as this were developed through public outreach events, which were critical given the extent of changes required to meet the 2050 target. The goal of reducing emissions by 80% requires dramatic changes in energy efficiency, energy sources, and travel behavior, such as a reduction from 18.5 to 6.8 passenger miles per day.

The 80% reduction in GHG emissions below 1990 levels by 2050 target is maintained in the 2015 climate action plan. One of the biggest changes in the latest update is a strengthened emphasis on social equity and health. While both points of emphasis are mentioned in the 2009 plan, the 2015 plan builds on this focus, expanding the breadth of strategies. The City released the document *Climate Action through Equity: The Integration of Equity in the Portland/Multnomah County 2015 Climate Action Plan* a year later in 2016. The focus on equity includes the engagement and inclusion of underserved and underrepresented communities. This was achieved through the establishment of the Climate Action Plan Equity Working Group to aid in the identification of issues and development of strategies.

Another critical change in the 2015 plan was a consumption-based or life-cycle GHG emissions inventory (see figure 9.1). This inventory

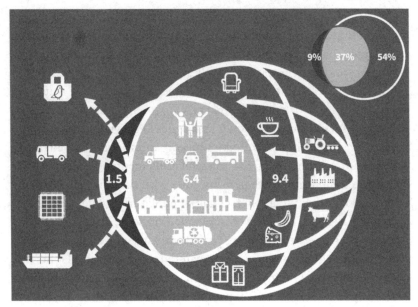

Figure 9-1 Global emissions as a result of local consumer demand as reported in the 2015 Portland and Multnomah County climate action plan
Source: City of Portland and Multnomah County, Climate Action Plan (2015), https://www.portlandoregon.gov/bps/49989.

includes all the upstream GHGs emitted as part of producing products consumed, purchased, or used in the city and county. This inventory allows consumption to be assessed and for Portland and Multnomah County's role in global GHG emissions to be more accurately understood.

Lessons Learned

The Portland city and region have engaged in a long, sustained effort to develop and implement planning policy to address climate change. Over the last 25 years, the city and region have achieved some remarkable GHG reductions. Some of the factors identified by the City as keys to this success include a focus on co-benefits, the development of partnerships to aid in implementation, and the integration of climate goals into all aspects of community policy.

Co-benefits can include improved air quality and human health, economic savings, and greater convenience. These co-benefits not only aid in fulfilling a range of other community goals but also yield unexpected collaborations and garner supporters of the plan. This has continued through the recent focus on equity and a 2016 document focused on the issue, specifically assessing and demanding that new approaches address unintended consequences, including investment strategies to alleviate displacement.

Forging partnerships with community organizations is viewed by city staff as a critical component of successful implementation. Portland has collaborated more closely than many cities with such entities. Not only has it relied on them to aid in facilitating public engagement, but it has even given the responsibility of implementing some strategies to local organizations. These partnerships provide resources necessary for implementation in the form of funding, material resources, and labor. This allows the City and County to implement more of the identified strategies in a timely manner because it expands the resources available to do so.

When asked what advice they would give a community just beginning a climate planning process, Portland staff identified two basic principles. The first is to start with the easy things. Choose lots of actions that can have an immediate impact. Demonstrating effectiveness quickly can build the momentum and gather the support necessary to take on larger, more expensive, and longer-term efforts. The second piece of advice is to learn from others. In the development of the 2009 plan, Portland staff read through the climate action strategies developed by other cities. The plan developers then repaid those from whom they learned by transparently reporting on the implementation progress of their most recent plan. The 2017 *Climate Action Plan Progress Report* not

Figure 9-2 The Portland and Multnomah County climate action plan, which identifies over 170 actions to be completed or significantly under way by 2020. The 2017 progress report indicates good progress on nearly 90% of the strategies identified.

Source: City of Portland and Multnomah County, Climate Action Plan (2015), https://www.portlandoregon.gov/bps/49989.

only keeps all participants in plan implementation accountable but also serves to build community support by demonstrating ongoing progress and provides lessons for other communities with similar aims.

City of Evanston, Illinois: Empowerment from the Grassroots[5]

To the citizens of the City of Evanston, Illinois, the decision to engage in climate action planning was the obvious and right thing to do (see box 9.2). The community has a long history of having an active and engaged citizenry who see the issue of sustainability as a key to a better future. Leaders in city hall recognized that waiting for the federal government to solve the problem was neither sufficient nor likely and that local action could be meaningful and effective.

In the late 1990s, a group of citizens interested in sustainability and the role of the faith community formed the Interreligious Sustainability Project. They held numerous public forums to present and discuss sustainability ideas, and they sought to build a network of interested citizens. This is often referred to as *building social capital*. The citizens of Evanston weren't organizing to specifically address climate change or any particular environmental issue at all. Instead, they were laying the groundwork for future action by educating, inspiring, and networking. This social capital paid dividends several years later with the formation

---

Box 9.2

City of Evanston, Illinois, Summary

Population: 74,486 (2010)

Key Climate Action Initiatives

- Evanston Climate Action Plan (2008, 2012)
- Evanston Livability Plan (2014)
- Evanston Climate Action and Resilience Plan (2018)

GHG Emissions

- 1,056,169 MT CO_{2e} in 2005
- 793,266 MT CO_{2e} in 2017

GHG Emissions Profile (2017)

- electricity (44%)
- natural gas (36%)
- transportation (17%)
- waste (2%)
- municipal operations (1%)

GHG Emissions Reduction Targets

- 50% reduction below 2005 levels by 2025
- 80% reduction below 2005 levels by 2035
- carbon-neutral by 2050

Climate Impacts

- increase in extremely hot days (over 95°F and 100°F)
- decrease in number of days below freezing
- increase in extreme precipitation events
- increase in drought conditions

---

of the Network for Evanston's Future. With the community coalescing under the group, the city government began the initial steps for climate action planning. In 2006, the Evanston city council voted unanimously to sign the U.S. Mayors Climate Protection Agreement, and state representative Julie Hamos committed some of her discretionary funds to support an Office of Sustainability in the mayor's office. With the City on board and the Network for Evanston's Future organizing the volunteer labor, Evanston was positioned to engage in climate action planning.

In 2008, the community completed the first *Evanston Climate Action Plan*; built on a cooperative effort among community organizations, businesses, religious institutions, and government, it showcased what communities can do when they come together to take responsibility for their actions and plan for a better future. Creation of the plan involved organizing these motivated citizens into teams to assist in inventorying the city's GHG emissions, developing potential strategies to reduce these emissions, and compiling them into a guiding document that could be successfully implemented. The mayor of Evanston, Elizabeth Tisdahl, described this as a "wonderful process." The wonder of Evanston was the community's ability to build coalitions of organizations and volunteers through a truly grassroots effort that was not controlled by city hall.

Over the next decade, the City updated the plan and GHG emissions inventory, released periodic progress reports, adopted the *Evanston Livability Plan*, and joined the Global Covenant of Mayors. In 2018, the City adopted the *Evanston Climate Action and Resilience Plan*, which establishes a goal of carbon neutrality by 2050. Other goals of the plan include the following:

- achieving 100% renewable electricity for all Evanston accounts by 2030
- achieving a 50% reduction in emissions by 2025 and an 80% reduction by 2035
- diverting 100% of waste from landfills (zero waste) by 2050
- securing 100% renewable electricity for municipal operations by 2020
- reducing vehicle miles traveled to 50% below 2005 levels by 2050 while increasing trips made by walking, bicycling, and public transit[6]

In addition to GHG emissions reduction, the 2018 Evanston plan for the first time addresses climate impacts. It contains numerous actions in six areas:

- green infrastructure
- health impacts of extreme heat
- resilience regulations

Evanston Climate Impacts

Climate Impact	By Mid-Century 2050	By End-Century 2075	Summary
Infrastructure Stress	↑	↑ ↑	With increased heat and sever storms physical infrastructure will be tested
Human Migration	?	?	The Chicago region may see an influx of climate refugees
Flooding	↑	↑ ↑	Higher risk of flooding and associated damage
Invasive Species/ Pests	↑	↑	Increase in invasive species and pests
Air Pollution	↑	↑	Poor air quality and increase in aeroallergens

Figure 9-3 Expected climate change impacts to the community of the City of Evanston, Illinois

Source: "Climate Change in Evanston," City of Evanston, https://www.cityofevanston .org/government/climate.

- community networks and education
- emergency preparedness and management
- vulnerable populations

All these strategies are evaluated through the lens of Evanston's three core guiding principles: equity-centered, outcome-focused, and cost-effective and affordable.

Evanston's planning has resulted in three notable actions. First, the City is leading by example by adopting aggressive municipal operations goals:

- 2020—100% renewable electricity for municipal operations
- 2030—achieve zero waste for municipal operations
- 2035—carbon neutrality for municipal operations

To achieve these goals, the City has identified 27 strategies, including for example, installing LED lighting, achieving net-zero emissions municipal buildings, transitioning to a zero-emissions fleet, planting trees, diverting construction waste, and advocating for state and national carbon markets.

Second, the City has secured commitments in the plan for climate action from leading employers in the city. For example, Northwestern University has adopted a net-zero emissions goal and Presence Saint Francis Hospital has committed to reducing GHG emissions levels 50% by 2025. The City has recognized that it cannot achieve its goals acting alone; it must have these partnerships with other leading entities in the community.

Third, the City's resiliency strategies are linked to public health services and emergency management. Agencies, companies, and organizations operating in these fields have a wealth of resources and knowledge on how to solve health and disaster problems. Evanston has wisely linked climate change with these other community challenges in its goal to build resilience. It is leading a new international movement to shift resilience thinking beyond just the issue of climate change and to include issues of social, economic, and environmental justice:

> The adoption of *Evanston's Climate Action and Resilience Plan* continues the City's leadership on climate and environmental issues. Since 2006, with the signing of the U.S. Conference of Mayors' Climate Protection Agreement, Evanston has achieved certification and recertification as a 4-STAR sustainable community, been named the World Wildlife Fund's 2015 U.S. Earth Hour Capital, joined the Global Covenant of Mayors, and served as a founding member of the Mayors National Climate Action Agenda (MNCAA). In 2017, Mayor Hagerty joined municipal leaders from across the world in signing the Chicago Climate Charter, pledging to uphold the commitments of the Paris Climate Agreement. The mayor has also committed to the Sierra Club's Mayors for 100% Clean Energy initiative, supporting a communitywide transition to 100 percent renewable energy.[7]

Lessons Learned

Evanston citizens felt like they could not wait for the state or federal government to take steps to alleviate the climate change problem. Before doing formal planning, they built social capital and collaborations, called on organizations already doing good climate action work, and began to build the political will in the community. They then organized and educated themselves and showed that motivated citizens, with support from city hall, can successfully engage in climate action planning.

The Evanston plan has many strategies that will be implemented by entities within the community, such as businesses, nonprofit organizations, and community groups. It is not clear at this point where the resources will come from to implement these strategies or how these entities can be held accountable. When depending on community-based entities rather than government agencies, there should be significant discussion of these implementation issues.

City of Boulder, Colorado: Innovative Financing for Implementation[8]

Boulder, Colorado, presents a different path in addressing climate change (see box 9.3). The City implemented programs to reduce GHG emissions for over 15 years without a formal climate plan. The City passed a resolution matching the terms of the Kyoto Protocol in 2002. This target served as

---

Box 9.3

City of Boulder, Colorado, Summary

Population: 108,507 (2018)

Key Climate Action Initiatives

• Climate Action Plan (CAP) Tax (2007)
• Boulder's Climate Commitment (2017)
• City of Boulder Resilience Strategy (2017)

GHG Emissions

• 1,848,741 MT CO_{2e} in 2015

GHG Emissions Profile (2017)

- commercial/industrial (53%)
- transportation (31%)
- residential (15%)
- miscellaneous (0.5%)

GHG Emissions Reduction Targets: Community-Wide

- 15% below 2005 levels by 2020
- 50% below 2005 levels by 2030
- 80% below 2005 levels by 2050

GHG Emissions Reduction Targets: Internal City Operations

- 50% below 2008 levels by 2020
- 80% below 2008 levels by 2030
- +90% below 2008 levels by 2050

Renewable Energy Goals

- 40% by 2020
- 100% by 2030

Climate Impacts

- increase in extreme events
- increase in temperatures
- increase in the length of drought cycles
- increase in wildfires

Sources: Adapted from City of Boulder, *City of Boulder's Climate Commitment* (Boulder, CO: Author, 2017), https://bouldercolorado.gov/climate; City of Boulder, *City of Boulder Resilience Strategy* (Boulder, CO: City of Boulder, 2017), https://bouldercolorado.gov/resilience.

the guiding aim for the next decade. The sustained progress, ongoing community support, and demonstrated effectiveness mean that Boulder can provide lessons to communities devising their approach to climate action.

In 2002, the City of Boulder's city council passed the Kyoto Resolution, which aimed to lower GHGs to 7% below 1990 levels by 2012. An inventory of local emissions was completed four years later, in 2006. A year after that, the City passed the nation's first voter-approved tax dedicated to addressing climate change, the climate action plan tax (CAP tax). The tax is levied on city residents and businesses based on the amount of electricity consumed. The CAP tax generates $1.8 million a year to be spent on programs, services, and incentive rebate programs in homes and businesses. Thus far the tax has raised $17.3 million to support climate action. It has worked. Boulder reports a 16% reduction in GHG emissions since 2005; over the same period, the city gained 7,500 more jobs and saw a 57% increase in gross domestic product.[9] Boulder voters approved a continuation of the tax in 2015, extending it to March 2023.

Over the last 10 years, Boulder has implemented many programs and strategies. The list below provides four such examples, but it is not exhaustive. Measures pursued by the City cover nearly all aspects of climate action, focused specifically on GHG emissions reduction from all sectors:

- *2011 SmartRegs Ordinance:* Boulder directly sought to affect one of the most difficult building types to address in any city, rental units. The city council adopted a SmartRegs Ordinance requiring energy performance in rental properties.[10] The ordinance set minimum energy efficiency standards for all rental properties (single and multifamily) to be met by 2019. In January 2019, rental properties had to prove compliance with SmartRegs to obtain new rental housing licenses, and noncompliant existing licenses expired.[11]

  Adopted in 2011, the ordinance afforded an eight-year period for rental property owners to comply. It was supported by three incentive or rebate programs to help owners and managers of rental properties: EnergySmart provided advice and access to funds for home energy and electric vehicle upgrades; the Water Conservation program provided assessment, low-cost upgrades, and incentives for water-use-reducing measures; and Excel Energy Incentives provided motivation for energy audits and for lighting, heating, and cooling upgrades.

- *2013 Energy Conservation Code:* First adopted in 2013 and updated in 2017, the City's building codes require new and remodeled residential and commercial buildings to meet net-zero emissions by 2031.[12] These codes build on international low-carbon building standards such as the American Society of Heating, Refrigerating, and Air-Conditioning Engineers (ASHRAE) and the GreenPoints program. The City conducted outreach, identified challenges with both programs, and devised an update to the building code to streamline the process and make the 2017 code even stronger from a GHG-emissions-reduction perspective.
- *2014 Marijuana Renewable Energy Offset Requirement:* In 2014, the State of Colorado legalized cannabis for both medical and recreational use. The Marijuana Renewable Energy Offset Requirement addresses the fact that the lighting and cooling systems that are used to grow marijuana plants indoors have been shown to disproportionately increase electricity consumption and associated GHG emissions. This offset asks marijuana facility owners to meet two requirements: to track energy use using the Environmental Protection Agency's Energy STAR portfolio manager (an online tool) and to prove that 100% of the energy used is offset using one or a combination of four methods, including renewable energy on site, participation in a verified solar garden, participation in one of Excel Energy's renewable energy programs, or offsets purchased through Excel Energy.[13]
- *2015 Universal Zero Waste Ordinance:* Boulder currently diverts 40% of its waste from a landfill (through recycling and composting) with an aim to move that number up to 85% by 2025. The Universal Zero Waste Ordinance has several requirements to support this aim, including the following: all single-family homeowners must subscribe to waste hauling, businesses must provide clearly marked receptacles for recycling and compost, and composting and recycling must be provided at all special events in the city.[14]

Boulder did not adopt a formal plan until 2017 with the release of *Boulder's Climate Commitment.* This plan is organized around four areas of action, and there are three sectors for each action area. For example, the energy action area includes buildings, mobility, and electricity. For each subsection, there are measures identified as "2017 to 2020 City Action Priorities." These short-term strategies are one way for the City to continue its success in implementing change and climate action. Further ensuring success, each section also identifies indicators to track progress and target dates for completion. Another critical aspect of the plan is a listing of supportive partnerships for each strategy subsection.

Beyond the measure-specific partnerships, the City of Boulder has pursued collaborative relationships both externally and internally. By joining the Carbon Neutral Cities Alliance, Boulder became part of a community of 20 cities from all over the world pursuing 80% to 100% GHG reduction by 2050. Having shared goals allows for information sharing that covers innovative approaches, strategies for overcoming barriers, and other lessons learned. Within the city, Boulder seeks ways to ensure that its climate actions are well understood and address the needs of all parts of the community. BoulderEarth is a coalition of local non-profits in partnership with the City that aims to inspire community action to address climate change and to support community engagement and input. The coalition keeps a calendar of community events—publicizing activities from local hikes, to speakers, to public hearings—and collects data to better understand local needs, concerns, and questions.

The CAP tax in Boulder is set to expire in 2023, and funding obtained from the local electrical utility will expire as well if the City successfully implements a city-owned electric utility, which would leave a $4.4 million shortfall each year if the City intends to meet the aggressive targets for GHG emissions reduction they have set. As a result, the City is considering a tax on new vehicles, called a vehicle registration efficiency tax. This is projected to alleviate all but $1.1 million of the projected shortfall. The City-owned electric utility may replace some of what Excel Energy provided, but it will not be generating revenue until at least 2024.[15] Boulder is a great lesson for communities with aspirations of aggressive climate policy, as they have creatively and effectively found ongoing ways to fund their strategies and engage the community.

Lessons Learned

Boulder's Climate Commitment states, "We need to change the system, not just the light bulbs." This commitment began in 2002 with the City's first formal action regarding climate change with the passage of the Kyoto Resolution, which committed Boulder to lowering GHG emissions 7% below 1990 levels by 2012. Since that time, Boulder has exemplified its commitment to ongoing, iterative implementation of climate goals with repeated updates, monitoring, and assessment, followed by even more new or updated strategies. This approach was not dependent on a climate plan; it was simply a comprehensive city goal. *Boulder's Climate Commitment* (the City's climate action plan) was adopted in 2017, 15 years into the City's pursuit of climate goals.

Ongoing pursuit of climate action strategies has led to the development and subsequent bolstering of many strategies. In several cases, Boulder is currently pursuing measures that would have been unthinkable 10 to 15 years ago but are now treated as an acceptable, even desirable, next steps given the ongoing efforts and commitments of the City. These include the following:

- *"Decarbonize, Democratize, and Decentralize":* Boulder has long pursued energy efficiency and adjustment to more renewable energy sources but now is pursuing community choice energy. Another critical and instructive aspect of this goal is that Boulder already has a backup plan that recognizes the need to keep improvising, adjusting, and moving forward: "If this effort is not successful, the city will redirect its efforts to partner with the current electric utility and/or explore other options."[16]
- *Buildings:* Already, the City has reduced building emissions by over 40% since 2010. Building on these achievements, the City is partnering with the county, the University of Colorado–Boulder, and the local school district to pursue strategies targeting rental and multifamily units as well as to implement net-zero building codes, with an aim toward all new buildings achieving net-zero energy by 2031.
- *Transportation:* Boulder set an initial goal of holding the 1996 VMT level steady as the city grew. That goal has been achieved despite other

communities in the Colorado Front Range experiencing continued growth in community VMT. No longer satisfied with holding VMT steady, Boulder now seeks overall reductions in transportation-generated GHG emissions. Similar to other focus areas, these goals will be achieved through several complementary measures, including an expanded transit program, increased ride-sharing, and a greater emphasis on bike and pedestrian transportation. Further supporting these actions, Boulder is pursuing various efforts to increase the number of electric vehicles used in the city.

While all the strategies are laudable, the other aspect of Boulder's approach to climate action planning that should be imitated is the focus on consistent funding to support these efforts. None of these efforts could be implemented without funding and staff. Boulder's CAP tax continues to provide funding to support climate action strategies. As mentioned above, the City continues to keep an eye to the future and plan ways to raise the required funds to support their ambitious climate aims.

City of Pittsburgh, Pennsylvania: The Power of Partnerships[17]

The 2018 *Pittsburgh Climate Action Plan* is the third plan by the City and continues to involve and rely on grassroots community effort and engagement rather than being a product exclusively of the municipal government (see box 9.4). Pittsburgh's initial climate action planning process was community initiated and catalyzed by several organizations. In 2006, the Green Building Alliance, with then mayor Bob O'Connor, convened the Green Government Task Force of Pittsburgh to begin discussions of addressing sustainability and climate change. At the same time, the Green Building Alliance partnered with Carnegie Mellon University students and faculty to develop the City's first GHG emissions inventory. In addition, the Surdna Foundation, a private grant-making foundation, helped bring in and fund the nonprofit Clean Air–Cool Planet to provide technical expertise and write the plan. The city government was a partner in the process but did not take the lead or an oversight role. In Pittsburgh, climate action planning was a stakeholder-based process to produce a plan with investment from all sectors.

Box 9.4

City of Pittsburgh, Pennsylvania, Summary

Population: 308,144 (2010)

Key Climate Action Initiatives

• Pittsburgh Climate Action Plan, Version 1.0 (2008)
• Pittsburgh Climate Action Plan, Version 2.0 (2012)
• One PGH: Pittsburgh's Resilience Strategy (2017)
• Pittsburgh Climate Action Plan, Version 3.0 (2018)

GHG Emissions

• 4,784,102 MT CO_{2e} in 2013

GHG Emissions Profile (2013)

• commercial (51%)
• residential (25%)
• transportation (17%)
• industrial (6%)
• waste (1%)

GHG Emissions Reduction Targets

• 20% below 2003 levels by 2023
• 50% below 2003 levels by 2030
• 80% below 2003 levels by 2050
• pursue a future carbon-neutral goal

Internal City Operations Goals

- 100% renewable electricity use
- 100% fossil fuel–free fleet
- divestment from fossil fuels

Community-Wide 2030 Climate Goals

- 50% energy use reduction
- 50% water use reduction
- 50% transportation emissions reduction
- zero waste—100% diversion from landfills

Climate Impacts

- increase in precipitation and flood events
- increase in number of major winter storms
- extreme temperatures—extended cold
- increase in landslides and subsidence incidents

Sources: Adapted from City of Pittsburgh, *City of Pittsburgh Climate Action Plan Version 3.0* (Pittsburgh, PA: Author, 2018), 81, https://pittsburgh.legistar .com/View.ashx?M=F&ID=5817176&GUID=075303EF-B062-46D5-A5EE -68A209C2B01A; City of Pittsburgh, *ONEPGH: Pittsburgh's Resilience Strategy* (Pittsburgh, PA: Author 2017), http://www.100resilientcities.org/wp-content/ uploads/2017/07/Pittsburgh_-_Resilience_Strategy.pdf.

The *Pittsburgh Greenhouse Gas Emissions Inventory* was completed in 2006 by a student and faculty research team from the Heinz School at Carnegie Mellon University. The baseline year for analysis was 2003 because this was the earliest year for which complete data were available. The City emitted about 6.6 million tons of CO_{2e} GHGs in 2003. The plan established a GHG emissions reduction target of 20% below 2003 by 2023 that was based on a review of peer communities and the task force's feasibility discussions. Another inventory was completed in 2013 and used as the basis for the 2018 plan, which includes new plans for annual updates of inventory data.

In 2012, the *Pittsburgh Climate Action Plan 2.0* was developed to review and revise the greenhouse gas emissions reduction efforts identified in the first plan and propose new measures that could be implemented to meet a greenhouse gas reduction target of 20% below 2003 levels by 2023. These targets were further bolstered and extended in the 2018 *Pittsburgh Climate Action Plan 3.0*. The 2018 plan has targets that align with those of the Paris Agreement: an 80% GHG emissions reduction below 2003 levels by 2050 and a companion goal of future carbon neutrality.[18] Two additions to the 2018 plan include a greater focus on local sustainability and resilience and new strategies centered on sequestration. With the creation of this plan, the community group that had been instrumental in the last two plans, now termed the Pittsburgh Climate Initiative group, reconvened, continuing the strong collaboration between the City and the community.

The *Pittsburgh Climate Action Plan 3.0* is organized into six sectors: energy generation and distribution, buildings and end-use efficiency, transportation and land use, waste and resource recovery, food and agriculture, and urban ecosystems. Development of the plan built on past success in its reliance on residents and community organizations, citing over 400 residents representing 90 organizations from the Pittsburgh business community, nonprofit sector, and local, state, and federal government partners. For each sector, goals, objectives, strategies, challenges, existing projects and previous work, and champions are identified. This level of detail and context and the full support of community partners illustrate a community vision and path forward that should lend confidence to future implementation effectiveness (e.g., see box 9.5).

In 2015, Pittsburgh was named one of the 100 Resilient Cities (100RC) pioneered by the Rockefeller Foundation.[19] The following year, the City named a chief resilience officer, who heads the new city department of Sustainability and Resilience. Pittsburgh was identified in 2018 as one of 20 cities that would receive a large monetary award ($70 million) as part of the Bloomberg American Cities Climate Challenge to support a two-year accelerated implementation program to reduce GHG emissions.[20] In addition, Pittsburgh has also received several grants and established partnerships to support the implementation of other parts of the plan, including $250,000 in funding from the Alternative Fuels

Box 9.5

Pittsburgh Climate Action Plan 3.0

Each chapter of the Pittsburgh Climate Action Plan 3.0 includes identification of goals, objectives, strategies, challenges, existing projects and previous work, and champions. The following example is from the energy generation and distribution chapter.

Energy Generation and Distribution

Goal: 50% Emissions Reduction below 2003 levels by 2030

Goal: Power all City facilities with 100% clean electricity by 2030

Objective:

• reduce natural gas fugitive emissions by 50% by 2030
• reduce line loss from electricity
• create a 21st Century energy system and support the utilities of the future
• install 200 Megawatts of local, clean power by 2030
• convert 50% of Pittsburgh customers to clean electricity

Strategies:

• calculate reasonable estimates for annual methane leakage volume
• calculate reasonable estimates for annual transmission loss for local grid
• improve gas line leak detection
• implement a long-term infrastructure plan to replace aging natural gas delivery lines and to optimize electricity delivery grids
• install smart meters to provide better customer data access

- Duquesne Light to install solar microgrid pilot at Woods Run facility
- support alternative utility ratemaking in Pennsylvania such as decoupling, formula rates, cost-recovery mechanisms, etc.
- develop and implement Pittsburgh's District Energy Plan
- create a local Energy Authority to enable community choice aggregation, power purchase agreements, and renewable regulatory approvals
- support Duquesne Light with the Public Utility Commission (PUC) to install local renewable power generation to meet Pennsylvania's Alternative Energy Portfolio Standards (AEPS) standards for Provider of the Last Resort (POLAR) customers
- support and allow for community source aggregation and renewable regulatory approvals (Big Opportunity)

Challenges:

- many regulations and policies regarding energy grids are enacted at the state level
- aging infrastructure
- population growth and new development will increase energy demands

Existing Projects and Previous Work:

- Ecoinnovation District
- District Energy Pittsburgh
- People's Gas Methane Mapping Project
- Duquesne Light Woods Run Microgrid
- NRG Fuel Cell

Energy Champions:

- University of Pittsburgh
- Carnegie Mellon University

> • National Energy Technology Laboratory
> • Green Building Alliance
> • People's Gas
> • Duquesne Light Company
> • Sustainable Pittsburgh
>
> *Source:* City of Pittsburgh, *City of Pittsburgh Climate Action Plan Version 3.0* (Pittsburgh, PA: Author, 2018), 81, https://pittsburgh.legistar.com/View .ashx?M=F&ID=5817176&GUID=075303EF-B062-46D5-A5EE-68A209C2B01A.

Incentive Grant Program (AFIG) run by the Pennsylvania Department of Environmental Protection.[21]

Lessons Learned

In Pittsburgh, strong leadership from the mayor and the formation of a community-based leadership group were important first steps in creating a climate action plan, and the City has maintained its reliance and collaborative relationship with the citizens and community groups that fostered the initiation of its climate action strategy development. These community leaders represented a diverse set of important sectors in the Pittsburgh economy. Forming this type of coalition of local partners built broad support for the plan and ultimately improved the quality of the plan.

Pittsburgh took a unique approach to implementation by assigning it to a new city department of Sustainability and Resilience, which can focus on and coordinate the varied strategies in the plan. To complement this department, each sector of the plan identifies critical collaborators and local champions, maintaining the close relationship between the City and the community.

Finally, Pittsburgh has already identified a projected time frame for development of climate action plan 4.0. Each iteration of the plan is stronger, more aggressive, and more integrative. This progress and explicit recognition of the ongoing process of implementation maintain community involvement, local commitment, and municipal staff commitment.

City of San Mateo, California: A Comprehensive Approach to Climate Action[22]

San Mateo is located south of San Francisco in Silicon Valley and is home to about 103,000 residents but is within a metropolitan area of nearly 2 million (see box 9.6). The City boasts a historic downtown and vibrant economy and is supportive of economic growth, infill, and mixed-use development. The City has a long-standing commitment to environmental stewardship and sustainability and was an early advocate of climate action planning. The City adopted its first sustainability plan in 2007 and has been working steadily to implement sustainable practices in its municipal operations and to reduce greenhouse gas emissions community-wide.[23] From 2005 to 2017, the community's GHG emissions decreased 18% while the City grew its population by 11% and increased jobs by 54%.[24]

The City's success in decreasing GHG emissions, expanding sustainability practices, and conserving natural resources can be attributed to long-standing commitments by the community and the city council in addition to a dedicated team of City staff and regional partnerships. The City considers itself to be "a progressive community that continuously considers the impact that today's actions will have on future generations. This is why sustainability is a top priority of the City. It is our goal to preserve the environment, provide economic well-being, and ensure social equity for our residents and businesses."[25]

Box 9.6

City of San Mateo, California, Summary

Population: 103,470 (2017)

Key Climate Action Initiatives

- Sustainable Initiatives Plan (2007)
- Climate Action Plan for Operations & Facilities (2008)

- Greenhouse Gas Emissions Reduction Program (2010)
- Climate Action Plan (2015)

GHG Emissions

- 660,600 MT CO_{2e} in 2005
- 541,960 MT CO_{2e} in 2017

GHG Emissions Profile (2017)

- transportation (50%)
- natural gas (25%)
- electricity (10%)
- off-road equipment (8%)
- waste (4%)
- stationary sources (3%)

GHG Emissions Reduction Targets

- 15% below 2005 levels by 2020
- 35% below 2005 levels by 2030
- 80% below 1990 levels by 2050

Climate Impacts

- decrease in supply of fresh water
- increase in sea level
- increase in severity and frequency of flood events
- increase in extremely hot days
- increase in drought conditions

The City has codified its sustainability goal through its environmental and land use planning processes, codes and ordinances, and funding commitments. The City adopted its first green building code in 2010. In 2013, the City adopted ordinances banning polystyrene containers in city restaurants and food stores and prohibiting single-use plastic bags in the city. The City was one of the first communities in California to integrate climate action into its comprehensive planning process. They have adopted and implemented many plans to increase mobility through alternative modes, including a *Pedestrian Master Plan*, a *Bicycle Master Plan*, a *Sustainable Streets Plan*, a Safe Routes to School program, and an *Active Transportation Plan*. The City's general plan promotes infill, mixed-use, and transit-oriented development.

The City's 2030 general plan, adopted in 2010, included the City's vision to be an environmentally, socially, and economically sustainable city and included goals and policies to reduce greenhouse gas emissions, a greenhouse gas emissions reduction implementation program based on the *Sustainable Initiatives Plan* adopted in 2007, and direction that all future development address climate change in accordance with the general plan. The general plan directed the City to reduce GHG emissions to 15% below 2005 levels by 2020, 35% below 2005 levels by 2030, and 80% below 1990 levels by 2050. At the time of adoption, the State of California's adopted statewide GHG reduction target was to reduce emissions to 1990 levels by 2020, which the State translated to be approximately equivalent to 15% below 2005–8 levels by 2020 for local government.

In 2014, the city council created a full-time sustainability coordinator staff position within the city manager's office to coordinate and expand the City's sustainability efforts. The sustainability coordinator position is funded by the City's general fund and has an allocated annual budget to implement new community-wide programs and projects in addition to capital projects, including energy retrofit projects, funded through the City's Capital Improvement Program, loans, and partnerships.

The City of San Mateo formed a sustainability commission in May 2014, which was renamed the sustainability and infrastructure commission in 2018. The commission is composed of five San Mateo residents appointed by the city council and is charged with making recommendations to the city council on policies and programs related to the long-term environmental, economic, and social health of the City. The first task assigned to the Sustainability Commission was to update the *General Plan 2030 Greenhouse Gas Reduction Plan*, later renamed the *Climate Action Plan* (CAP). Since the adoption of the CAP, the sustainability commission has supported implementation.[26] The commission's work plan includes serving in an advisory role to staff during the implementation and update of the climate action plan.

In 2014, the City hired a consultant to prepare a climate action plan in partnership with city staff and the community, guided by the newly designated sustainability coordinator, the newly appointed sustainability commission, and community stakeholders. In April 2015, the city council adopted the CAP to serve as the City's comprehensive community-wide strategy to reduce GHG emissions to achieve the 2020, 2030, and 2050 reduction targets adopted in the 2030 general plan.

Many of the City's GHG reduction measures rely on the city government to initiate and lead implementation. As such, interdepartmental engagement was essential in the development of the CAP to ensure that goals and strategies were attainable and appropriate for each responsible department. The City formed a CAP technical advisory committee (TAC) to support the consultant's and sustainability manager's review of existing programs and evaluation of new programs. The TAC included staff from multiple city departments, including public works, community development, parks and recreation, the city attorney's office, and the city manager's office. Drawing on the expertise of these departments helped define actions.

The City invited residents, business owners, and other stakeholders to contribute ideas and concerns throughout the CAP development process. The project team facilitated engagement outreach activities at its Concerts in the Park events, an online town hall website, and a community forum at the San Mateo Public Library. Community engagement was supported by graphics and materials that sought to present the CAP in an accessible and engaging manner (see figure 9.4). The City's online town hall website provided ongoing open dialogue on key questions and topics important to plan preparation. In addition, all sustainability commission meetings, planning commission hearings / study sessions, and city council public hearings allowed opportunities for public comment.

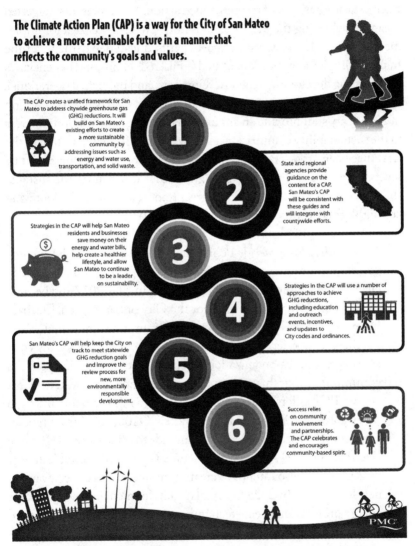

Figure 9-4 The City of San Mateo's prepared and distributed education materials, including a "What is a CAP?" poster, part of its community engagement program during preparation of the 2015 CAP

Source: City of San Mateo, *City of San Mateo Climate Action Plan* (2014), https://www.cityofsanmateo.org/DocumentCenter/View/44698/San-MateoCAP-PublicReviewDraft_2-23-15_Clean?bidId=.

The 2015 CAP includes 28 implementation measures organized into categories such as energy efficiency, renewable energy, alternative transportation and fuels, solid waste, wastewater, and off-road equipment. Each measure has a list of recommended actions that represents suggested means of achieving the measure but is not a prescriptive path for implementation. Each also identifies co-benefits, a lead department, a time frame for implementation, quantified GHG reductions, and beneficiaries (i.e., existing development, new development, and municipal operations).

The City has sustained implementation of the CAP since its adoption in 2015. City staff provide an annual update of implementation progress to the sustainability commission and city council. Implementation of the CAP has been cross-cutting, with projects and programs carried out by several city departments and throughout the community. The sustainability coordinator's 2018 CAP Progress Report identified the following key highlights of the work completed since 2015:

- *Community choice energy:* Peninsula Clean Energy (PCE), a community choice energy (CCE) program, completed enrollment of all electricity accounts in San Mateo County in May 2017 and became the default electricity provider for the City of San Mateo. Electricity in the city was previously provided by an investor-owned utility, Pacific Gas & Electric Company (PG&E). PCE is a locally controlled community organization that procures electricity and provides community programs to support energy efficiency and renewable energy. PCE offers two options: ECOplus, a minimum of 50% from renewables and 90% carbon free; and ECO100, 100% from renewables and 100% carbon free. PCE intends to offer 100% GHG-free electricity by 2021, which will be sourced by 100% renewable energy by 2025. PCE also intends to create a minimum of 20 megawatts of new local power by 2025 to stimulate development of new renewable energy projects and clean-tech innovation in San Mateo County, to expand local green jobs, and to invest in electric vehicles, energy efficiency, and demand response programs. The City's draft for its 2017 Community-Wide GHG Inventory reflected the impact of PCE on the community's emissions, with GHG emissions from electricity use having decreased approximately 50% since 2015.

- *Streetlight retrofits:* The City converted 80% of streetlights to LED bulbs—approximately 5,000 traditional streetlights to LED lights. The first phase was completed in July 2014 and consisted of the conversion of 900 cobra-head streetlights to LED lights through a turnkey on-bill financing partnership with PG&E. The second phase included the LED retrofit of 4,400 cobra-head and low-voltage decorative streetlights funded by a loan from the California Energy Commission.
- *Energy efficiency retrofits at City facilities:* The City entered into a contract with PG&E for the Sustainable Solutions Turnkey program and completed an energy assessment for retrofits at major municipal City facilities. Retrofits are planned to begin in 2019.
- *Community-wide energy and water conservation and efficiency programs:* The City has led or partnered in many energy and water conservation and efficiency programs with positive results.
  - The City has approved several Property Assessed Clean Energy (PACE) financing programs—including California First, HERO, Alliance NRG, Ygrene, Figtree, and OpenPACE—to provide financing options for residents and business owners. PACE programs support energy efficiency, renewable energy, and water efficiency projects by property owners.
  - In 2010, the Bay Area Regional Energy Network (BayREN) formed to provide regional-scale energy efficiency programs, services, and resources. BayREN is a collaboration of the nine counties that make up the San Francisco Bay Area, led by the Association of Bay Area Governments. BayREN is funded by California utility ratepayers under the auspices of the California Public Utilities Commission. The City partnered with BayREN to promote energy efficiency rebate programs, issuing rebates to 85 single-family homes and 887 multifamily units from 2014 to 2017.
  - The City collaborated with San Mateo County to provide home energy and water-saving toolkits at San Mateo branch libraries with free supplies.
  - The City participated in the Georgetown University Energy Prize (GUEP) competition from January 1, 2015, through December 31, 2016. The GUEP was a two-year-long friendly

national competition among 50 small and medium-sized cities to lower energy use in the residential, municipal, and public school sectors. While San Mateo was not a GUEP finalist, the City reduced overall electricity consumption by 6.4% and gas consumption by 17.4% from 2013 usage.

- The City provided supplemental funding to El Concilio, a local nonprofit, to target energy efficiency upgrades for low-income households through the Energy Savings Assistance Program. Energy specialist ambassadors canvassed door to door for the program in both English and Spanish.

- In 2008, the City joined San Mateo County Energy Watch, which formed as a partnership between PG&E and the City/County Association of Governments of San Mateo County to provide energy efficiency services to local governments, schools, small businesses, nonprofits, and low-income residents in the county. The services provided by San Mateo County Energy Watch include no-cost energy audits, special incentives, benchmarking services, and hosted classes and trainings about energy efficiency.

- *Reach codes:* The city council adopted green building and energy code amendments that require items that are above and beyond what is included in state codes.[27] The City's adopted reach codes, which went into effect on January 1, 2017, require the following:

  - *Mandatory EV readiness:* The green building code amendment requires that one space in all multifamily buildings with 3–16 units and 10% of the parking spaces in all other multifamily and nonresidential projects be EV-ready.[28]

  - *Mandatory Laundry-to-Landscape diverter valve:* The green building code amendment includes a mandate for new single-family homes to install a diverter valve to more easily allow for future gray water reuse from their laundry machines.

  - *Mandatory solar installations:* The energy code amendment requires the inclusion of minimum-size solar photovoltaic installations for all new construction.[29]

  - *Mandatory cool roof installations:* The energy code amendment requires cool roof installations for new multifamily and nonresidential projects with low-sloped roofs.

- *Bike share:* The City operated the Bay Bikes bike-share program, a fleet of dockable bicycles. It grew to over 1,000 members and 8,700 unique trips. The City also currently offers a dockless fleet of bicycles and electric bicycles through a private provider at no cost to the city.
- *City-promoted infill and transit-oriented development projects:* Transit-oriented projects are located near Caltrain stations and/or bus routes. Many new development projects are required to implement transportation demand management (TDM) practices to reduce vehicle trips generated by the development. Sample TDM strategies include providing free transit passes for residents or employees, paying into a shuttle program, encouraging carpooling, and providing on-site car-sharing vehicles.
- *CAP consistency checklist:* All new development subject to discretionary review and the State's California Environmental Quality Act must prepare a CAP Consistency Checklist for submittal with land use permit applications. City staff consider the project's implementation of GHG reduction programs part of discretionary review.

Lessons Learned

The 2015 CAP provided a strategic plan to achieve the City's 2020 GHG reduction target. The City has implemented the CAP since adoption and has seen steady reductions in emissions. The CAP included an implementation program and a commitment to monitoring, annually reporting, and updating at least every five years. The City's success with CAP implementation can be attributed to a team of climate champions:

- a dedicated sustainability coordinator, who has provided time and technical expertise to facilitate implementation, monitoring, reporting, and community engagement;
- oversight by the sustainability and infrastructure commission, which provides transparency and accountability;
- ongoing support by the city council; and
- multiple regional partners and programs that support GHG reductions in all sectors.

The community's achievement of its 2020 GHG reduction target is a result of its successful implementation of the CAP; its commitment to the use of its general fund and external grants and loans to fund energy efficiency retrofits, renewable energy projects, waste reduction programs, clean and alternative transportation projects and programs, and water conservation programs; and its participation in a regional community choice energy program. While the community's conservation and efficient use of resources have contributed to its decline in GHG emissions, the community has also significantly benefited from increases in clean energy and a transition to carbon-free and renewable energy. Peninsula Clean Energy, the community choice energy program, appears to be the most impactful program to reduce local and regional GHG emissions to date.

In addition, the City, like all communities in California, has benefited from the policies and programs of recent state governors and legislatures that have prioritized and funded statewide GHG reductions in all sectors. The noticeable local benefits are from the expansion of clean fuels and the renewable energy supply.

In fall of 2018, the City initiated an update to the CAP with an expectation that the 2020 CAP will include a more aggressive 2030 reduction target than the one currently adopted and a decarbonization pathway to 2030 and beyond. Its challenges will be to sustain and increase reductions through significant decarbonization in the transportation and energy sectors.

Miami-Dade County, Florida, and the Southeast Florida Regional Climate Change Compact: Cooperating for Regional Action

Miami-Dade County, Florida, is one of the 12 original members of the ICLEI Cities for Climate Protection Campaign founded in 1990 (see box 9.7). They have a 30-year history of acknowledging and addressing

---

Box 9.7

Miami-Dade County, Florida, Summary

Population: 2,751,796 (2017)

Key Climate Action Initiatives

- A Long Term CO_2 Reduction Plan for Metropolitan Miami-Dade County, Florida (1993, 2006)
- GreenPrint: Our Design for a Sustainable Future (2010)
- Mayor's Response to County Commission's Resolutions on Sea Level Rise (2016)

GHG Emissions

- 23.4 million MT CO_{2e} in 1988
- 30.7 million MT CO_{2e} in 2005

GHG Emissions Profile (2005)

- transportation (43%)
- commercial (25%)
- residential (25%)
- industrial (3%)
- waste (4%)

GHG Emissions Reduction Target

- 20% below 2008 levels by 2020
- 80% below 2008 levels by 2050

Climate Impacts

- extreme temperatures
- extreme levels of precipitation
- increase in saltwater intrusion into the water supply
- increase in coastal erosion and shallow coastal flooding
- increase in inland flooding and stormwater damage
- extreme storms and damage

the issue of climate change. When the County started, they were one of the few local governments taking action, but they realized that they could not tackle the issue alone. As more local governments in southeast Florida began climate action planning, it became clear that a cooperative regional approach would help accelerate action and enhance implementation.

In 1993, the County became one of the first communities in the world to engage in climate action planning. They developed *A Long Term CO$_2$ Reduction Plan for Metropolitan Miami-Dade County, Florida,* which set a GHG emissions reduction target of 20% below 1988 levels by 2005 and identified 13 areas for emissions reduction. Also, it notably called on the state and federal governments to adopt measures to improve vehicle gas mileage and energy conservation.

In 2006, the County updated the plan and reported that as a direct result of its implementation, the County's CO$_2$ emissions reductions averaged 2.5 million tons per year.[30] However, Miami-Dade County's 27% population growth over the 13 years of the planning time frame resulted in an overall increase in emissions. Although the plan kept the emissions lower than they might have been otherwise, the County realized the challenge of reducing emissions in a fast-growing community. The County also cited the failure of the state and federal governments to take more aggressive action as part of the problem.

Also in 2006, the County created the Miami-Dade County Climate Change Advisory Task Force (CCATF), made up mostly of technical experts in the climate change field, to advise the mayor (the County is a municipal county) and the board of county commissioners. The task force produced annual reports and investigated new strategies for reducing emissions. Most importantly, the task force kept the County moving forward with climate action planning that would lead to the next evolution of progressive action on energy and environmental issues.

In 2009, ICLEI chose Miami-Dade County as one of only three communities to pilot test its new Sustainability Planning Toolkit. The County saw this as an opportunity to revisit the CO$_2$ reduction plan, broaden its scope, and use it to coordinate a variety of ongoing and new activities across departments and the community. The result of this process was the *GreenPrint: Our Design for a Sustainable Future* (GreenPrint) plan, released in December 2010,[31] which addressed climate change as well as a broader set of environmental and sustainability initiatives. GreenPrint contains 137 separate initiatives that will reduce and avoid 4.6 MMT of GHG emissions.

In 2010, Miami-Dade, Broward, Monroe, and Palm Beach Counties formed the Southeast Florida Regional Climate Change Compact to coordinate climate action—both mitigation and adaptation. The compact includes 35 municipalities that have signed onto the Mayors' Climate Action Pledge in support of the compact as well as a variety of nonprofit partners.

The compact calls on the counties to work cooperatively to do the following:

- develop annual legislative programs and jointly advocate for state and federal policies and funding
- dedicate staff time and resources to create a Southeast Florida Regional Climate Action Plan, which outlines recommended mitigation and adaptation strategies to help the region pull in one direction and speak with one voice
- meet annually at the Southeast Florida Regional Climate Leadership Summits to mark progress and identify emerging issues[32]

The compact's signature achievements have been the development of a common set of regional sea-level-rise projections for use by members, the creation of a regional climate action plan, and the hosting of an annual summit. As a member of the compact, Miami-Dade County sought to link the local efforts identified in the GreenPrint to a broader, regional initiative: "Through the Compact, the County also contributed to the development of the Regional Climate Action Plan. This plan contains over 100 recommendations which focus on sustainable communities, transportation planning, water supply, management and infrastructure, natural systems, agriculture, energy and fuel, risk reduction and emergency management, and outreach and public policy. Compact members, both municipalities and counties, track the implementation of these recommendations and share best practices through work groups, publication of case studies, regular implementation workshops and accompanying guidance documents, which have focused on issues such as transportation, water supply planning, stormwater management, and Adaptation Action Areas."[33]

Most recently, the County has prioritized accelerating action on sea-level rise by forming the Sea Level Rise Task Force. In 2013, the task force reviewed the science and existing policy and issued seven recommendations. The County then adopted resolutions to direct action on these recommendations. Most notable were the creation of adaptation action areas to focus resources and implementation and the creation of the Enhanced Capital Plan to integrate climate risks into capital improvements planning.

Lessons Learned

According to Miami-Dade County, one of the most important lessons learned was that an issue could be studied for years but that this should not delay addressing it. To get started, the County secured strong and vocal support from the mayor and board, created a sustainability director position, and staffed it with someone good at planning, organization, and task management. This was critical for the success of climate action planning in a complex urban county with so many regional assets.

Building peer relationships and community partnerships proved to be key for Miami-Dade County. The County reached out to numerous communities that had completed sustainability plans and CAPs to learn about their experiences and get advice. In particular, the County received great help from the City of New York, which has recently completed its *PlaNYC* sustainability and climate action plan. Furthermore, starting in 2010, the County formalized regional cooperation through the Southeast Florida Regional Climate Change Compact.

Many communities struggle with determining how to get people interested in and supportive of climate action planning. Although the impacts of climate change seem like they would constitute an important motivator, the County found that this tended to scare or put people off. Instead, the County focused on energy efficiency and quality of life benefits and found the public and officials much more receptive. Figuring out what is important to the community when starting the process is a key to success.

Finally, the County found the process to be very iterative. In other words, as staff moved through the process and tried things or learned new information, they sometimes had to back up and do things over. The County has continued to update and revise GreenPrint, track implementation of the 137 measures, and publicize a "sustainability scorecard." It continues to seek new ways to build cooperative relations and act on climate change.

City of Copenhagen, Denmark: Racing toward Carbon Neutrality[34]

Although this book is focused on climate action planning in the United States, there is much to be learned from global cities. Over 9,000 cities around the world have made commitments to address climate change.[35] Copenhagen is a global leader not only in climate action planning but in a number of specific areas of climate action, such as green energy, bicycle transportation, and coastal adaptation (see box 9.8).

In 2009, Copenhagen established a goal to be the world's first carbon-neutral capital by 2025—the mayor considers this a realistic goal that will be achieved. The City developed and updated climate action plans in 2002, 2009, and 2012. It has also developed a climate adaption plan (2011) to build resilience, especially around the issues of rainfall-driven urban flooding and sea-level rise.

Copenhagen's 2012 emissions were 1.9 million metric tons (MMT) of CO_2 with a goal of 1.2 MMT by 2025 (about 1.8 MT per person). They will then achieve carbon neutrality by offsetting the remaining 1.2 MMT through exporting excess green energy. This is a common strategy for carbon neutrality; often it is very difficult to eliminate all GHG emissions, so some offset or carbon sequestration strategies must be used to close the remaining gap. Copenhagen has already demonstrated success by reducing emissions from 3.2 MMT in 1990 to 2.5 MMT in 2005 to 1.45 MMT in 2015. A significant part of Copenhagen's success in reducing GHG emissions has been due to two factors: investment in and commitment to bicycling, walking, and transit and a district heating system.

Copenhagen's role as a world leader in bicycle transportation is well documented, but its other success—in district heating—is less well known

Box 9.8

City of Copenhagen, Denmark, Summary

Population: 602,481 (2017)

Key Climate Action Initiatives

- Plan for CO_2 Reduction in Copenhagen, 1990–2010 (2002)
- CPH 2025 Climate Plan (2009, 2012)
- Copenhagen Climate Adaptation Plan (2011)
- CPH 2025 Climate Plan Roadmap, 2017–2020 (2016)

GHG Emissions

- 3.2 MMT CO_{2e} in 1990
- 2.5 MMT CO_{2e} in 2005
- 1.9 MMT CO_{2e} in 2012
- 1.45 MMT CO_{2e} in 2015

GHG Emissions Profile

- energy (~80%)
- transport (~18%)
- other (~2%)

GHG Emissions Reduction Target

- carbon-neutral by 2025

Climate Impacts

- increase in urban flooding due to increased rainfall
- increase in sea levels
- increase in incidence of heat waves and urban-heat-island effect
- increase in groundwater loss

and can serve as a model for other dense cities in colder climates. District heating (rather than individual heating of residences and businesses) now serves 99% of the city population, making use of waste heat from power plants, industry, and wastewater treatment.[36] These power plants have run on coal, but the City (in cooperation with a private utility) is working to convert them to sustainable biomass. The goal is 100% renewable energy for the district heating system by 2020.

In addition to energy from biomass, the City is collaborating with the utility and the federal government to support the expansion of wind turbines for generating electricity. This is expected to contribute the largest share of future emissions reduction—over 300,000 MT CO_{2e}. Since much of this is out of the hands of the City, it raises issues of uncertainty.

As part of its climate action planning, the City examined the economic implications of implementation. It looked at impacts to the municipal budget, cost increases to private investments, cost savings, and jobs creation. The analysis showed a positive return on the investments, especially those that result in energy conservation and efficiency. The analysis also showed the potential for 28,000 to 35,000 new jobs. The lord mayor of Copenhagen, Frank Jensen, and the mayor of technical and environmental administration, Ayfer Baykal, write, "Copenhageners will have so much to gain from the implementation of the Climate Plan. With the Climate Plan, we invest in growth and quality of life: clean air, less noise and a green city will improve everyday life for Copenhageners. The investments will secure jobs here and now—and the new solutions will create the foundation for a strong, green sector."[37]

Copenhagen's goal of being carbon-neutral by 2025 is ambitious and has received much attention, but the City has also recognized that it is being impacted by climate change and must seek to build a resilient city as well as a carbon-neutral one. In 2011, the City adopted the *Copenhagen Climate Adaptation Plan*. The plan prioritizes four strategies:

1. Development of methods to discharge during heavy downpours
2. Establishment of green solutions to reduce the risk of flooding
3. Increased use of passive cooling of buildings
4. Protection against flooding from the sea

Notable among all these strategies is a commitment to using natural systems and approaches as much as possible.

The *Copenhagen Climate Adaptation Plan* acknowledges three levels of adaptation based on the nature of the risk and city capabilities: "If the risk assessment shows that the risk is so high that it cannot be tolerated, the strategy of the City of Copenhagen is to choose actions that first of all prevent a climate-induced accident from happening [Level 1]. If this cannot be done—for either technical or economic reasons—actions that reduce the scale of the accident will be preferred [Level 2]. The lowest priority goes to measures that are only capable of making it easier and/ or cheaper to clean up after the accident. [Level 3]."[38] These three levels of adaptation are applied to different geographic scales to develop strategies for action. Figure 9.5 shows this approach applied to the issue of rainfall-driven flooding.

The City's climate adaptation plan, like its climate action plan, identifies the co-benefits of action. The City establishes that adaptation

	Level 1	Level 2	Level 3
Geography/Measure	Reduce likelihood	Reduce scale	Reduce vulnerability
Region	Delay of quantities of rain in catchment, pumping of water to sea	Delaying of volumes of rain in catchment, pumping of water to sea	
Municipality	Dikes, raised building elevations, increased sewer capacity, pumping of water to sea	Emergency preparedness Warning Securing of infrastructure	Information, moving of vulnerable functions to safe places
District	Dikes, "plan B", raised building elevation/ threshold	"Plan B" securing of infrastructure	Moving of vulnerable functions to safe places
Street	Control of stormwater runoff, raised building elevation/threshold, local management of stormwater	Control of stormwater runoff, raised building elevation/threshold, sandbag	Moving of vulnerable functions to safe places
Building	Backwater valve, raised building elevation/ threshold	Sandbags	Moving of vulnerable functions to safe places

Figure 9-5 Copenhagen Climate Adaptation Plan. It shows three levels of risk management for flooding at different spatial scales.

Source: City of Copenhagen, *Copenhagen Climate Adaptation Plan* (Copenhagen: Author, 2011), https://international.kk.dk/artikel/climate-adaptation.

strategies must not only address climate change but also improve the quality of life of the current and future residents. Specifically, it identifies more recreational opportunities, new jobs, and an improved local environment with more green elements.

Copenhagen's climate planning is ambitious in scope and detailed in implementation. Climate planning is seen as supporting the broad goal of a more livable city and is integrated throughout city planning and operations. The City's climate planning not only has produced the plans discussed but also has integrated the *Municipal Master Plan 2011 "Green Growth and Quality of Life,"* the Agenda 21 plan, the *Action Plan for Green Mobility*, the *City of Copenhagen Resources and Waste Plan*, *Cycling Strategy 2025*, and *Eco-Metropolis 2015*. If anyone has a chance of achieving carbon neutrality in the next decade, it is Copenhagen.

Lessons Learned

Copenhagen shows that an aggressive GHG emissions reduction target is achievable but that it requires significant investment and the willingness to transform transportation and energy systems in a relatively short time. This transformation is facilitated by a careful strategy of ensuring that these changes provide economic and social benefits, especially ones that have a positive economic return. The lord mayor of Copenhagen has been an effective champion in communicating the City's vision.

In regards to climate adaptation, Copenhagen sees necessary infrastructure projects as an opportunity not just to make the city more resilient but to actually make it more livable. Projects to reduce street flooding also seek to improve the streets for biking and walking and to provide additional parks and open space in dense neighborhoods. As it states in its plan, "A greener Copenhagen is a climate-proof Copenhagen."[39]

Chapter 10

Time to Act

As we continue to tackle our environmental challenges, it's clear that change won't come from Washington alone. It will come from Americans across the country who take steps in their own homes and their own communities to make that change happen.

—U.S. president Barack Obama in the speech "A New Foundation for Energy and the Environment"

C ommunities around the world have set goals to be low-carbon and resilient by reducing greenhouse gas (GHG) emissions and adapting to unavoidable climate impacts. The development and implementation of climate action policies and strategies represent a unique opportunity for communities not only to contribute to solving a global problem but to position themselves to thrive well into the future. Climate action planning should be seen as a chance for communities to control their own destinies in the face of shifting conditions and to act as leaders in the formation of effective, innovative climate policy.

The Case for Immediate Action

We humans have been contributing GHG emissions to the atmosphere for generations. Communities may ask, Why take action now? Why not wait until we know more? We offer three reasons for communities to take immediate action to reduce their GHG emissions and prepare for the local impacts of climate change.

The Longer We Wait, the Harder It Will Get

The accumulation of GHGs in the atmosphere has only been recognized as tied to climate change in the last several decades, partly because the concentrations have reached levels where the outcomes are more directly observable. Just as it has taken many decades to create the problem, the solution will require prolonged effort. Climate action planning seeks to reduce emissions that are contributing to the problem and reduce vulnerability to those impacts that are unavoidable. The benefits from emissions reductions will not be felt for many decades. This alone should be motivation to act sooner rather than later; however, it can also be viewed as an excuse to delay action.

The need for local climate action is increasingly recognized by the global community. In 2018, the IPCC released a special report on the impacts of 1.5°C of global warming. It concluded that current commitments to GHG emissions reduction by the global community, as submitted under the Paris Agreement, would still lead to a global increase in GHG emissions by 2030 that would not limit global warming to 1.5°C. It stated that global CO_2 emissions must start to decline well before 2030—only 11 years away from the publication of this book. We are almost out of time.

The most recent rounds of negotiation at the United Nations Framework Convention on Climate Change (UNFCCC) have included calls for subnationals (meaning states, regions, and cities) to commit to action, most notably in the Marrakech Partnership for Global Climate Action. As of 2019, nearly 10,000 cities and regions around the world had formally submitted their ambitions and commitments to GHG emissions reduction to the United Nations.[1] In addition, organizations like ICLEI–Local

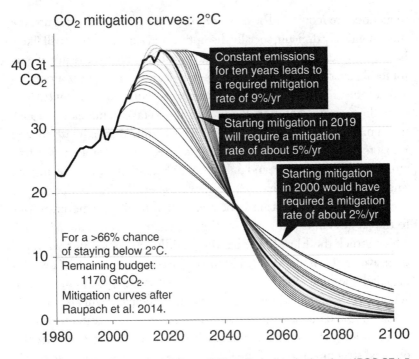

Figure 10-1 Mitigation curves required to meet 2°C target based on different starting years

Source: Robbie Andrew, "Figures from the Global Carbon Budget 2018," CICERO Center for International Climate Research, Creative Commons Attribution 4.0 International license, http://folk.uio.no/roberan/t/global_mitigation_curves.shtml. See website for methods and limitations.

Governments for Sustainability, C40 Cities, the Urban Sustainability Directors Network, and the Global Covenant of Mayors have emerged as leaders in the global climate action movement, catalyzing local climate action.

The longer a community waits to act, the more aggressive these actions will need to be to meet stated goals. Figure 10.1 shows that if we had been more aggressive in bending the global GHG emissions curve in the year 2000, the annual reduction rate needed to stay below 2°C would be 2%. Given that the GHG emissions curve shows no sign of bending down soon, we could be in a situation a decade from now where 9% or more annual reductions are required. The more dramatic the required future cuts, the more politically difficult, socially disruptive, and expensive they will likely be. It is also likely that they will be mandatory and carry more requirements for local governments. Communities that act now are best positioned to satisfy future requirements and maintain local control and flexibility.

In the case of adaptation, the motivation to take immediate action is much more urgent. Many communities face immediate climate change impacts that could have far-reaching consequences for a city's infrastructure, economic base, and public safety. Scientists are now seeing the fingerprints of climate change on major disasters. The recent destructive fire seasons in California are associated with drought and modifications to the jet stream exacerbated by climate change. Hurricane Michael, which struck the Florida Panhandle, rapidly intensified in a warmer-than-average Gulf of Mexico, and the storm surge rode on top of decades of global-warming-driven sea-level rise. What should prompt immediate action is the fact that addressing some of these changes will take considerable time and investment. For example, if a city's wastewater treatment facility is located near a shoreline, sea-level rise or flooding may place the physical structure at risk. If the facility is viewed as so vulnerable that it should be moved, a community would have to identify a new site, obtain funding, build the new facility, and reroute sewer infrastructure to reach the new facility. These steps will all take time and money. A community facing projected climate change impacts cannot afford to delay planning.

Communities Can Achieve Long-Term Success

Acting now to develop GHG emissions reduction and climate adaptation strategies allows communities to control their own destinies. Climate action planning has the power not only to reduce vulnerability to the hazards associated with climate change but to position a community to thrive economically, environmentally, and socially well into the future. The needs to reduce GHG emissions and adapt to unavoidable consequences are likely to be considerations in policy development for many decades. These goals are compatible with the many other goals of local governments, such as housing, environmental protection, and economic development. The development of comprehensive, integrated climate strategies presents an opportunity for communities to meet a range of local needs now and well into the future.

The emission of GHGs is a result of how our energy is produced and the efficiency with which it is used, the way people move around a community, the products purchased and the manner in which they were made, and the methods of solid waste disposal. These choices are influenced by local urban form, climate, culture, economic conditions, values, the local employment base, and a host of other characteristics. While the overarching goals of climate policy may be shared, the most effective and lasting climate planning strategies will acknowledge and build on this local context. Accounting for the environmental, economic, political, and social settings in the development of climate actions provides a great opportunity to incorporate strategies that not only meet the global needs of climate change but situate a community for long-term livability. For example, a shift in transportation mode share from single-occupancy vehicles to bus, bike, and pedestrian travel to reduce GHG emissions is also likely to improve public health due to increased physical activity and improved air quality. Improved energy efficiency in homes reduces the utility bills of residents. Strategies that seek to foster a green business community are likely not only to reduce the emissions associated with the commercial and industrial sector but also to create economic stimulus and foster job creation.

Sustained collaboration on climate action can foster community support and security. Community members experience the outcomes of actions, from safer streets to greater economic stability. Over time, these actions yield a slow shift in local culture and understanding. The implementation of climate planning strategies can yield an improved global condition as well as a community that is vital, livable for all residents, and economically resilient. Climate action planning becomes, simply, good community planning.

Communities Are Positioned to Innovate and Lead

The federal government has largely ignored its responsibility to formulate and pass climate change legislation. Even when countries or international organizations succeed, the policies represent a compromise. This is to be expected given the diversity of interests and issues at large spatial scales; actions taken at these scales are often broad in scope and less able to be experimental or innovative. Local communities are the entities best positioned to innovate in the realm of climate action planning.

A community that makes a long-term commitment to climate planning goals should treat strategy development as an adaptive process. Some strategies may not work, but others will prove effective. Each community represents a unique local setting from the biophysical to the sociopolitical. Strategy development built from a laundry list of actions used elsewhere will only be successful if adapted to the specific challenges and opportunities presented by any given community. Local governments have the opportunity to be incubators for new climate actions that can be tailored or adjusted to meet the needs of others.

Climate action planning is a new enough area of policy development that innovative ideas and approaches are critical to ensure widespread success. The long-term nature of climate planning efforts gives communities room to experiment. However, experimentation requires a firm commitment to monitoring. The feedback loop provided by monitoring GHG emissions and climate vulnerability allows for adjustments to be made and areas of success or failure to be identified.

Many areas of climate action planning rely on voluntary behavior, such as the choice to drive or walk or of housing type. Climate action strategies can render some behaviors inconvenient or expensive and others easier or more cost-effective, but these behaviors cannot be directly addressed through policy. Community culture and values change with time. Engaging in a climate action planning process represents a long-term commitment. As local culture changes, there are strategies that may have been ineffective in the past that prove effective in the present. The implementation of strategies and community acceptance or support of climate policy evolve together. Demonstrated or observed policy effectiveness can lead to shifts in community views.

The case study of Portland and Multnomah County in Oregon illustrates a slow evolution in transportation choices that occurred as the government focused on providing greater opportunity and convenience with an expansion of transit, bike infrastructure, and pedestrian safety. As residents began to use these services and opportunities, the societal view of them began to shift.

Over time, sustained implementation and monitoring of climate action planning strategies will likely begin to inform the policies that govern many areas of community operation. In the long term, climate planning goals should be integrated into all areas of government. Once such policies are normalized, the goals of minimizing GHG emissions and exposure to hazards associated with climate change will become standard considerations in all decision-making processes.

Who and for Whom?

Anyone who asks the question "Who should do climate action planning for our community?" should consider themselves a candidate for the answer. As shown in the case studies in chapter 9, climate action planning can be done in city hall, it can be done by nonprofits in the community, and it can be done by a dedicated and informed citizenry that comes together

---

Box 10.1

Ten Things Your Community Should Do Right Now
(Even before Starting Climate Action Planning)

1. Switch to energy-efficient lighting such as LEDs.
2. Upgrade insulation in older residences, businesses, and government buildings.
3. Install solar panels where feasible.
4. Provide electrical vehicle charging stations.
5. Start or enhance recycling programs.
6. Provide and promote transit, bike, micromobility, and pedestrian infrastructure and services.
7. Use local, sustainably produced products, especially food.
8. Purchase renewable energy (if available).
9. Conserve water through retrofit of fixtures, low-water landscaping, and rainwater catchment.
10. Plant trees.

for this specific purpose. Those motivated to do climate action planning in their communities should immediately begin to make connections and develop partnerships, as described in chapter 2. Everyone should be represented in climate action planning; a community is only resilient when all its members are resilient. Any community can and should do climate action planning. Moreover, communities can even begin reducing emissions immediately while waiting for the climate action planning process to get started (see box 10.1).

Our goal with this book is to inspire, inform, and facilitate local action on the global climate crisis. This crisis will compromise the social, cultural, and economic integrity of many communities around the globe. If we as a global community are to achieve all our hopes and dreams for our children and grandchildren, then we must act now to create low-carbon, resilient communities.

Appendix A

Climate Science

The effort to organize and interpret the hundreds of scientific studies about various aspects of climate change is being led internationally by the Intergovernmental Panel on Climate Change (IPCC) and in the United States by the U.S. Global Change Research Program (USGCRP). Communities can use the data and summary reports from these entities to establish the scientific basis for taking local action. The IPCC was "established by the United Nations Environment Programme (UNEP) and the World Meteorological Organization (WMO) to provide the world with a clear scientific view on the current state of climate change and its potential environmental and socio-economic consequences."[1] The IPCC is made up of thousands of scientists from around the world who review and assess the latest science and publish a report every several years, most recently in 2014. The USGCRP was established by the Global Change Research Act of 1990 (P.L. 101-606), which called for "a comprehensive and integrated United States research program which will assist the Nation and the world to understand, assess, predict, and respond to human-induced and natural processes of global change."[2] It is composed of 13 federal agencies and departments and periodically publishes a National Climate

Assessment. The scientific reports on climate change prepared by these organizations are the best defendable science available to inform local climate action planning.

Based largely on these reports, this appendix summarizes the science of greenhouse gas emissions and climate change. This summary provides local government staff with strategies for communicating climate change, which will be needed to engage the various participants in the climate action planning process.

Planning typically begins with identifying and defining a problem that needs to be solved. For climate action planning, the problem is global warming, which drives climate change (explained in the next section). Communities choose to address climate change for a variety of reasons, as explained in chapter 1, but once they commit to taking action, they must all be clear about how they define the problem. Good problem definition helps the public and decision-makers understand the challenges presented by climate change and the role of a local response.

A Primer on Greenhouse Gas Emissions and Climate Change

The presence of gases in Earth's atmosphere, such as carbon dioxide (CO_2) and water vapor, creates a natural greenhouse effect that traps heat generated by the sun. The greenhouse effect maintains a warm enough temperature for life to survive. Scientists have observed that Earth's climate has been warming since the late 1800s, most rapidly in the last few decades. The observations include an "increase in global average air and oceans temperatures, widespread melting of snow and ice, and rising global average sea level."[3] This warming is primarily attributed to an increase in greenhouse gases in the atmosphere caused by the burning of fossil fuels.[4] The rate of this warming is unprecedented and threatens to warm the planet by as much as 4.8°C (8.6°F) by 2100. The potential impacts of this level of warming are numerous but most notably include the rise of sea level threatening low-lying coastal communities; an increase in the occurrence of extreme weather-related events such as heat waves, storms, floods, droughts, and wildfires; and the loss of native plants and wildlife. These impacts potentially threaten the social, economic, and cultural stability of many of the planet's communities.

How Do We Know the Earth Is Warming?

Extensive datasets gathered by multiple scientific organizations track a range of climate indicators, such as temperature. Together, these data provide compelling evidence of global warming. The U.S. Environmental Protection Agency (EPA) tracks 37 indicators of climate change and includes on their website background information, maps and graphics, indicator descriptions, data sources, and technical documentation. The EPA concludes the following: "All of the indicators are based on observations over time and consist of the best available peer-reviewed, publicly available data. Some indicators show trends that can be more directly linked to human-induced climate change than others. Together, these indicators present credible and compelling evidence that climate change is happening now in the United States and globally."[5] The following is a summary of these indicators provided by the EPA:

- *Atmospheric Concentrations of Greenhouse Gases:* Historical measurements show that the current global atmospheric concentrations of carbon dioxide are unprecedented compared with the past 800,000 years, even after accounting for natural fluctuations.
- *U.S. and Global Temperature:* Average temperatures have risen across the contiguous 48 states since 1901. Global temperatures show a similar trend, and all of the top 10 warmest years on record worldwide have occurred since 1998.
- *Coastal Flooding:* Flooding is becoming more frequent along the U.S. coastline as sea level rises. Nearly every site measured has experienced an increase in coastal flooding since the 1950s. The rate is accelerating in many locations along the East and Gulf coasts.
- *Snowpack:* Snowpack in early spring has decreased at more than 90 percent of measurement sites in the western United States between 1955 and 2016.
- *Heat-Related Deaths:* Since 1979, more than 9,000 Americans were reported to have died as a direct result of heat-related illnesses such as heat stroke. However, considerable year-to-year variability and certain limitations of the underlying data make it difficult to determine

whether the United States has experienced long-term trends in the number of deaths classified as "heat-related."

- *Marine Species Distribution:* The average center of biomass for 105 marine fish and invertebrate species along U.S. coasts shifted northward by about 10 miles between 1982 and 2015. These species also moved an average of 20 feet deeper.[6]

Many reported measures of climate change represent a global average. In any specific area of the globe at any specific time, these trends may be different. For example, in 2009 Europe experienced warmer than usual average temperatures, whereas the American Midwest experienced cooler than average temperatures. In addition, year to year, the average global surface temperature varies up and down, but the long-term trend is upward. These year-to-year changes are due to annual variability in a variety of climate-related systems, particularly ocean currents, that affects global temperatures. This raises the issue of "weather" versus "climate." Weather typically refers to changes over a shorter period of time, and climate refers to changes over a longer period of time. A particularly cold week, month, or year is not evidence against global warming, nor is a particularly hot week, month, or year evidence supporting global warming. The longer-term indicators established by the EPA (listed earlier) constitute the best evidence to date of global warming.

What Causes Global Warming?

The greenhouse effect is a natural phenomenon that has caused the temperature of the planet to be warmer than it otherwise would be if it had no atmosphere. If the natural greenhouse effect did not occur, the average temperature of the planet would be about 60°F colder than it is currently. The natural greenhouse effect is a process wherein solar energy heats the planet, and some of this heat is radiated back toward space only to be absorbed by atmospheric gases and reradiated back toward the planet's surface. In other words, the planet is essentially heated by two phenomena: the direct heating of the surface and atmosphere by the sun and the "captured" heat (that would have radiated back out to space) by the atmosphere. Although the term *greenhouse effect* is used, the phenomenon is not exactly like a greenhouse; still, the analogy works well enough. Earth can be thought of as a giant greenhouse, with an atmosphere that contains certain gases that act as the glass.

The naturally occurring greenhouse gases are carbon dioxide (CO_2), water vapor (H_2O), methane (CH_4), nitrous oxide (N_2O), and ozone (O_3). There are also several human-made chemicals that are released into the atmosphere and that act as greenhouse gases. These are generically called halocarbons (see box A.1). The addition of these human-made chemicals and of naturally occurring greenhouse gases beyond their natural levels have contributed to anthropogenic (human-caused) global warming. In other words, humans have enhanced the natural greenhouse effect that made the planet a livable temperature. We have created thicker layers of glass in our greenhouse. As noted earlier, this additional warming could have a serious impact on the planet.

Box A.1

Greenhouse Gases

Carbon Dioxide (CO_2)

A naturally occurring gas that is also a by-product of burning fossil fuels and biomass, as well as land use changes and other industrial processes. It is the principal anthropogenic (human-made) greenhouse gas that affects Earth's radiative balance between incoming and outgoing heat. It is the reference gas against which other greenhouse gases are measured and therefore has a global warming potential of 1.

Fluorocarbons

Carbon-fluorine compounds that often contain other elements such as hydrogen, chlorine, or bromine. Common fluorocarbons include chlorofluorocarbons (CFCs), hydrochlorofluorocarbons (HCFCs), hydrofluorocarbons (HFCs), and perfluorocarbons (PFCs). These compounds can be found in a variety of materials and processes such as air conditioning, building materials, and industrial operations.

Halocarbons

Compounds containing chlorine, bromine or fluorine, and carbon. Such compounds can act as powerful greenhouse gases in the atmosphere. The chlorine- and bromine-containing halocarbons are also involved in the depletion of the ozone layer. While there are natural sources of halocarbons, the addition of anthropogenic sources has led to warming. Halocarbons have many uses including as solvents, pesticides, refrigerants and adhesives as well as specialized industrial uses.

Methane (CH_4)

A hydrocarbon with a global warming potential most recently estimated at 28 times that of carbon dioxide (CO_2). Methane is produced through anaerobic (without oxygen) decomposition of waste in landfills, animal digestion, decomposition of animal wastes, production and distribution of natural gas and petroleum, coal production, and incomplete fossil fuel combustion.

Nitrous Oxide (N_2O)

A powerful greenhouse gas with a global warming potential most recently estimated at 265 times that of carbon dioxide (CO_2). Major sources of nitrous oxide include soil cultivation practices, especially the use of commercial and organic fertilizers; fossil fuel combustion; nitric acid production; and biomass burning.

Ozone (O_3)

A gaseous atmospheric constituent. Its contribution to global warming varies depending on the atmospheric layer in which it is located. In the troposphere, it is created both naturally and by photochemical reactions (pollutants + sunlight) involving gases resulting from human activities (smog). Tropospheric ozone acts as a greenhouse gas, with higher concentrations resulting in warming. In the stratosphere, ozone is created by the interaction between solar ultraviolet radiation and molecular oxygen (O_2). Stratospheric ozone plays a decisive role in the stratospheric radiative balance. Depletion of stratospheric ozone allows increased solar radiation to reach Earth. In other words, ozone in the stratosphere reduces warming, and ozone in the troposphere increases it.

Water Vapor (H_2O)

The most abundant greenhouse gas, it is the water present in the atmosphere in gaseous form. Water vapor is an important part of the natural greenhouse effect. While humans are not significantly increasing its concentration, it contributes to the enhanced greenhouse effect because the warming influence of greenhouse gases leads to increased levels of water vapor. In addition to its role as a natural greenhouse gas, water vapor plays an important role in regulating the temperature of the planet because clouds form when excess water vapor in the atmosphere condenses to form ice and water droplets and precipitation.

Source: Compiled from the U.S. Environmental Protection Agency's "Glossary," http://www.epa.gov/climatechange/glossary.html.

Each of these greenhouse gases does not have the same effect on the energy balance (or heat transfer) of the atmosphere (called "radiative forcing"). Some of these greenhouse gases have more global warming potential (GWP) and are thus of more concern than others. This is because of their physical properties, their quantities in the atmosphere, and their longevity in the atmosphere. Carbon dioxide (CO_2) in the atmosphere has the highest relative radiative forcing and is considered a long-lived greenhouse gas, meaning that the carbon dioxide being put into the atmosphere will remain there for a long time. There are also several factors working to reduce anthropogenic global warming. These include surface albedo (the ability of Earth's surface to reflect sunlight back into space before it causes warming) and aerosols, especially clouds (that also can reflect sunlight). Human activities have increased Earth's surface albedo in some areas, especially where forests (darker areas) have been converted to other uses (usually lighter) and decreased in others, especially where sea ice (lighter areas) has been converted to open ocean.

What Is the Difference between Global Warming and Climate Change?

The terms *global warming* and *climate change* have essentially become interchangeable in contemporary usage. In general, *climate change* has become the preferred term partly to avoid the confusion that occurs with people who assume *global warming* means that every place will be warmer all the time. Climate change could be considered more accurate, since the phenomenon will result in greater temperature variability and volatility, not just uniform warming in all parts of the globe. This book uses both terms but most often prefers *climate change*.

What Are the Levels and Sources of Greenhouse Gases?

To develop a common metric for all greenhouse gases, scientists often refer to emissions in CO_2 equivalent units (CO_{2e}; also abbreviated CO_{2eq}, eCO_2, or *CDE*) based on their GWP. Only 82% of the greenhouse gas emissions reported for the United States in 2016 were specifically CO_2, whereas the remainder were primarily methane and nitrous oxide.[7] Researchers convert the non-CO_2 gases into CO_{2e} for convenience of reporting and understanding the overall effect of greenhouse gas emissions. It is important to note that the GWP reported for various greenhouse gases varies depending on the source. GWP cannot be known precisely, which explains the variation seen in the climate science literature. While there is variation, the relative scale tends to be consistent. For example, methane is always reported as having a GWP between 21 and 28, and nitrous oxide ranges from 265 to 310. For the GWP of common greenhouse gases, see table A.1.

Table A.1. Common greenhouse gases' global warming potential (GWP)

Greenhouse gas	Global warming potential (GWP) of one molecule of the gas over 100 years (relative to carbon dioxide)
Carbon dioxide	1
Methane	28
Nitrous oxide	265
CFC-12	10,200
CFC-11	4,660
HFC-134a	1,300
Sulfur hexafluoride	23,500
Nitrogen trifluoride	16,100

Note: Carbon dioxide's lifetime is poorly defined because the gas is not destroyed over time but instead moves between different parts of the ocean–atmosphere–land system. Some of the excess carbon dioxide will be absorbed quickly (e.g., by the ocean surface), but some will remain in the atmosphere for thousands of years.

Source: Greenhouse gas protocol using AR5 standards, https://www.ghgprotocol .org/sites/default/files/ghgp/Global-Warming-Potential-Values%20%28Feb%2016 %202016%29_1.pdf

Atmospheric measures of CO_2 and CO_{2e} are usually made in parts per million volume (ppm). As of 2019, atmospheric CO_2 was over 410 ppm as measured by NOAA at the Mauna Loa Observatory, Hawaii (this roughly translates to 480 ppm CO_{2e}). This is up from 317 ppm in 1960 as measured at the same station. In addition, the IPCC states the following: "Current concentrations of atmospheric CO_2 and CH_4 far exceed pre-industrial values found in polar ice core records of atmospheric composition dating back 650,000 years."[8] The IPCC describes the implication of atmospheric concentration for temperature: "A limited number of studies provide scenarios that are more likely than not to limit warming to 1.5°C by 2100; these scenarios are characterized by concentrations below 430 ppm $CO_{2\text{-}eq}$ by 2100 and 2050 emission reduction between 70% and 95% below 2010."[9]

The primary source, but not the only source, of anthropogenic greenhouse gases is the burning of fossil fuels for energy and transportation.

Net U.S. greenhouse gas emissions in 2016 were 5,796 teragrams of CO_{2e} (an increase of 4.7% since 1990), most of which came from the burning of petroleum for transportation (see figure 1.1 in chapter 1).[10] The combustion of coal for electricity production is a close second in total emissions. As a result, these two sectors are usually the focus of climate action planning; they represent the largest part of the global warming problem. In addition, emissions occur from natural gas combustion, solid waste decomposition, and agriculture, among other sources. These categories translate to the activities occurring every day in communities across the United States. People drive their cars and trucks; fly in airplanes; turn on electrical and gas appliances in their homes, especially for heating and cooling; eat food grown on farms; and throw away their garbage. Businesses, industries, farms, and government agencies do similar things and provide people with the goods and services they demand. All these activities result in the production of greenhouse gases.

In addition to the direct emission of greenhouse gases, human activities can contribute to global warming by adversely impacting carbon sinks. A *sink* is anything that absorbs more carbon than it releases. Oceans, soils, and forests all store carbon and can act as sinks. The degree to which they serve as sinks varies seasonally within the global carbon cycle. Changes in climate and human development practices can influence the degree to which carbon can be stored. For example, increasing water temperature in oceans reduces the carbon storage capacity. A reduction in the carbon uptake rate of the ocean is equivalent to direct emissions of CO_2 into the atmosphere. Similarly, deforestation and soil degradation both reduce the CO_2 uptake and storage capacity of ecosystems and result in increased atmospheric greenhouse gas concentrations.

What Are the Projected Climate Impacts?

Climate change directly alters temperature, sea-level, and precipitation patterns. These changes result in a much wider range of consequences, including drought, wildfire, flooding, and species migration disruption. Each of these events has the potential to disrupt or damage local resources and systems, such as the built environment (infrastructure and buildings), economic and social resources, and ecosystems. Climate change impacts can be expressed on large spatial scales as alteration in the probability and magnitude of event occurrence (e.g., a 100-year flood or extended heat wave). The impacts experienced by communities will vary widely. This is a challenge for local jurisdictions, which must communicate the likely local consequences of climate change and formulate policy to reduce local vulnerability. Brief summaries of the climate change impacts projected for the United States and some of the consequences of these changes follow.[11]

Sea-Level Rise

Two processes drive sea-level rise: the melting of glaciers and the thermal expansion of marine waters. Sea level has risen nine inches in the last 100 years and is projected to continue at nearly double the historic rate. Melting of Antarctic or Greenland ice sheets may result in much more extensive impacts, but the likelihood and timing of these events are uncertain. Sea-level rise poses a series of consequences, such as coastal flooding (gradual coastal inundation and coastal stream flooding), extreme high tide, increased erosion, ecosystem loss (of estuaries), and saltwater intrusion into groundwater.

These changes can have a range of impacts on community resources along the coast. Many critical components of a coastal community's infrastructure can be located near the coast. Transportation infrastructure such as roads, marine ports, airports, and train lines located in low-lying coastal areas are potentially vulnerable to the impacts of sea-level rise. In addition to transportation networks, populations often concentrate near coastal areas. This concentration of structures results in sea-level rise threatening not only buildings but also the safety of inhabitants. Sea-level rise can also pose a threat to local water supplies through intrusion into groundwater resources and damage to local ecosystems. These two impacts may have economic consequences, from the decreased viability of drinking water sources to the loss of recreation areas.

Temperature Variation

Changes in the temperature can result in different outcomes depending on location. In some locations, this may mean a higher frequency of high-temperature days (> 90° or 100°F) and prolonged periods of extreme heat (heat waves). In others, it may not result in extreme heat but will alter the timing and duration of seasons, such as shorter winters with fewer cold days. These changes have the potential to result in a wide range of community outcomes. Heat has direct consequences for human health, from lethargy, to heat stroke, to even death. Heat can result in increased formation of ground-level ozone, which is associated with many respiratory ailments. There are also interactions between heat outcomes. Heat may result in increased water and energy use. It may also increase fire frequency and severity. Fire can pose a direct threat to human safety and structures as well as reduce air quality and threaten ecosystems.

Changes in annual temperature patterns can result in changes in natural systems and processes. Chemical reactions such as those in water change with temperature, meaning water quality could shift. In addition, changing seasons will alter growing seasons, which have consequences for overall ecosystem function and agricultural production. Altered season lengths and average temperatures can also result in increased pest and/ or invasive species presence.

Precipitation Variation

Similar to the other climate impacts, changes in the annual amount and timing of precipitation vary based on location. The total amount of precipitation may change, as well as the timing, intensity, and form (e.g., snow to rain). These changes can result in reductions in rainfall or extended periods without rain (e.g., drought). Conversely, climate change can result in intensive storms that can cause flooding and erosion. The change in precipitation type can result in a reduction in snow and an increase in rain totals.

These changes, particularly when paired with alterations in temperature, can result in water scarcity for drinking and agricultural uses. The intensive rain can damage flood-prone areas, threatening structures, inhabitants, and infrastructure in low-lying areas. Alteration in precipitation can also impact ecosystem function, such as by changing the availability of water that supports plant life in stream ecosystems. Changing the amount and timing of precipitation will impact not only high flows but also low flows in rivers. Reduced flow conditions can make habitat unsuitable for aquatic species such as anadromous fish.

Glossary of Terms[12]

The following list includes some of the key terms often found in climate science articles and reports. Planners faced with communicating with the public and decision-makers about the challenge presented by climate change should be familiar with these terms.

Albedo   The fraction of incoming solar radiation reflected by a surface or object, often expressed as a percentage. Snow-covered surfaces have a high albedo, indicating a high level of reflectivity. The albedo of soils ranges from high to low, and vegetation-covered surfaces and oceans have a low albedo. Earth's albedo is influenced by varying levels of cloudiness, snow, and ice, as well as by leaf area and land cover changes.

Anthropogenic   Made by people or resulting from human activities. Usually used in the context of emissions that are produced as a result of human activities.

Atmosphere   The gaseous envelope surrounding Earth. The dry atmosphere consists almost entirely of nitrogen (78.1% volume mixing ratio) and oxygen (20.9% volume mixing ratio), together with a number of trace gases, such as argon (0.93% volume mixing ratio), helium, and radiatively active greenhouse gases. Radiatively active gases such as carbon dioxide (0.035% volume mixing ratio) and ozone influence how much energy leaves the atmosphere. In addition, the atmosphere contains water vapor, the amount of which is highly variable (but is typically 1% volume mixing ratio).

Carbon dioxide equivalent (CO_{2e}, CO_{2eq}, eCO_2, and CDE)   A measure used to compare the emissions from various greenhouse gases based on their global warming potential (GWP). Carbon dioxide equivalents are commonly expressed as million metric tons of carbon dioxide equivalents (MMTCDE) or million short tons of carbon dioxide equivalents (MSTCDE). The carbon dioxide equivalent for a gas is derived by multiplying the tons of the gas by the associated GWP: MMTCDE = (million metric tons of a gas) × (GWP of the gas). For example, the GWP for methane is 21. This means that emissions of 1 million metric tons of methane are equivalent to emissions of 21 million metric tons of carbon dioxide.

Climate   In a narrow sense, this is usually defined as the "average weather." A more rigorous statistical description is the mean and variability of quantities such as temperature, precipitation, and wind over a period of time ranging from months to thousands of years. The most commonly used period is three decades.

Climate change   Any significant change in measures of climate (such as temperature, precipitation, or wind) lasting for an extended period (decades or longer). Climate change may result from natural factors (e.g., changes in the sun's intensity or slow changes in Earth's orbit around the sun), natural processes within the climate system (e.g., changes in ocean circulation), and human activities that change the atmosphere's composition (e.g., through burning fossil fuels) and the land surface (e.g., deforestation, reforestation, urbanization, desertification, etc.).

Global warming   An average increase in the temperature of the atmosphere near Earth's surface and in the troposphere, which can contribute to changes in global climate patterns. Global warming can occur due to a variety of causes, both natural and human induced. In common usage, this often refers to the warming that can occur as a result of increased emissions of greenhouse gases from human activities.

Global warming potential (GWP)   The cumulative radiative forcing effects from the emission of a unit mass of gas relative to a reference gas. The GWP-weighted emissions of direct greenhouse gases in the U.S. GHG Emissions Inventory are presented in terms of equivalent emissions of carbon dioxide.

Greenhouse effect   The trapping and buildup of heat in the atmosphere (troposphere) near Earth's surface. Some of the heat flowing back toward space from Earth's surface is absorbed by water vapor, carbon dioxide, ozone, and several other gases in the atmosphere and then radiated back toward Earth's surface. If the atmospheric concentrations of these greenhouse gases rise, the average temperature of the lower atmosphere will gradually increase. Greenhouse gases include, but are not limited to, water vapor, carbon dioxide (CO_2), methane (CH_4), nitrous oxide (N_2O), chlorofluorocarbons (CFCs), hydrochlorofluorocarbons (HCFCs), ozone (O_3), hydrofluorocarbons (HFCs), perfluorocarbons (PFCs), and sulfur hexafluoride (SF_6).

Enhanced greenhouse effect   The enhanced or amplified greenhouse effect due to anthropogenic emissions of greenhouse gases. Increased concentrations of carbon dioxide (CO_2), methane (CH_4), nitrous oxide (N_2O), chlorofluorocarbons (CFCs), hydrochlorofluorocarbons (HCFCs), perfluorocarbons (PFCs), sulfur hexafluoride (SF_6), nitrogen trifluoride (NF_3), and other heat-trapping gases caused by human activities such as fossil fuel consumption have trapped more infrared radiation, thereby exerting a warming influence on the climate.

Radiative forcing   Radiative forcing refers to actions that impact the energy balance of the planet. In equilibrium, the same amount of energy that enters the system (sunlight) would leave (emitted as heat). If there is any imbalance in the energy entering and leaving the atmosphere, the earth would be heating or cooling. The presence or absence of this balance is most meaningfully measured at the boundary between the troposphere (the lowest level of the atmosphere) and the stratosphere (the thin upper layer). Radiative forcing is a way to measure the impact of human activities on global temperature. It is influenced by the level of greenhouse gases present as well as changes in albedo (surface reflectivity), clouds, and solar input. (Additional detail on radiative forcing and its measurement can be found in chapter 6 of the 2001 IPCC Third Assessment Report, "Working Group I: The Scientific Basis.")

Troposphere   The lowest part of the atmosphere from Earth's surface to about 10 km in altitude in midlatitudes (ranging from 9 km in high latitudes to 16 km in the tropics, on average) where clouds and weather phenomena occur. In the troposphere, temperatures generally decrease with height.

Weather   Atmospheric condition at any given time or place. It is measured in terms of such things as wind, temperature, humidity, atmospheric pressure, cloudiness, and precipitation. In most places, weather can change from hour to hour, day to day, and season to season. Climate can be defined as the "average weather." A simple way of remembering the difference is that climate is what you expect (e.g., cold winters) and weather is what you get (e.g., a blizzard).

Appendix B

The Public Participation Program

This section provides an outline for a model public participation program that can be tailored based on the public participation approach desired and the answers to the key questions presented in chapter 3. This example assumes preparation of a climate action plan (CAP) but can be tailored for other climate action programs. Similar to the climate action planning process, a public participation program can be seen as including three phases with several actions in each phase:

1. Preliminary phase
   a. Establish goals for the program.
   b. Develop a target audience list and identify stakeholders.
   c. Create key messages and an "identity."
   d. Publicize the climate action planning process (via media, websites, social media, email, events).
2. Planning phase
   a. Host a kickoff event.
   b. Communicate with the community.
   c. Hold workshops / task force meetings / focus groups.

3. Adoption and implementation phase
   a. Arrange adoption meetings.
   b. Throw celebration events.
   c. Organize implementation activities.

Preliminary Phase

The preliminary phase includes the tasks that should be completed before engaging the public in the planning process.

Goals for the Program

The goals of the public participation program for the climate action plan include the following:

- communicate to the community the purpose of the CAP and the impacts of CAP implementation on the three primary greenhouse gas (GHG) emissions sectors (energy, transportation, waste) and climate change impacts, providing opportunities for the community to give input about how emissions reduction and adaptation goals should be reached
- promote the CAP according to a message or issue of importance to the community rather than that of the project
- position the planning organization as the best resource for information about the CAP
- generate interest and identify early supporters
- ensure community empowerment, buy-in, and long-term success

Target Audience

While the whole community is ultimately the outreach target, subpopulations of the whole are concerned about different issues and will require different techniques of engagement. The following are some of the key populations:

- local business owners
- environmental advocacy groups

- homeowners
- retirees
- residents who rent their homes
- utilities
- partner agencies
- community-based organizations
- ethnic and cultural groups
- development stakeholders
- vulnerable populations

Key Message and "Identity"

Key messages are the main points to convey to all audiences, from residents to policy makers. These messages are crafted to move the community to action—in this case, to attend public meetings and provide input on GHG emissions reduction and adaptation policies. How these issues relate to the community's response to the potential impacts of climate change is of paramount importance. Key messages should remain simple and straightforward. To achieve this, they can also be divided into primary and secondary messages if necessary.

Important to the completion of the CAP will be communicating these messages to the local and regional community. One highly effective way to do this is by creating an identity or "look and feel" through design choices, slogans, and iconic images, and a corresponding outreach program that promotes the CAP. There is an important distinction to be made between the development of an identity and key messages. An identity typically includes a graphic representation that conveys something permanent about the CAP. Unlike key messages, which are nimble and vary depending on the issue and the target audience, an identity would be set in place to convey one message to every target audience for a lifetime of at least five years.

Publicity

The CAP process should be publicized in a diverse manner to reach the maximum number of community members. This process should begin with the identification of local social and cultural hubs, local events, and familiar communication networks. Press releases, announcements, and supporting materials should be developed to include non-English-speaking populations and to ensure equitable access by all stakeholders in the community. Announcements should be made using the radio, the internet, posters at community gathering points, and displays at local events.

A website or webpage should be developed after identification of the CAP's identity and messaging. The decision to create a stand-alone project site or a webpage integrated into the agency's existing website is based on the agency's existing online tools and resources. If the agency has a known presence online, such as the provision of green or sustainability resource webpages, then the CAP should be integrated into existing resources. If the agency is using the CAP to launch a larger sustainability effort, then a stand-alone website would be beneficial.

Planning Phase

In the planning phase, the public is engaged through several measures to educate them on climate change and solicit their input on the CAP.

Kickoff Event

The CAP should be launched at a high-profile and interactive event. Depending on the community, the launch or kickoff event could include a town hall–style meeting or workshop, a mobile workshop or booth at an established event (i.e., a weekly farmer's market or other regular community event), or an open house. The event should be heavily promoted; media outreach as well as public outreach will be necessary to reach a broad spectrum of stakeholders.

The goal of the kickoff event is to inform community stakeholders of the CAP and the planning process. Objectives should be to provide a meeting approach that balances education, engagement, and input. Tools may include a mix of traditional large-group presentations and non-traditional polling and small-group exercises. The kickoff event should occur early in the project, often in the first two months. The event should provide an overview of the CAP—the planning process and project objectives—as well as any relevant local background information, such as the results of the community-wide greenhouse gas (GHG) inventory or potential impacts/risks of climate change. The event should include opportunities to present information (i.e., to educate or inform) and to receive input. Information should be presented with visual aids, including PowerPoint presentations, boards with graphics, or videos. Opportunities for participants to provide input or engage include real-time polling, question-and-answer sessions, small-group facilitated tables, or information stations. A computer-based polling system may be used to gather anonymous and immediate feedback on existing conditions and future policy direction.

Communications

Organize a speakers' bureau following the kickoff event and in advance of the additional workshops that will enable plan managers to connect with key stakeholder groups on important issues. The speakers' bureau should include development of a PowerPoint presentation on the CAP sectors and process. Speakers should be selected carefully, as they will be the ambassadors of the project. The plan proponent should provide training to all speakers and opportunities for feedback and support.

Develop a stakeholder database and send a minimum of two blast emails (e-blasts) in advance of the kickoff event and all workshops to promote community attendance. Developing the list to include a cross section of stakeholders in the community will be important. The stakeholder list will also require regular updating as people sign up via the website, Facebook, or public meetings. Also send e-blasts to announce website updates, releases of drafts, and public hearings. Stakeholder and media outreach should begin four to six weeks in advance of the kickoff event (and all workshops).

Develop an online or telephone survey to accompany the initial planning process. The survey will alert participants and stakeholders to the CAP planning process and provide an opportunity for stakeholders to offer their level of education about the CAP, climate change, and the contribution of their individual behaviors to GHGs. The survey can also assess willingness to change and priorities for GHG reduction strategies.

The online survey should use a standardized online survey software program. Online surveys are not usually statistically valid; however, they do offer useful information to the planning process. Telephone surveys provide statistically valid results and could be more applicable to high-profile or sensitive topics. The survey should activate concurrent with the public outreach for the kickoff event. The survey should end prior to the development of draft GHG reductions strategies, at least one month prior to the second event.

Workshops / Task Force Meetings / Focus Groups

The second event should focus on measures and strategies and be a more traditional public workshop in which participants engage in a variety of activities where they can provide input and feedback on the GHG reduction measures and/or adaptation strategies. Opportunities for facilitated small-group discussions should be provided for discussion of specific issues. For this workshop, consider providing up to six large-format posters for use during small-group discussions and handouts that summarize the reduction measures by sector.

If resources allow, host separate workshops for GHG reduction measures and adaptation strategies, as each topic can be complex and worthy of dedicated time for information sharing and discussions.

In addition to the main workshops, stakeholder roundtables or mini-workshops provide an opportunity for key stakeholders to provide input on specific sectors in a facilitated setting. The meetings are suitable for up to 20 participants and are most productive when stakeholders are separated by the sectors of the GHG inventory and CAP—energy, land use, transportation, agriculture, business, and climate hazards. For each meeting, participants should receive an information packet including background information and preliminary strategies (or best practices), questions for discussion, and ground rules for participation. The meeting format should include a presentation and facilitated brainstorming and discussion. The objectives and next steps should be clear to all participants.

Consider also holding informal opportunities for engagement, including "coffee and climate" chats in local coffee shops, community centers, or even living rooms. Gatherings in community coffee shops or community facilities can be open to the public, while gatherings in private homes can be by invitation. The goal of these discussions is to have an open and comfortable discussion about the CAP in a nontraditional, drop-in setting. These types of gatherings can attract stakeholders who might not normally attend large events or who prefer a more intimate or one-on-one engagement.

If a task force, steering committee, or commission is convened to support plan preparation, it should meet regularly during the planning phase. All meetings should be noticed publicly. Members of the task force, committee, or commission can also serve as project ambassadors and support speakers' bureaus, workshops, and "coffee and climate" chats. These meetings should provide dedicated time for public comment and provide a detailed agenda and meeting materials in advance of the meeting.

Dispute resolution is needed in cases of disagreement or conflict over an issue. Bring in professional mediators to help the parties resolve their dispute.

For facilitated brainstorming and consensus-building, bring in professional facilitators to help the citizens brainstorm ideas and develop agreements about the best ideas.

A subsequent workshop should review the draft CAP and follow a format similar to those described above. The objective of this workshop is to provide an opportunity for the public to provide input and feedback on the draft CAP before the public hearing process. Opportunities for facilitated small-group discussions should be provided for discussion of specific issues. Again, consider providing up to six large-format posters for use during small-group discussions or setting up information stations and handouts that summarize the reduction measures, GHG reductions, adaptation strategies, and co-benefits by sector.

Adoption and Implementation Phase

The adoption and implementation phase includes the tasks to be completed once a draft of the plan is ready for review and adoption by decision-makers.

Adoption Meetings

Schedule at least two open, noticed public meetings or hearings before the adopting government board or entity. In some cases, a joint study session of the planning commission and city council provides an opportunity for questions and discussions prior to an adoption hearing. Prepare presentations and handouts summarizing the CAP. Provide electronic copies of the CAP online. Ensure that the draft CAP is available at least one month prior to the meetings.

Celebration

After adoption, create a community event to celebrate the CAP, inform the public about actions they can take, and kick off key implementation strategies. The event should be scheduled for a Saturday in a public area and include activities for all ages.

Implementation Activities

Continue to involve the public in decisions about implementation. Develop an annual reporting or review process that informs the public about progress and obtains feedback. Maintaining the participation of key community stakeholders throughout implementation will require a mix of online and traditional information sharing, education, and interactive tools. Online tools allow the agency to report on implementation progress and allow for individual tracking of contributions to the overall target.

Develop or support community-based or peer-to-peer education and networking forums to facilitate implementation of reduction measures that rely on changes in business-as-usual practices.

Additional Resources

Chapter 1: Climate Action Planning

Climate Change Science General Background

Robert Henson, *The Thinking Person's Guide to Climate Change* (Boston: American Meteorological Society, 2014)

This book is an introduction to the science of climate change that is appropriate for citizens and public officials. In addition to the science, it includes a section on what individuals can do to reduce their carbon footprints.

Intergovernmental Panel on Climate Change (IPCC)
    http://www.ipcc.ch/
    The IPCC website provides the organization's various assessment reports covering physical science; impacts, adaptation, and vulnerability; and mitigation. The most recent reports are the 2014 Fifth Assessment Report (AR5) series. The most accessible of these is the AR5 Synthesis Report.

U.S. Global Change Research Program (USGCRP)
    http://www.globalchange.gov/
    The USGCRP website contains numerous reports on the science of climate change, including the National Climate Assessment, a key report for understanding the expected impacts of climate change.

National Oceanic and Atmospheric Administration (NOAA) Climate.gov
    https://www.noaa.gov/climate
    NOAA provides timely and authoritative information about climate. They promote public understanding of climate science and climate-related events through videos, stories, images, and data visualizations; they make common data products and services easy to access and use;

and they provide tools and resources that help people make informed decisions about climate risks, vulnerability, and resilience.

Sustainable Community Planning

Peter Newman, Timothy Beatley, and Heather Boyer, *Resilient Cities: Overcoming Fossil Fuel Dependence*, 2nd ed. (Washington, DC: Island Press, 2017)

Resilient Cities shows that climate change will force cities to become more resilient or face the potential for collapse. It describes creating cities that are not only resilient but striving to become regenerative, and it is organized around the characteristics of a resilient city.

Stephen Wheeler, *Planning for Sustainability: Creating Livable, Equitable and Ecological Communities*, 2nd ed. (New York: Routledge, 2013)

Planning for Sustainability defines and makes the argument for sustainability as a key component of city planning. It is primarily a resource book for ideas on implementing sustainability in planning at several different levels of governance.

Climate Action Organizations

ICLEI USA–Local Governments of Sustainability
    http://icleiusa.org
    This site provides members with tools and resources for climate action, including ClearPath.

C40 Cities
    https://www.c40.org
    C40 is a network of the world's megacities committed to addressing climate change. C40 supports cities to collaborate effectively, share knowledge, and drive meaningful, measurable, and sustainable action on climate change.

Carbon Neutral Cities Alliance
    https://carbonneutralcities.org

Member cities collaborate to share lessons in planning for and implementing deep carbon reductions, as well as opportunities to accelerate best practices in deep decarbonization.

Center for Climate and Energy Solution (C2ES)
https://www.c2es.org
C2ES's mission is to advance strong policy and action to reduce greenhouse gas emissions, promote clean energy, and strengthen resilience to climate impacts.

Global Covenant of Mayors
https://www.globalcovenantofmayors.org
The Global Covenant of Mayors for Climate & Energy is an international alliance of cities and local governments with a shared long-term vision of promoting and supporting voluntary action to combat climate change and move to a low-emission, resilient society.

Urban Sustainability Directors Network
https://www.usdn.org/
The Urban Sustainability Directors Network supports peer exchange and collaboration between local government sustainability leaders to catalyze the creation and implementation of urban sustainability solutions.

Chapter 2: Creating a Framework for Community Action

United Nations Human Settlements Programme (UN-Habitat), *Guiding Principles for City Climate Action Planning, Version 1.0* (Nairobi, Kenya: Author, 2015)
https://unhabitat.org/books/guiding-principles-for-climate-city-planning-action/
This guidance document reviews typical steps in the city-level climate action planning process in light of a proposed set of globally applicable principles.

Chapter 3: Community Engagement and Collaboration

ecoAmerica, *Let's Talk Communities and Climate: Communication Guidance for City and Community Leaders* (Washington, DC: Path to Positive Communities, 2016)

> http://icleiusa.org/wp-content/uploads/2015/06/EcoAmerica-Lets-Talk-Communities-and-Climate.pdf

This guide features research-proven practices for successful climate communication. It includes talking points, counterpoints, dos and don'ts, proven steps to create custom messages, and a model speech.

Don Knapp and Amruta Sudhalkar, *Climate Extremes Communications Guidebook* (ICLEI–Local Governments for Sustainability USA and World Wildlife Fund, 2014)

> http://icleiusa.org/wp-content/uploads/2015/06/ExtremeWeatherGuidebook-0109.pdf

This is a resource to help local governments communicate about weather and climate extremes in the context of climate change.

Center for Research on Environmental Decisions, *The Psychology of Climate Change Communication: A Guide for Scientists, Journalists, Educators, Political Aides, and the Interested Public* (New York: Columbia University, 2009)

> http://guide.cred.columbia.edu

This guide provides information on how to communicate with the general public about climate change. It also addresses small-group participation and behavior change and is useful in communities where understanding of climate change may be low.

International Association for Public Participation (IAP2)

> http://www.iap2.org/

IAP2 is an international membership-based association that promotes and improves the practice of public participation. It provides numerous tools for developing and implementing public participation as well as training and access to the latest research on public participation.

ClimateLab

https://www.universityofcalifornia.edu/climate-lab

ClimateLab provides short videos appropriate for the general public on sustainability, green living, and climate change.

Chapter 4: Greenhouse Gas Emissions Accounting

GHG Inventory Accounting Protocols

Local Government Operations Protocol for the Quantification and Reporting of Greenhouse Gas Emissions Inventories, Version 1.1 (May 2010)

http://www.theclimateregistry.org/tools-resources/reporting -protocols/local-goverment-operations-protocol/

The LGO Protocol was developed with the collaboration of the California Climate Action Registry, the California Air Resources Board, ICLEI–Local Governments for Sustainability, and The Climate Registry.

U.S. Community Protocol for Accounting and Reporting of Greenhouse Gas Emissions, Version 1.1 (July 2013)

http://icleiusa.org/ghg-protocols/

ICLEI–Local Governments for Sustainability developed the U.S. Community Protocol.

Global Protocol for Community-Scale Greenhouse Gas Emission Inventories

https://ghgprotocol.org/greenhouse-gas-protocol-accounting -reporting-standard-cities

The Global Protocol was developed by the World Resources Institute, the C40 Cities Climate Leadership Group, and ICLEI–Local Governments for Sustainability. The Global Protocol is available in both English and Spanish.

GHG Inventory Tools and Software

ClearPath Basic and ClearPath Pro

http://icleiusa.org/clearpath/

ClearPath is an online software platform for GHG inventories and related climate action planning activities developed by ICLEI–Local Governments for Sustainability. ClearPath is free to ICLEI members, regional affiliates such as the Statewide Energy Efficiency Collaborative (SEEC), and their consultants. Local governments in California can use ClearPath at no cost through the SEEC program. Nonmembers can purchase ClearPath Pro annual subscriptions.

CURB—Climate Action for Sustainability

http://www.worldbank.org/en/topic/urbandevelopment/brief/
the-curb-tool-climate-action-for-urban-sustainability

CURB is an Microsoft Excel–based interactive tool for quantifying emissions reduction measures and assessing their cost and feasibility. CURB was developed through collaboration among the World Bank Group, the C40 Cities Climate Leadership Group, Bloomberg Philanthropies, and AECOM Consulting.

California Air Pollution Control Officers Association (CAPCOA), *Quantifying Greenhouse Gas Emissions Measures: A Resource for Local Government to Assess Emission Reductions from Greenhouse Gas Mitigation Measures* (Sacramento, CA: Author, August 2010)

http://www.capcoa.org/

This guide provides detailed quantification methods that can be used throughout California and adapted for use outside of the state. It contains a series of fact sheets on particular types of reduction strategies and accompanying guides on how to use the fact sheets.

Chapter 5: Strategies for Creating Low-Carbon Communities

Rocky Mountain Institute, *The Carbon-Free City Handbook* (Aspen, CO, 2017)

https://www.rmi.org/insight/the-carbon-free-city-handbook/

The handbook describes 22 actions—and associated resources—for cities globally to move toward climate neutrality and see results within a year.

Project Drawdown
https://www.drawdown.org/
Project Drawdown gathers and facilitates a broad coalition of researchers, scientists, graduate students, PhDs, postdocs, policy makers, business leaders, and activists to assemble and present the best available information on climate solutions in order to describe their beneficial financial, social, and environmental impact over the next 30 years.

ICLEI–Local Governments for Sustainability USA Localizing the Paris Agreement (2017)
http://icleiusa.org/localizing-the-paris-agreement/
This guide is intended to help local governments go beyond pledges and move toward action on implementing the Paris Agreement.

California Climate Action Portal Map (CAP-Map)
https://webmaps.arb.ca.gov/capmap/
CAP-Map is an open data tool developed by the California Air Resources Board to promote the sharing of creative ideas to tackle climate change. Users—including those outside of California—can quickly access the climate action planning details of local jurisdictions, including an inventory of climate plans created, greenhouse gas (GHG) inventory information and reduction targets, the local strategies planned to meet these targets, and more. CAP-Map consists of both an interactive web map and a GHG reduction strategy search tool.

Funding Wizard (CCI + CARB)
https://fundingwizard.arb.ca.gov/
The Funding Wizard is a searchable database of grants, rebates, and incentives to help pay for sustainable projects. Non-California communities can filter for federal grants that are available nationwide.

Chapters 6 and 7: Climate Change Vulnerability Assessment and Strategies for Creating Resilient Communities

U.S. Climate Resilience Toolkit
https://toolkit.climate.gov/

The U.S. Climate Resilience Toolkit is a website that provides tools, information, and subject matter expertise to build climate resilience.

U.S. Climate Explorer

https://toolkit.climate.gov/tool/climate-explorer

The Climate Explorer offers downloadable maps, graphs, and data tables of observed and projected temperature, precipitation, and climate-related variables dating back to 1950 and projected out to 2100. Built to accompany the U.S. Climate Resilience Toolkit, the Climate Explorer helps community leaders, business owners, municipal planners, and utility and resource managers understand how environmental conditions may change over the next several decades.

Adaptation Clearinghouse

https://www.adaptationclearinghouse.org/

Content in the Adaptation Clearinghouse is focused on the resources that help policy makers at all levels of government reduce or avoid the impacts of climate change for communities in the United States. The Clearinghouse was developed by the Georgetown Climate Center through the support of the MacArthur Foundation, Rockefeller Foundation, Kresge Foundation, Federal Highway Administration, and other funders. The Georgetown Climate Center works with several organizations, including the Urban Sustainability Directors Network, the U.S. Society of Adaptation Professionals, and the U.S. Environmental Protection Agency, to ensure that the content of the Adaptation Clearinghouse is relevant and that the site is user-friendly for practitioners working in the field of adaptation.

California Adaptation Planning Guide

http://resources.ca.gov/climate/safeguarding/local-action/

The Adaptation Planning Guide (APG) provides guidance to support regional and local communities in proactively addressing the unavoidable consequences of climate change. It was developed cooperatively by the California Natural Resources Agency and the California Emergency Management Agency, with support from California Polytechnic State University–San Luis Obispo, and with funding through the Federal Emergency Management Agency and the

California Energy Commission. The APG provides a step-by-step process for local and regional climate vulnerability assessment and adaptation strategy development. Usage of the APG is meant to allow for flexibility in the commitment of time, money, and effort to suit the needs of the community.

Climate Adaptation Knowledge Exchange (CAKE)
https://www.cakex.org/
CAKE, managed by EcoAdapt, provides case studies, a virtual library, tools, and community forums.

ICLEI Canada—Local Governments for Sustainability "Adaptation Methodology"
http://www.icleicanada.org/resources/item/79-adaptation-methodology
ICLEI provides a straightforward approach to adaptation planning using a five-milestone framework.

California Adaptation Clearinghouse
https://resilientca.org/
The California Adaptation Clearinghouse allows users to navigate a searchable database of adaptation and resilience resources that have been organized by climate impact, topic, and region. The types of resources in the Clearinghouse include, but are not limited to, assessments; plans or strategies; communication or educational materials; planning and/or policy guidance; data, tools, and research; and case studies, projects, or examples. These can be helpful resources to users inside and outside of California.

Chapter 8: Pathways to Successful Implementation

Eugene Bardach, *A Practical Guide for Policy Analysis: The Eightfold Path to More Effective Problem Solving* (Washington, DC: CQ Press, 2015)
The book provides a basic, straightforward approach to evaluating proposed public policies. It can be used to inform the development and application of evaluation criteria to emissions reduction and climate adaptation policies.

Notes

Chapter 1: Climate Action Planning

1. "27 Cities Have Reached Peak Greenhouse Gas Emissions Whilst Populations Increase and Economies Grow," Global Climate Action Summit, September 13, 2018, https://www.globalclimateactionsummit.org/27-cities-have-reached-peak/.

2. U.S. Global Change Research Program, *Fourth National Climate Assessment* (Washington, DC: Author, 2018), https://nca2018.globalchange.gov.

3. "27 Cities Have Reached Peak Greenhouse Gas Emissions Whilst Populations Increase and Economies Grow," Global Climate Action Summit, September 13, 2018, https://www.globalclimateactionsummit.org/27-cities-have-reached-peak/.

4. Ibid.

5. "Looking Forward: Chief Resilience Officers Share Their Hopes for the Next 5 Years," 100 Resilient Cities, May 15, 2018, http://www.100resilientcities.org/looking-forward-chief-resilience-officers-share-their-hopes-for-the-next-5-years/.

6. "Five Milestones of Emissions Management," ICLEI–Local Governments for Sustainability, http://icleiusa.org/programs/emissions-management/5-milestones/.

7. Compiled from Natural Capital Solutions, *Climate Protection Manual for Cities* (Eldorado Springs, CO: Author, 2007); American Planning Association, *Policy Guide on Planning and Climate Change* (Washington, DC: Author, 2008); National Wildlife Federation, *Guide to Climate Action Planning: Pathways to a Low-Carbon Campus* (Reston, VA: Author, 2008); International Council for Local Environmental Initiatives, *U.S. Mayors' Climate Protection Agreement: Climate Action Handbook*, http://www.seattle.gov/climate/docs/ClimateActionHandbook.pdf; International Council for Local Environmental Initiatives, *ICLEI Climate Program*, http://www.iclei.org/index.php?id=800.

8. "Greenhouse Gas Emissions Inventory and Climate Action Plan," City of Hoboken, New Jersey, https://www.hobokennj.gov/resources/greenhouse-gas-emissions-inventory-and-climate-action-plan.

9. The Global Protocol for Community-Scale Greenhouse Gas Emission Inventories, https://ghgprotocol.org/greenhouse-gas-protocol-accounting-reporting-standard-cities.

10. U.S. Community Protocol for Accounting and Reporting of Greenhouse Gas Emissions, http://icleiusa.org/ghg-protocols/.

11. Local Government Operations Protocol (LGO Protocol), http://icleiusa.org/ghg-protocols/.

12. City of Cincinnati, *Climate Protection Action Plan: The Green Cincinnati Plan* (Cincinnati, OH: Office of Environmental Quality, 2008).

13. New York Climate Change Science Clearinghouse, https://nyclimatescience.org.

14. California Adaptation Clearinghouse, https://resilientca.org/.

15. California Adaptation Planning Guide, http://resources.ca.gov/climate/safeguarding/local-action/.

16. Stephen M. Wheeler, "State and Municipal Climate Change Plans: The First Generation," *Journal of the American Planning Association* 74, no. 4 (2008): 481–96; American Planning Association, *Policy Guide on Planning and Climate Change* (Washington, DC: Author, 2008); International Council for Local Environmental Initiatives, *U.S. Mayors' Climate Protection Agreement: Climate Action Handbook*, http://www.seattle.gov/climate/docs/ClimateActionHandbook.pdf.

17. "Knoxville—Knoxville Extreme Energy Makeover," C40 Cities, https://www.c40.org/awards/2017-awards/profiles/130.

18. "Organization," Intergovernmental Panel on Climate Change, http://www.ipcc.ch/organization/organization.htm.

19. Intergovernmental Panel on Climate Change, *Climate Change 2014: Synthesis Report Summary for Policymakers, Fifth Assessment Report of the Intergovernmental Panel on Climate Change*, https://www.ipcc.ch/site/assets/uploads/2018/02/AR5_SYR_FINAL_SPM.pdf.

20. U.S. Global Change Research Program, *Impacts, Risks, and Adaptation in the United States: Fourth National Climate Assessment*, vol. 2, ed. D. R. Reidmiller, C. W. Avery, D. R. Easterling, K. E. Kunkel, K. L. M. Lewis, T. K. Maycock, and B. C. Stewart (Washington, DC: Author, 2018), 1515, doi: 10.7930/NCA4.2018.

21. "What Will Climate Change Mean to Alaska?," State of Alaska, http://www.climatechange.alaska.gov/cc-ak.htm.

22. State of South Carolina, Department of Natural Resources, *Climate Change Impacts to Natural Resources in South Carolina*, http://www.dnr.sc.gov/pubs/CCINatResReport.pdf.

23. Fredrich Kahrl and David Roland-Holst, *California Climate Risk and Response, Research Paper No. 08102801* (Berkeley: University of California, Department of Agricultural and Resource Economics, 2008).

24. "Climate Change," Miami-Dade County, https://www.miamidade.gov/green/climate-change.asp.

25. City of Aspen, *Canary Initiative: Climate Action Plan* (2007).

26. United Nations Framework Convention on Climate Change, *National Greenhouse Gas Inventory Data for the Period 1990–2007* (2009), http://unfccc.int/resource/docs/2009/sbi/eng/12.pdf.

27. See various reports from C2ES at https://www.c2es.org/.

28. Peter Newman, Timothy Beatley, and Heather Boyer, *Resilient Cities: Responding to Peak Oil and Climate Change* (Washington, DC: Island Press, 2009).

29. Lawrence D. Frank, Sarah Kavage, and Bruce Appleyard, "The Urban Form and Climate Change Gamble," *Planning* 73, no. 8 (2007): 18–23.

30. Stephen Pacala and Robert Socolow, "Stabilization Wedges: Solving the Climate Problem for the Next 50 Years with Current Technologies," *Science* 305, no. 5686 (2004): 968–72.

31. The source for this case is the City of Des Moines "Sustainability Efforts" website, https://www.dmgov.org/Departments/CityManager/Pages/SustainabilityEfforts.aspx.

32. The sources for this case include the City of Atlanta Office of Resilience website, https://www.atlantaga.gov/government/mayor-s-office/executive-offices/office-of-resilience; City of Atlanta, *Resilient Atlanta* (2017), http://www.100resilientcities.org/wp-content/uploads/2017/11/Atlanta-Resilience-Strategy-PDF-v2.pdf; City of Atlanta, *Clean Energy Atlanta: A Vision for a 100% Clean Future* (2018), https://atlantabuildingefficiency.com/clean-energy-atlanta-a-vision-for-a-100-clean-energy-future/; City of Atlanta, Atlanta Climate Action Plan (2015), https://atlantaclimateactionplan.wordpress.com.

33. City of Atlanta, *Resilient Atlanta* (2017), http://www.100resilientcities.org/wp-content/uploads/2017/11/Atlanta-Resilience-Strategy-PDF-v2.pdf.

34. The sources for this case include the authors' personal knowledge and "Sustainability," City of San Luis Obispo, https://www.slocity.org/government/department-directory/community-development/sustainability.

35. The sources for this case include "Sea Level Rise Strategy," City of Charleston, https://www.charleston-sc.gov/index.aspx?NID=1432; "Green Plan," City of Charleston, https://www.charleston-sc.gov/index.aspx?NID=904.

36. City of Charleston, *Charleston Green Plan* (2010), https://www.charleston-sc.gov/DocumentCenter/View/1458.

Chapter 2: Creating a Framework for Community Action

1. J. Carlson, J. Cooper, M. Donahue, M. Neale, and A. Ragland, "City of Detroit Greenhouse Gas Inventory: An Analysis of Citywide and Municipal Emissions for 2011 and 2012" (master's thesis, University of Michigan, Ann Arbor, 2014), 60, http://css.umich.edu/publication/city-detroit-greenhouse-gas-inventory-analysis-citywide-and-municipal-emissions-2011-and.

2. "What Is the RCAP?," Southeast Florida Regional Compact (2019), http://www.southeastfloridaclimatecompact.org/about-us/what-is-the-rcap/.

3. U.S. Environmental Protection Agency, *Inventory of U.S. Greenhouse Gas Emissions and Sinks: 1990–2016* (Washington, DC: Author, 2018), 655, https://www.epa.gov/sites/production/files/2018-01/documents/2018_complete_report.pdf.

Chapter 3: Community Engagement and Collaboration

1. Pew Partnership for Civic Change, *Ready, Willing, and Able: Citizens Working for Change* (Charlottesville, VA: Author, 2000), http://www.pew-partnership.org/.

2. Public opinion statements based on the following surveys: "Yale Climate Opinion Maps 2018," Yale Program on Climate Change Communication (2018), http://climatecommunication.yale.edu/visualizations-data/ycom-us-2018/; "Majorities See Government Efforts to Protect the Environment as Insufficient," Pew Research Center, http://www.pewinternet.org/2018/05/14/majorities-see-government-efforts-to-protect-the-environment-as-insufficient/; "Global Warming Age Gap: Younger Americans Most Worried," Gallup, https://news.gallup.com/poll/234314/global-warming-age-gap-younger-americans-worried.aspx.

3. E. Maibach, C. Roser-Renouf, and A. Leiserowitz, *Global Warming's Six Americas 2009: An Audience Segmentation Analysis* (New Haven, CT: Yale Project on Climate Change and the George Mason University Center for Climate Change Communication, 2009).

4. Samuel D. Brody, David R. Godschalk, and Raymond J. Burby, "Mandating Citizen Participation in Plan Making: Six Strategic Planning Choices," *Journal of the American Planning Association* 69, no. 3 (2003): 245–64.

5. U.S. Department of Energy, *How to Design a Public Participation Program* (Washington, DC: Author, n.d.).

6. Jeffrey M. Berry, Kent E. Portney, and Ken Thomson, *The Rebirth of Urban Democracy* (Washington, DC: Brookings Institution Press, 1993), 55.

7. Sherry Arnstein, "A Ladder of Citizen Participation," *Journal of the American Institute of Planners* 35, no. 4 (1969): 216–24.

8. PublicVoice maintains a good list here: https://www.publicvoice.co.nz/lets-get -digital-52-tools-for-online-public-engagement/.

Chapter 4: Greenhouse Gas Emissions Accounting

1. To help build capacity in local-level climate planning, the World Bank and global partners developed the City Climate Planner program. The program is an overarching name to represent the distinct scopes, or professional areas of practice, that aim to increase the global talent base of climate planning professionals. The areas of practice will include at minimum the following: urban greenhouse gas inventory specialist, city climate action planning specialist (mitigation), city climate action planning specialist (adaptation and resilience), and possibly additional scopes in other areas to be determined. See https://cityclimateplanner.org.

2. In addition to community-level GHG inventories, there are national, state, regional, corporate, facility, project, and product (i.e., life cycle) GHG inventories. These types of inventories are not discussed in this chapter.

3. ICLEI is the leading network of cities, towns, and regions committed to building a sustainable future. See http://icleiusa.org.

4. The Global Covenant of Mayors for Climate & Energy is an international alliance of cities and local governments with a shared long-term vision of promoting and supporting voluntary action to combat climate change and move to a low-emission, resilient society. See https://www.globalcovenantofmayors.org.

5. U.S. Environmental Protection Agency State and Local Climate and Energy Program, *From Inventory to Action: Putting Greenhouse Gas Inventories to Work*, EPA 430-F-09-002 (Washington, DC: Author, 2009).

6. California Air Resources Board, California Climate Action Registry, ICLEI–Local Governments for Sustainability, and The Climate Registry, *Local Government Operations Protocol for the Quantification and Reporting of Greenhouse Gas Emissions Inventories Version 1.1* (May 2010).

7. Access to all listed protocols is available through ICLEI USA (http://icleiusa .org/ghg-protocols).

8. The California Climate Registry and The Climate Registry protocols are not discussed separately, as their general reporting protocol for governments is the Local Government Operations Protocol.

9. The California Climate Action Registry was a program of the Climate Action Reserve and served as a voluntary greenhouse gas (GHG) registry to protect and promote early actions to reduce GHG emissions by organizations. The California Climate

Action Registry accepted its last emissions inventory reports and officially closed in December 2010.

10. Established in 2007, The Climate Registry (TCR) was formed to continue the work of the California Climate Action Registry. TCR is a nonprofit collaboration among North American states, provinces, territories, and Native Sovereign Nations that sets consistent and transparent standards to measure, report, and verify greenhouse gas emissions into a single registry.

11. World Resources Institute, C40 Cities Climate Leadership Group, and ICLEI–Local Governments for Sustainability, *Global Protocol for Community-Scale Greenhouse Gas Emission Inventories* (2014), https://ghgprotocol.org/greenhouse-gas -protocol-accounting-reporting-standard-cities.

12. California Air Resources Board, California Climate Action Registry, ICLEI–Local Governments for Sustainability, and The Climate Registry, *Local Government Operations Protocol for the Quantification and Reporting of Greenhouse Gas Emissions Inventories Version 1.1* (May 2010).

13. Portions of this section were modified from Michael R. Boswell, Adrienne I. Greve, and Tammy L. Seale, "An Assessment of the Link between Greenhouse Gas Emissions Inventories and Climate Action Plans," *Journal of the American Planning Association* 76, no. 4 (2010): 451–62.

14. United Nations, *Paris Agreement* (2015), https://unfccc.int/process-and-meetings/ the-paris-agreement/the-paris-agreement.

15. Johan Rockstrom, Will Steffen, Kevin Noone, Asa Persson, F. Stuart Chapin, Eric F. Lambin, Timothy M. Lenton, et al., "A Safe Operating Space for Humanity," *Nature* 461, no. 7263 (2009): 472–75.

16. CO2Now.org, accessed July 31, 2010, http://www.co2now.org/.

17. Malte Meinshausen, Nicolai Meinshausen, William Hare, Sarah C. B. Raper, Katja Frieler, Reto Knutti, David J. Frame, and Myles R. Allen, "Greenhouse-Gas Emission Targets for Limiting Global Warming to 2°C," *Nature* 458, no. 7242 (April 30, 2009): 1158–62; Intergovernmental Panel on Climate Change, *Climate Change 2007: Impacts, Adaptation and Vulnerability. Contribution of Working Group II to the Fourth Assessment Report of the Intergovernmental Panel on Climate Change*, ed. M. L. Parry, O. F. Canziani, J. P. Palutikof, P. J. van der Linden, and C. E. Hanson (Cambridge: Cambridge University Press, 2007), 776.

18. The Climate Group, *Under2Coalition*, https://www.under2coalition.org.

19. For examples of state and international targets, see pewclimate.org/what_s _being_done/targets.

20. California Air Resources Board, *California's 2017 Climate Change Scoping Plan* (2017), https://www.arb.ca.gov/cc/scopingplan/scoping_plan_2017.pdf.

21. Intergovernmental Panel on Climate Change, *Global Warming of 1.5°C*, special report (2018), https://www.ipcc.ch/sr15/.

22. "The CURB Tool: Climate Action for Urban Sustainability," World Bank, http://www.worldbank.org/en/topic/urbandevelopment/brief/the-curb-tool-climate -action-for-urban-sustainability.

23. California Air Pollution Control Officers Association (CAPCOA), *Quantifying Greenhouse Gas Emissions Measures: A Resource for Local Government to Assess Emission*

Reductions from Greenhouse Gas Mitigation Measures (Sacramento, CA: Author, August 2010), 3.

24. Ibid., 33–34.

25. Ibid., 3.

26. Thomas R. Karl, Jerry M. Melillo, and Thomas C. Peterson, eds., *Global Climate Change Impacts in the United States* (New York: Cambridge University Press, 2009).

27. California produces periodic scientific assessments on the potential impacts of climate change in California and reports potential adaptation responses. Required by Executive Order #S-03-05, these assessments influence legislation and inform policy makers. See https://www.climatechange.ca.gov/climate_action_team/reports/climate_assessments.html.

Chapter 5: Strategies for Creating Low-Carbon Communities

1. Sustainable Development Solutions Network and the Institute for Sustainable Development and International Relations, *Pathways to Deep Decarbonization* (2015), http://deepdecarbonization.org.

2. County of Santa Barbara, Energy and Climate Action Plan (2015), https://www.countyofsb.org/csd/asset.c/173.

3. "Inventory of U.S. Greenhouse Gas Emissions and Sinks," U.S. Environmental Protection Agency, https://www.epa.gov/ghgemissions/inventory-us-greenhouse-gas-emissions-and-sinks.

4. Cambridge Systematics, *Moving Cooler: An Analysis of Transportation Strategies for Reducing Greenhouse Gas Emissions* (2009), http://www.movingcooler.info/.

5. Ibid., 17.

6. Ibid., 2.

7. For additional information, see the National Complete Streets Coalition at https://smartgrowthamerica.org/program/national-complete-streets-coalition/.

8. Regina R. Clewlow and Gouri S. Mishra, *Disruptive Transportation: The Adoption, Utilization, and Impacts of Ride-Hailing in the United States*, Institute of Transportation Studies, University of California, Davis, Research Report UCD-ITS-RR-17-07 (2017).

9. A. Henao and W. E. Marshall, "The Impact of Ride-Hailing on Vehicle Miles Traveled," *Transportation* 45, no. 5 (2018): https://doi.org/10.1007/s11116-018-9923-2.

10. R. Lal, "Soil Carbon Sequestration Impacts on Global Climate Change and Food Security," *Science* 304 (2004): 1623–27.

11. U.S. Environmental Protection Agency, https://www.epa.gov/ghgemissions/sources-greenhouse-gas-emissions.

12. H. Steinfeld, P. Gerber, T. Wassenaar, V. Castel, M. Rosales, and C. de Haan, *Livestock's Long Shadow: Environmental Issues and Options* (Rome: Food and Agriculture Organization of the United Nations, 2006), 26.

13. Ibid.

14. Ibid.

15. See https://sfenvironment.org/carbon-fund.

16. See https://energydistrict.org/services/carbon-offsets/.

Chapter 6: Climate Change Vulnerability Assessment

1. U.S. Global Change Research Program, *Impacts, Risks, and Adaptation in the United States: Fourth National Climate Assessment*, vol. 2, ed. D. R. Reidmiller, C. W. Avery, D. R. Easterling, K. E. Kunkel, K. L. M. Lewis, T. K. Maycock, and B. C. Stewart (Washington, DC: Author, 2018), 1515, doi: 10.7930/NCA4.2018.

2. Intergovernmental Panel on Climate Change, *Climate Change 2014: Impacts, Adaptation, and Vulnerability. Contribution of Working Group II to the Fifth Assessment Report of the Intergovernmental Panel on Climate Change*, ed. C. B. Field, V. R. Barros, D. J. Dokken, K. J. Mach, M. D. Mastrandrea, T. E. Bilir, M. Chatterjee, K. L. Ebi, Y. O. Estrada, R. C. Genova, B. Girma, E. S. Kissel, A. N. Levy, S. MacCracken, P. R. Mastrandrea, and L. L. White (Geneva, Switzerland: Author, 2014).

3. California Natural Resources Agency, *Safeguarding California Plan: 2018 Update—California's Climate Adaptation Strategy* (2018), accessed on December 1, 2018, http://resources.ca.gov/docs/climate/safeguarding/update2018/safeguarding-california-plan-2018-update.pdf.

4. National Atmospheric and Oceanic Administration, *National Coastal Population Report—Population Trends from 1970 to 2020* (2013), accessed on December 1, 2018, https://aamboceanservice.blob.core.windows.net/oceanservice-prod/facts/coastal-population-report.pdf.

5. J. A. Ekstrom and S. C. Moser, *Vulnerability and Adaptation to Sea-Level Rise: An Assessment for the City of Hermosa Beach* (Hermosa Beach, CA: City of Hermosa Beach, 2014), 88, http://www.hermosabch.org/modules/showdocument.aspx?documentid=9181.

6. "Japan Heatwave Declared Natural Disaster as Death Toll Mounts," BBC World News, July 24, 2018, https://www.bbc.com/news/world-asia-44935152.

7. "Deaths Rose 650 above Average during UK Heatwave—with Older People Most at Risk," *Guardian*, August 3, 2018, https://www.theguardian.com/society/2018/aug/03/deaths-rose-650-above-average-during-uk-heatwave-with-older-people-most-at-risk.

8. "Estimated 70 Deaths Linked to Canada's Heat Wave," *NPR*, July 10, 2018, https://www.npr.org/2018/07/10/627687639/estimated-70-deaths-linked-to-canadas-heat-wave.

9. "Ground Level Ozone Pollution," U.S. Environmental Protection Agency, accessed on December 1, 2018, https://www.epa.gov/ground-level-ozone-pollution.

10. California Energy Commission, *Cal-Adapt* (2018), http://cal-adapt.org/.

11. Los Angeles County Metropolitan Transportation Authority, *Limited English Proficiency Plan 4 Factor Analysis* (2012), 38, http://media.metro.net/projects_studies/sustainability/images/Climate_Action_Plan.pdf.

Chapter 7: Strategies for Creating Resilient Communities

1. Federal Emergency Management Agency, *Local Mitigation Planning Handbook* (Washington, DC: Author, 2013), 162.

2. U.S. Congressional Budget Office, *Potential Cost Savings from the Pre-Disaster Mitigation Program*, Pub. No. 2926 (2007), 20; Multihazard Mitigation Council, *Natural Hazard Mitigation Saves 2017 Interim Report: An Independent Study*, principal investigator K. Porter; coprincipal investigators C. Scawthorn, N. Dash, J. Santos; investigators M. Eguchi, S. Ghosh, C. Huyck, M. Isteita, K. Mickey, T.

Rashed; and director, MMC, P. Schneider (Washington, DC: National Institute of Building Sciences, 2017).

3. B. Smit, I. Burton, R. J. T. Klein, and J. Wandel, "An Anatomy of Adaptation to Climate Change and Variability," *Climatic Change* 45 (2000): 223–51; R. de Loe, R. Kreutzwiser, and L. Moraru, "Adaptation Option for the Near Term: Climate Change and the Canadian Water Sector," *Global Environmental Change* 11 (2001): 231–45; B. Smit and J Wandel, "Adaptation, Adaptive Capacity and Vulnerability," *Global Environmental Change* 16 (2006): 282–92.

4. "What Is a Pathways Approach to Adaptation?," Coast Adapt, National Climate Change Adaptation Research Facility (2017), accessed on December 5, 2018, https://coastadapt.com.au/pathways-approach.

5. "Ground-Level Ozone Basics," U.S. Environmental Protection Agency (2018), accessed on December 5, 2018, https://www.epa.gov/ground-level-ozone-pollution/ground-level-ozone-basics.

6. A. Kingsborough, E. Borgomeo, and J. W. Hall, "Adaptation Pathways in Practice: Mapping Options and Trade-Offs for London's Water Resources," *Sustainable Cities and Society* 27 (2016): 386–97.

7. B. Smit, I. Burton, R. J. T. Klein, and J. Wandel, "An Anatomy of Adaptation to Climate Change and Variability," *Climatic Change* 45 (2000): 223–51; J. B. Smith, J. M. Vogel, and J. E. Cromwell III, "An Architecture for Government Action on Adaptation to Climate Change: An Editorial Comment," *Climate Change* 95 (2009): 53–61.

8. California Emergency Management Agency and California Department of Natural Resources, *California Adaptation Planning Guide—Planning for Adaptive Communities* (Sacramento, CA: Author, 2012), 60.

9. New York City, "Appendix G," in *New York City Building Code* (2008), accessed on December 15, 2018, https://www2.iccsafe.org/states/newyorkcity/Building/PDFs/Appendix20G_Flood-Resistant%20Construction.pdf.

10. New York City, *PlaNYC: A Stronger, More Resilient New York* (New York: Author, 2013), 445, http://s-media.nyc.gov/agencies/sirr/SIRR_singles_Lo_res.pdf.

Chapter 8: Pathways to Successful Implementation

1. 100 Resilient Cities, "100 Resilient Cities" (2019), http://www.100resilientcities.org/our-impact/.

2. Maggie Hernandez, "Fort Lauderdale Creates Groundbreaking Climate Training for Employees," Dream in Green, July 14, 2015, http://dreamingreen.org/fort-lauderdale-conducts-groundbreaking-climate-training-for-employees/.

3. Brent Toderian (@BrentToderian), Twitter, February 28, 2016, 7:37 p.m., https://twitter.com/BrentToderian/status/704148379182366720.

4. City of Cincinnati, *2018 Green Cincinnati Plan* (2018).

5. City of Atlanta, *Clean Energy Atlanta* (2019), http://www.100atl.com/.

6. City of San Mateo, CAP Progress Updates, https://www.cityofsanmateo.org/3962/CAP-Progress-Updates.

Chapter 9: Communities Leading the Way

1. Sources for this case include the identified planning documents and an interview with Michael Armstrong, senior sustainability manager, City of Portland Office of Sustainability.

2. T. Wheeler, "Portland Will Keep Paving the Way for Action on Climate Change," *Oregonian*, October 3, 2018, accessed on December 5, 2018, https://www.oregonlive.com/opinion/index.ssf/2018/10/ted_wheeler_portland_will_keep.html.

3. "Portland's Green Dividend," CEO for Cities, http://www.ceosforcities.org/files/PGD%20FINAL.pdf.

4. City of Portland Bureau of Planning and Sustainability and Multnomah County Sustainability Program, *City of Portland and Multnomah County Climate Action Plan* (2009), 39, http://www.portlandonline.com/bps/index.cfm?c=49989&a=268612.

5. Sources for the case include the identified planning documents, the City of Evanston climate change website (https://www.cityofevanston.org/about-evanston/sustainability/climate-change), and interviews with the mayor of Evanston, Elizabeth Tisdahl; Paige K. Finnegan, chief operating officer at e-One, LLC, and cochair of the Evanston environment board; and Dr. Stephen A. Perkins, senior vice president of the Center for Neighborhood Technology.

6. "Evanston Targets 100 Percent Renewable Electricity," City of Evanston, December 11, 2018, https://www.cityofevanston.org/Home/Components/News/News/3219/17.

7. Ibid.

8. Sources for the case include the identified planning documents and the City of Boulder's climate program website (https://bouldercolorado.gov/climate/).

9. City of Boulder, Climate Action Tax (2018), accessed on December 5, 2018 https://bouldercolorado.gov/climate/climate-action-plan-cap-tax.

10. City of Boulder, *SmartRegs Guidebook + The Rental License Handbook* (Boulder, CO: Author, 2011), 68, https://www-static.bouldercolorado.gov/docs/smartregs-guidebook-rental-license-handbook-1-201601111513.pdf.

11. City of Boulder, *SmartRegs* (2019), accessed on January 3, 2019, https://bouldercolorado.gov/plan-develop/smartregs.

12. City of Boulder, Energy Conservation Code (Boulder, CO: Author, 2017), 97, accessed on January 3, 2019, https://www-static.bouldercolorado.gov/docs/2017_City_of_Boulder_Energy_Conservation_Code_2nd-1-201711151002.pdf?_ga=2.101686401.1214223683.1546708670-1442822913.1546614853.

13. City of Boulder, *Boulder Marijuana Facility Energy Requirements* (2019), accessed on January 3, 2019, https://bouldercolorado.gov/planning/boulder-marijuana-facility-energy-requirements.

14. City of Boulder, *Universal Zero Waste Ordinance* (2019), accessed on January 3, 2019, https://bouldercolorado.gov/zero-waste/universal-zero-waste-ordinance.

15. S. Castle, "Boulder Eyes New Car Fee to Combat Climate Change," *Daily Camera—Boulder News*, October 23, 2018, accessed on December 5, 2018, http://www.dailycamera.com/news/boulder/ci_32226398/boulder-eyes-new-car-fee-combat-climate-change.

16. City of Boulder, *Boulder's Climate Commitment* (Boulder, CO: Author, 2017), 60.

17. Sources for the case include the identified planning documents and an interview with Lindsay Baxter, the City of Pittsburgh sustainability coordinator.

18. City of Pittsburgh, *City of Pittsburgh Climate Action Plan Version 3.0* (Pittsburgh, PA: Author, 2018), 81, https://pittsburgh.legistar.com/View.ashx?M=F&ID=5817176 &GUID=075303EF-B062-46D5-A5EE-68A209C2B01A.

19. City of Pittsburgh, *Resilient Pittsburgh*, accessed January 2019, http://pittsburghpa .gov/dcp/resilientpgh.

20. Tribune Staff Wire Reports, "Philly among 4 Cities to Get Funding for Climate Change Efforts," *Philadelphia Tribune*, October 22, 2018, http://www.phillytrib .com/news/philly-among-cities-to-get-funding-for-climate-change-efforts/ article_f7669456-d960-5d9a-b975-00783a57cc20.html.

21. City of Pittsburgh, *City of Pittsburgh Climate Action Plan Version 3.0* (Pittsburgh, PA: Author, 2018), 81, https://pittsburgh.legistar.com/View.ashx?M=F&ID=5817176 &GUID=075303EF-B062-46D5-A5EE-68A209C2B01A.

22. Sources for this case include the identified planning documents.

23. The City of San Mateo's sustainability plans and policies are available online at https://www.cityofsanmateo.org/2738/Plans-and-Policies.

24. Accessed from a presentation and administrative report provided by city staff and their consultant team of PlaceWorks and DNV GL to the City of San Mateo Sustainability Commission during its regularly scheduled meeting on January 9, 2019, and a follow-up memo from the City to staff and the commission on January 15, 2019.

25. See the City of San Mateo website, https://www.cityofsanmateo.org/709/ Sustainability.

26. In 2018, the sustainability commission and the public works commission merged to become the sustainability and infrastructure commission.

27. The California Energy Commission (CEC) requires that a cost-effectiveness study be conducted and filed in the case of local amendments to the California Energy Code. It is required that the City demonstrate to the CEC, using a cost-effectiveness study, that the amendments to the code are financially responsible and do not present an unreasonable burden to nonresidential and residential applicants. A cost-effectiveness study is not required for amendments to the green building code.

28. To be EV-ready is to have adequate electrical capacity and conduits installed to allow for EV charger installations.

29. New single-family buildings are required to have a minimum 1 kilowatt photovoltaic system, new multifamily buildings containing 3 to 16 units are required to have a minimum 2 kilowatt photovoltaic system, and new multifamily buildings containing 17 or more units are required to have a minimum 3 kilowatt photovoltaic system. New nonresidential buildings of less than 10,000 square feet are required to have a minimum 3 kilowatt photovoltaic system, and new nonresidential buildings 10,000 square feet or larger are required to have a minimum 5 kilowatt photovoltaic system. As an alternative, all projects may provide a solar hot water (solar thermal) system with a minimum collector area of 40 square feet.

30. Miami-Dade County, *A Long Term CO_2 Reduction Plan for Miami-Dade County, Florida* (December 2006), http://www.miamidade.gov/derm/library/air_quality/CO2 _Reduction_Final_Report.pdf.

31. Miami-Dade County, *GreenPrint: Our Design for a Sustainable Future* (2010), https://www.miamidade.gov/green/climate-change.asp.

32. Southeast Florida Regional Climate Change Compact, http://www.southeast floridaclimatecompact.org/about-us/what-is-the-compact/.

33. Miami-Dade County, *Mayor's Response to County Commission's Resolutions on Sea Level Rise* (2016), 14, https://www.miamidade.gov/green/library/sea-level-rise -executive-summary.pdf.

34. Sources for this case include the identified planning documents.

35. Global Covenant of Mayors for Climate & Energy, https://www.globalcovenant ofmayors.org.

36. C40 Cities, *27 C40 Cities Have Peaked Their Emissions* (n.d.), https://www.c40 .org/press_releases/27-cities-have-reached-peak-greenhouse-gas-emissions-whilst -populations-increase-and-economies-grow.

37. City of Copenhagen, *CPH 2025 Climate Plan* (2012), https://urbandevelopment cph.kk.dk/artikel/cph-2025-climate-plan.

38. Ibid.

39. Ibid.

Chapter 10: Time to Act

1. "Global Climate Action: NAZCA," United Nations Framework Convention on Climate Change, http://climateaction.unfccc.int.

Appendix A: Climate Science

1. "Organization," Intergovernmental Panel on Climate Change, http://www.ipcc .ch/organization/organization.htm.

2. "Program Overview," U.S. Global Change Research Program, http://www.global change.gov/about.

3. Intergovernmental Panel on Climate Change, "Summary for Policy Makers," in *Climate Change 2007: The Physical Science Basis. Contribution of Working Group I to the Fourth Assessment Report of the Intergovernmental Panel on Climate Change*, ed. S. Solomon, D. Qin, M. Manning, Z. Chen, M. Marquis, K. B. Averyt, M. Tignor, and H. L. Miller (Cambridge: Cambridge University Press, 2007), 5.

4. Ibid.

5. "Climate Change Indicators in the United States," U.S. Environmental Protection Agency, https://www.epa.gov/climate-indicators.

6. U.S. Environmental Protection Agency, *Climate Change Indicators in the United States*, fact sheet, EPA 430-F-16-071 (Washington, DC: Author, October 2016), https://www.epa.gov/sites/production/files/2016-11/documents/climate-indicators -2016-fact-sheet.pdf.

7. U.S. Environmental Protection Agency, *Inventory of U.S. Greenhouse Gas Emissions and Sinks: 1990–2016*, EPA 430-R-18-003 (Washington, DC: Author, 2018).

8. S. Solomon, D. Qin, M. Manning, R. B. Alley, T. Berntsen, N. L. Bindoff, Z. Chen, A. Chidthaisong, J. M. Gregory, G. C. Hegerl, M. Heimann, B. Hewitson, B. J. Hoskins, F. Joos, J. Jouzel, V. Kattsov, U. Lohmann, T. Matsuno, M. Molina, N. Nicholls, J. Overpeck, G. Raga, V. Ramaswamy, J. Ren, M. Rusticucci, R. Somerville,

T. F. Stocker, P. Whetton, R. A. Wood, and D. Wratt, "Technical Summary," in *Climate Change 2007: The Physical Science Basis. Contribution of Working Group I to the Fourth Assessment Report of the Intergovernmental Panel on Climate Change*, ed. S. Solomon, D. Qin, M. Manning, Z. Chen, M. Marquis, K. B. Averyt, M. Tignor, and H. L. Miller (Cambridge: Cambridge University Press, 2007).

9. Intergovernmental Panel on Climate Change, *Climate Change 2014: Synthesis Report. Contribution of Working Groups I, II and III to the Fifth Assessment Report of the Intergovernmental Panel on Climate Change*, ed. core writing team, R. K. Pachauri, and L. A. Meyer (Geneva, Switzerland: Author, 2014), 21.

10. U.S. Environmental Protection Agency, *Inventory of U.S. Greenhouse Gas Emissions and Sinks: 1990–2016*, EPA 430-R-18-003 (Washington, DC: Author, 2018).

11. Summary of impacts and consequences is based on the following reports: Thomas R. Karl, Jerry M. Melillo, and Thomas C. Peterson, eds., *Global Climate Change Impacts in the United States* (New York: Cambridge University Press, 2009); National Research Council, *Adapting to the Impacts of Climate Change* (Washington, DC: National Academies Press, 2010); U.S. Global Change Research Program, *Fourth National Climate Assessment* (Washington, DC: Author, 2017).

12. Compiled from the U.S. Environmental Protection Agency (http://www.epa.gov/climatechange/glossary.html) and California Energy Commission (https://www.arb.ca.gov/cc/inventory/faq/ghg_inventory_glossary.htm).

Index

Page numbers followed by *f* and *t* refer to figures and tables, respectively.

wildland–urban interface (WUI), 182, 190,
    214, 249
wind, 173, 178, 214
    See also energy: wind
wind turbines, 293
Winneshiek Energy District (Iowa), 170–71
WMO. *See* World Meteorological
    Organization
workshops, 58–59, 89, 326–27
    roving, 92
    See also community workshops

World Bank, 125
World Business Council for Sustainable
    Development (WBCSD), 103
World Conference on the Changing
    Atmosphere, 254
World Meteorological Organization (WMO),
    18, 305
World Resources Institute (WRI), 103, 104
WUI. *See* wildland–urban interface

zoning. *See under* land use